ROUTLEDGE LIBRARY EDITIONS:
INTERNATIONAL SECURITY STUDIES

Volume 23

T0313296

WEAPONS OF MASS DESTRUCTION
AND THE ENVIRONMENT

WEAPONS OF MASS DESTRUCTION AND THE ENVIRONMENT

SIPRI
STOCKHOLM INTERNATIONAL PEACE
RESEARCH INSTITUTE

Routledge
Taylor & Francis Group

LONDON AND NEW YORK

First published in 1977 by Taylor & Francis Ltd., London

This edition first published in 2021
by Routledge
2 Park Square, Milton Park, Abingdon, Oxon OX14 4RN

and by Routledge
52 Vanderbilt Avenue, New York, NY 10017

Routledge is an imprint of the Taylor & Francis Group, an informa business

British Library Cataloguing in Publication Data
A catalogue record for this book is available from the British Library

ISBN: 978-0-367-68499-0 (Set)
ISBN: 978-1-00-316169-1 (Set) (ebk)
ISBN: 978-0-367-71624-0 (Volume 23) (hbk)
ISBN: 978-0-367-71630-1 (Volume 23) (pbk)
ISBN: 978-1-00-315297-2 (Volume 23) (ebk)

Publisher's Note
The publisher has gone to great lengths to ensure the quality of this reprint but
points out that some imperfections in the original copies may be apparent.

Disclaimer
The publisher has made every effort to trace copyright holders and would welcome
correspondence from those they have been unable to trace.

Weapons of Mass Destruction and the Environment

sipri

Stockholm International Peace Research Institute

Taylor & Francis Ltd
London
1977

Crane, Russak & Company, Inc.
New York

First published 1977 by Taylor & Francis Ltd., London
and Crane, Russak & Company, Inc., New York

Copyright © 1977 by SIPRI
Sveavägen 166, S-113 46 Stockholm

ISBN 0 8448 1295 1

Library of Congress Catalog Card Number 77-15308

Printed and bound in the United Kingdom by
Taylor & Francis (Printers) Ltd, Rankine Road,
Basingstoke, Hampshire RG24 0PR

Preface

Given the present state of the world, it is essential to the future well-being of mankind that nuclear, chemical, biological and other weapons of mass destruction be eliminated from the arsenals of the world. A substantial fraction of the research effort of SIPRI has been devoted to providing objective information that would help to create an appropriate climate for relevant disarmament efforts and that would also prove useful to the negotiators themselves.

The present book is the product of one of the several recent and current SIPRI projects devoted to the environmental aspects of arms control and disarmament, a hitherto neglected area of concern in this context. A partial listing of related SIPRI publications will be found on page 88. It is hoped that these documents will contribute to the success of the special session on disarmament of the UN General Assembly scheduled for May–June 1978.

This book was written by Dr Arthur H. Westing, a senior research fellow at SIPRI. He is on leave from Windham College in Putney, Vermont, where he is professor of botany.

July 1977

Frank Barnaby
Director

Contents

Tables

Chapter 1. Nuclear weapons
Tables

Chapter 2. Chemical and biological weapons
Table

Chapter 3. Geophysical and environmental weapons
Table

Conventions and units of measure

As far as possible, the names of plants conform to Lawrence (1951), of the mammals to Walker *et al.* (1964), of the bacteria to Buchanan *et al.* (1974), and of the protozoa to Kudo (1966). The chemical nomenclature follows that of Stecher *et al.* (1968) or, secondarily, of Weast (1974: B–C). All units of measure follow the *Système Internationale d'Unités* (SI) (Page and Vigoureux, 1974); conversions to customary US and British units are from Weast (1974: F:282–304).

References to publications in the text provide information sufficient to locate the full bibliographic citation in the alphabetical listing of 'References', that is, author and date. Different publications by the same author that were published during the same year are distinguished by the arbitrary assignment of a series of lower case letters appended to the year of publication. Additional numbers are in some instances provided in the text immediately following the year of publication (being separated from it by a colon). These refer to specific portions or locations within the publication. Roman numerals signify chapters and Arabic numerals signify pages.

The units of measure used in the text follow:

a	= are = 10^2 square metres = 1076.39 square feet
d	= day = 86 400 seconds
°C	= degree Celsius (to obtain temperature in degrees Fahrenheit, multiply by 1.8 and then add 32)
Ci	= curie = 37×10^9 disintegrations per second = 2.22×10^{12} disintegrations per minute (dpm)
g	= gram = 10^{-3} kilogram = $2.204\,62 \times 10^{-3}$ pound
g/kt	= gram per kilotonne = 0.002 pound per 10^3 US (short) tons
g/m³	= gram per cubic metre = $8.345\,40 \times 10^{-6}$ pound per US gallon = $10.022\,4 \times 10^{-6}$ pound per British gallon
h	= hour = 3600 seconds
h-	= hecto- = $10^2 \times$
ha	= hectare = 10^4 square metres = 10^{-2} square kilometre = 2.471 05 acres
J	= joule = 0.238 846 calorie
J/kg	= joule per kilogram = 0.108 339 calorie per pound
k-	= kilo- = $10^3 \times$
kCi	= kilocurie = 37×10^{12} disintegrations per second
kCi/kg	= kilocurie per kilogram = 453.592 4 curies per pound
kCi/kt	= kilocurie per kilotonne = 907.184 7 curies per 10^3 US (short) tons

kCi/Mt = kilocurie per megatonne = 907.184 7 curies per 10^6 US (short) tons

kg = kilogram = 2.204 62 pounds

kg/ha = kilogram per hectare = 0.892 179 pound per acre

kg/kt = kilogram per kilotonne = 2 pounds per 10^3 US (short) tons

kg/m^3 = kilogram per cubic metre = $8.345\,40 \times 10^{-3}$ pound per US gallon
= $10.022\,4 \times 10^{-3}$ pound per British gallon = 1.685 55 pounds per cubic yard

kJ = kilojoule = 10^3 joules = 238.846 calories

kJ/m^2 = kilojoule per square metre = 238.846 calories per square metre
= 0.154 094 calorie per square inch

km = kilometre = 10^3 metres = 0.621 371 mile

kPa = kilopascal = $9.869\,23 \times 10^{-3}$ atmosphere = 0.145 038 pound per square inch

kR = kiloröntgen = 10^3 röntgens, which see

ks = kilosecond = 10^3 seconds = 16.666 7 minutes

kt = kilotonne = 10^6 kilograms = 1102.31 US (short) tons = 984.207 British (long) tons. See also Chapter 1, note 2

m = metre = 3.280 84 feet

m- = milli- = $10^{-3} \times$

m^2 = square metre = 10.763 9 square feet = 1550.00 square inches

m^3 = cubic metre = 10^3 litres = 264.172 US gallons = 219.969 British gallons = 1.307 95 cubic yards

m^3/ha = cubic metre per hectare = 55.846 6 board feet per acre

mg = milligram = 10^{-6} kilogram = $2.204\,62 \times 10^{-6}$ pound

mg/m^3 = milligram per cubic metre = $8.345\,40 \times 10^{-9}$ pound per US gallon
= $10.022\,4 \times 10^{-9}$ pound per British gallon

min = minute = 60 seconds

mol = mole = that amount of substance which contains as many elementary entities as there are atoms in 12 grams of ^{12}C, that is, 602.252×10^{21} elementary entities

mm = millimetre = 10^{-3} metre = 0.039 370 1 inch

mmol = millimole = 10^{-3} mole, which see

m/s = metre per second = 3.6 kilometres per hour = 2.236 94 miles per hour

M- = mega- = $10^6 \times$

MCi = megacurie = 37×10^{15} disintegrations per second

MCi/kg = megacurie per kilogram = 453.592 4 kilocuries per pound

MCi/kt = megacurie per kilotonne = 907.184 7 kilocuries per 10^3 US (short) tons

MCi/Mt = megacurie per megatonne = 907.184 7 kilocuries per 10^6 US (short) tons

Ms = megasecond = 10^6 seconds = 11.574 1 days

Mt = megatonne = 10^9 kilograms = $1.102 31 \times 10^6$ US (short) tons = $0.984 207 \times 10^6$ British (long) ton. See also chapter 1, note 2.

μ = micro- = $10^{-6} \times$

μg = microgram = 10^{-9} kilogram = $2.204 62 \times 10^{-12}$ pound

μg/kg = microgram per kilogram = part per 10^9 parts, by weight

μg/m^3 = microgram per cubic metre = $1.685 55 \times 10^{-12}$ pound per cubic yard

n- = nano- = $10^{-9} \times$

nm = nanometre = 10^{-9} metre = $39.370 1 \times 10^{-9}$ inch = 10 Ångströms

Pa = pascal = $9.869 23 \times 10^{-6}$ atmosphere = 145.038×10^{-6} pound per square inch

R = röntgen = a unit of X or gamma radiation exposure producing a charge of 258×10^{-6} coulomb per kilogram of air; for biota it is numerically equivalent to *ca.* 1 'rad', a unit of ionizing radiation absorption of 10^{-2} joule per kilogram of body weight (Arena, 1971: 215–218)

s = second

t = tonne = 10^3 kilograms = 1.102 31 US (short) tons = 0.984 207 British (long) ton

Foreword

The arms race between the USA and the USSR continues unabated. This unholy race is spreading ever more widely and rapidly among the other nations of the world. These two powers each maintain enormous nuclear arsenals plus the systems to deliver them. Four further nations have a demonstrated nuclear capability and several others probably have similar capabilities. Substantial numbers of nations have the chemical and microbiological expertise and production facilities to suggest that they could be maintaining chemical and biological arsenals. And a number of additional weapons of mass destruction could be available to certain nations in special locations or circumstances.

The inhumane aspects of weapons of mass destruction are widely recognized and underlie the continuing efforts in many quarters to abolish or restrict their use. Their impact on the environment, usually an ancillary aspect of their employment, has, on the other hand, been of much less general concern or interest. This is regrettable. Whereas concern for ecological disruption during warfare may to some appear misdirected or even callous, especially when such disruption appears to be in partial substitution for human destruction, it can be justified on a number of grounds. First, it is in the long-run self-interest of the human race to protect the natural environment from which it ultimately derives its sustenance. Second, all living things deserve a measure of respect and protection in their own right. Third, an exposition of the environmental damage associated with weapons of mass destruction might serve to bolster the argument to control their use, especially so in the light of today's growing environmental awareness. And fourth, a concern over ecological consequences of war does not preclude the direct traditional human concerns. It may, in fact, enhance such concerns via a civilizing influence and also perhaps by awakening a wider public to war-related concerns.

1

1. Nuclear weapons

Superior numerals, thus [5], refer to notes on pages 24–30.

I. Introduction

Nuclear weapons exist, they have been employed and they can have a tremendous ecological impact. No treatment of the interaction between weapons of mass destruction and the environment would be complete without an examination of nuclear weapons.[1]

Nuclear weapons come in all sizes or yields[2] and can be delivered in a variety of ways. The bomb that destroyed Hiroshima had an energy yield of about 13 kt and the one which destroyed Nagasaki a yield of about 21 kt (US Atomic Energy Commission, priv. comm., 9 Jan. 1974; see also Penney *et al.*, 1970). Although a nuclear device of over 50 Mt has been detonated (Glasstone, 1964: 681 a), one gathers that likely sizes for use as strategic nuclear weapons would be in the range of 1 Mt to 10 Mt. Hundreds if not thousands of such weapons might be expended within a period of days during some major nuclear exchange of the future. By way of partial contrast, the total energy yield of all the munitions expended during $8\frac{1}{2}$ years of the Second Indochina War comes to less than 4 Mt (note 3).

Nuclear weapons are awe-inspiring not only for their total energy yield, but also for the several forms in which this energy is dissipated, as will be seen in the following section. The ecological consequences of nuclear war are covered in section III of this chapter.

II. Description

General

The effects of a nuclear attack depend not only upon the number of devices detonated and their types and sizes, but also upon how they are distributed in time and space. The effects are strongly influenced by whether a burst occurs at or near ground level, substantially below ground, under water, in the denser portions of the atmosphere (that is, below about 30 km), or even in the very rarified upper atmosphere.[4]

2

The character of the terrain, weather conditions and other factors also modify the character and magnitude of the effects.

A nuclear bomb that bursts in the troposphere high enough that its fire-ball does not reach the ground[5] will dissipate about half of its energy in the form of a blast or shock wave (Table 1.1). Another third of the energy will be released in the form of thermal radiation. The remaining energy will be expended in the form of nuclear radiation, about one third of this within the initial minute and the rest over a much longer period of time.

A burst in the very thin air above the stratosphere[4] will translate significantly less of its energy into blast and more into thermal radiation. Surface and sub-surface bursts, either terrestrial or aquatic, produce far more radioactive fall-out than do air bursts. Underwater bursts are a class by themselves. Their effects differ markedly depending upon how far below the surface the bomb is detonated, how deep and how large the body of water is and other factors. The reader is referred to Glasstone (1964: VI) for further information on underwater nuclear explosions.

In the sections that follow can be found separate descriptions of the blast (shock) wave of a nuclear detonation, of its pulse of thermal radiation and of its nuclear radiation. The tabulated data are usually presented for three bomb sizes: 18 kt, 0.91 Mt and 9.1 Mt (note 2). The smallest of these is roughly comparable to the Hiroshima and Nagasaki shots, whereas the larger two sizes are likely to be employed in any future nuclear war.

The ecological consequences of nuclear attack will in many respects be similar to those of conventional warfare or other major environmental disturbance. The consequences will differ, however, owing to the novel stresses imposed upon the involved ecosystems by nuclear (and perhaps also ultra-violet) radiation. And, depending upon the magnitude of the nuclear exchange, they can differ dramatically in scale.

Blast (shock) wave

Within seconds of detonation, a nuclear bomb dissipates about half of its tremendous energy in the form of a blast or shock wave (Table 1.1). This wave, which initially propagates outward at many times the speed of sound (and eventually turns into a sound wave), is responsible for much of the physical damage brought about by a nuclear explosion. Since the parameters of a blast wave are highly complex even under idealized conditions, the data on damage presented below are based largely on empirically gathered information (Glasstone, 1964: III–V).

Table 1.1. Distribution of energy release by a nuclear bomb exploded in the troposphere

Energy form		Energy released		
		$(10^{12}$ J$)$	$(10^{15}$ J$)$	$(10^{15}$ J$)$
	Bomb size:	18 kt	0.91 Mt	9.1 Mt
Blast (shock)		41.9	2.28	22.8
Thermal radiation		29.3	1.59	15.9
Nuclear radiation, first min		4.2	0.10	1.0
Nuclear radiation, residual		8.4	0.21	2.1
Total		**83.7**	**4.19**	**41.9**

Notes:

(a) For an explanation of bomb size designations, see note 2.

(b) The data are derived from those of Glasstone (1964: 7–9).

(c) The 18 kt bomb is a fission bomb, whereas the 0.91 Mt and 9.1 Mt bombs are half fission and half fusion. The explosions are so-called typical air bursts.[5] Comparable data for surface bursts are difficult to generalize about.

Table 1.2. Blast damage to forests from a nuclear bomb exploded in the troposphere

Level of damage		Size of damaged area		
	Bomb size:	18 kt	0.91 Mt	9.1 Mt
30% Blowdown				
Diameter (km)		4.0	18.3	46.9
Area (ha)		1 270	26 300	173 000
90% Blowdown				
Diameter (km)		2.7	13.4	32.3
Area (ha)		565	14 100	82 000

Notes:

(a) For an explanation of bomb size designations, see note 2.

(b) The data are derived from those of Glasstone (1964: 169, 174–175). They compare well with those of Fons et al. (1957).

(c) The data refer to what was described as an 'average' coniferous forest growing under 'unfavourable' conditions, but were asserted to be equally applicable to a dicotyledonous forest in leaf.

(d) To bring about equal damage by a steady wind would require a velocity of 40–45 m/s to blow down 30 per cent of the trees and 58–63 m/s to blow down 90 per cent. These steady wind velocities are roughly comparable to the transient ones at the shock front which can be theoretically derived for the distances involved (Glasstone, 1964: 107, 135).

(e) The explosions are so-called typical air bursts.[5] Comparable data for surface bursts would have diameters roughly 80 per cent and areas 64 per cent of those presented (Glasstone, 1964: 632, 107).

With respect to trees, the destructive force of a blast wave from a nuclear detonation is best related to the peak transient wind (or particle) velocity at the shock front. The effect (known as drag loading) caused by this transient wind is more destructive than one might expect from a knowledge of blast waves initiated by conventional explosives, because of its relatively long duration. The greater the distance from the explosion, the longer is the duration of this positive phase, varying from roughly 0·5 s to 1 s for an 18 kt bomb, from 2 s to 4 s for a 0.91 Mt bomb and from 4 s to 8 s for a 9.1 Mt bomb. Thus the increasing duration with distance compensates in part for the decreasing velocity of the peak transient wind. A 0.91 Mt bomb will blow down most of the trees on 14×10^3 ha if it is an air burst, or on 9×10^3 ha if a surface burst (Table 1.2).

With respect to wildlife, the destructive force of a blast wave from a nuclear detonation is best related to the peak transient overpressure at the shock front, that is, the transient maximum pressure above atmospheric. Significant damage can occur to the lungs of large mammals (including humans) at a point where the nuclear blast wave, with its lengthy positive phase, has a peak transient overpressure of about 100 kPa (Glasstone, 1964: 557). Approximately 1 per cent of such

Table 1.3. **Blast damage to wildlife from a nuclear bomb exploded in the troposphere**

		Size of damaged area		
	Bomb size:	18 kt	0.91 Mt	9.1 Mt
Lung damage				
Diameter (km)		1.4	5.1	10.9
Area (ha)		148	2 010	9 330
Lethal to 50 %				
Diameter (km)		0.7	2.7	5.9
Area (ha)		43	591	2 740

Notes:

    (a) For an explanation of bomb size designations, see note 2.

    (b) The data are derived from those of Glasstone (1964: 135). Lung damage is considered to occur at a transient overpressure of 100 kPa or more, and 50 per cent lethality at 345 kPa or more (Glasstone, 1964: 557).

    (c) The above figures are based only on the incident or free-field overpressures which develop. These are, in fact, augmented by reflected overpressures which (depending upon height of burst, terrain, etc.) can more than double the total (so-called Mach front) overpressures experienced at any distance.

    (d) The explosions are so-called typical air bursts.[5] Comparable data for surface bursts would have diameters roughly 75 per cent and areas 56 per cent of those presented (Glasstone, 1964: 632, 638).

exposed animals will be killed at an overpressure of 275 kPa, 50 per cent at 345 kPa and 99 per cent at 415 kPa. Through the transient over-pressure it generates, a 0.91 Mt bomb will kill more than half the wildlife on about 590 ha if it is an air burst, or on 330 ha if a surface burst (Table 1.3).

It is important to note that these wildlife mortality data are based only on the incident or free-field overpressures that develop. The area of blast fatalities is, however, enlarged in a number of ways. First, the incident overpressures are augmented by reflected overpressures. And second, a very high, though variable, proportion of animal deaths and injuries is not attributable to the blast *per se* (the so-called primary blast effects), but rather to flying missiles (so-called secondary blast effects) and to body displacement, that is, to having the body slammed into some object (so-called tertiary blast effects). Depending especially on the terrain, these indirect effects on the blast wave can considerably intensify and enlarge the zone of wildlife casualties.

The shock wave of a surface or sub-surface burst will blast out an immense crater. For example, a 0.91 Mt bomb detonated at or near ground level will produce in dry soil a crater having a surface area of about 12 ha and a maximum depth of about 90 m (Table 1.4). The

Table 1.4. Size of crater produced by a nuclear bomb exploded at the surface

		Crater dimensions		
	Bomb size:	18 kt	0.91 Mt	9.1 Mt
Diameter (m)		108	396	854
Surface area (ha)		1	12	57
Maximum depth (m)		25	91	197
Volume (10^3 m^3)		75	3 760	37 600
Displaced mass (10^6 kg)		199	9 960	99 600

Notes:

(a) For an explanation of bomb size designations, see note 2.

(b) The data are derived from those of Glasstone (1964: 276–277). (See also Brode (1968: 193–198).)

(c) Volume is based on the assumption that crater shape is conical. Displaced mass is based on the assumption that soil and rock weigh 2650 kg/m^3 (Lutz and Chandler, 1946: 236; Daly *et al.*, 1966).

(d) The data presented are for explosions at or near the surface of dry soil. If the material were rock in lieu of soil, then the diameters and depths would be roughly 80 per cent of those given, the areas 64 per cent and the volumes (and masses) 51 per cent (Glasstone, 1964: 292).

(e) Subsurface bursts at optimal depth would, roughly speaking, double the diameters presented, quadruple the areas, triple the depths and increase the volumes (and masses) by a factor of twelve (Glasstone, 1964: 293). A so-called typical air burst[5] would not produce a crater (Glasstone, 1964: 277).

6

volume of such a crater is thus almost 4×10^6 m^3 in size. It is estimated that roughly 0.5 per cent of the material blown out of the crater is injected into the stratosphere for a residence time of perhaps one to three years (Nier *et al.*, 1975: 54). The implications of this contamination are discussed below.

Finally one should add that there is a remote possibility that underground nuclear detonations might trigger an earthquake or related seismic event in a location that is tectonically unstable (Bolt, 1976: X; Boucher *et al.*, 1969).

Thermal radiation

Fires are virtually certain following an above-ground nuclear detonation. This is because approximately one-third of the bomb's immense energy is dissipated during the initial several seconds after the burst as an immense pulse of thermal energy that propagates outward at almost the speed of light (Table 1.1). Under appropriate site and weather conditions, there will be large wildfires, some of which may develop into so-called mass fires or fire storms.[6]

The amount of thermal energy or radiant exposure from a nuclear bomb required to ignite vegetation varies not only with the type of

Table 1.5. Pulse of radiant exposure required for igniting plant materials from a nuclear bomb explosion

Plant material (dry)		Radiant exposure required for ignition (kJ/m^2)		
	Bomb size:	18 kt	0.91 Mt	9.1 Mt
Rotted conifer wood (*Abies*; Pinaceae)		150	250	330
Dicotyledonous leaves (*Fagus*; Fagaceae)		150	250	330
Grass (*Bromus*; Gramineae)		180	330	420
Sedge (*Carex*; Cyperaceae)		220	380	460
Brown conifer needles (*Pinus*; Pinaceae)		360	670	880

Notes:
  (*a*) For an explanation of bomb size designations, see note 2.
  (*b*) The data are derived from those of Glasstone (1964: 332).
  (*c*) As bomb size increases, a higher level of radiant exposure is required to achieve the same effect. This is because as bomb size increases, a given amount of energy delivered to a given point in space is spread over a longer period of time (Glasstone, 1964: 571).

Table 1.6. Pulse of radiant exposure required for burn damage from a nuclear bomb explosion

		Radiation exposure required (kJ/m^2)		
	Bomb size:	18 kt	0.91 Mt	9.1 Mt
First-degree burn		100	130	150
Second-degree burn		180	270	380
Burns lethal to 50%		380	590	750

Notes:

    (*a*) For an explanation of bomb size designations, see note 2.

    (*b*) The data for first-degree and second-degree burns are derived from those of Glasstone (1964: 571); the data for 50 per cent lethality are from the US Department of Defense (priv. comm., 25 Feb. 1976). (See also Defense Civil Preparedness Agency (1973: III: 2).)

    (*c*) The data are for flash burns of the exposed skin of pigs (*Sus;* Suidae) or humans.

    (*d*) As bomb size increases, a higher level of radiant exposure is required to achieve the same effect. This is because as bomb size increases, a given amount of energy delivered to a given point in space is spread over a longer period of time (Glasstone, 1964: 571).

plant material, its size and state of moisture content, but also with the duration of exposure. A given amount of radiant exposure is more effective in igniting a potential fuel if delivered in a briefer span of time. On the other hand, the larger a nuclear bomb, the more protracted is its pulse of energy. Thus, by way of example, for an 18 kt bomb to ignite dry conifer needles requires only $360 \, kJ/m^2$, for a 0.91 Mt bomb the comparable value is $670 \, kJ/m^2$ and for a 9.1 Mt bomb it is $880 \, kJ/m^2$ (Table 1.5).

With direct injury to wildlife in mind, it can be noted that 50 per cent or more of those exposed would be burnt to death by a pulse of radiant exposure of $380 \, kJ/m^2$ from an 18 kt bomb, of $590 \, kJ/m^2$ from a 0.91 Mt bomb and of $750 \, kJ/m^2$ from a 9.1 Mt bomb (Table 1.6). There would be additional wildlife damage from the wildfires started.

When a nuclear bomb's zone of likely ignitions (approximately that zone experiencing a radiant exposure of at least $500 \, kJ/m^2$ from an 18 kt bomb, $750 \, kJ/m^2$ from a 0.91 Mt bomb or $1\,000 \, kJ/m^2$ from a 9.1 Mt bomb) overlaps a forested region, under reasonably dry conditions the initiation of many small and several large fires is virtually certain. Depending upon the fuel and weather conditions, the burning areas within this zone could in large part coalesce during the course of the first day (Chandler *et al.*, 1963). For a 0.91 Mt bomb, this zone would on a clear day extend over some 33×10^3 ha if it is an air burst, or over 21×10^3 ha if a surface burst (Table 1.7), and fire might spread beyond this initial zone of ignitions, particularly if the attack occurred during the so-called fire season.

Table 1.7. Pulse of radiant exposure from a nuclear bomb exploded in the troposphere

Radiant exposure Bomb size:	Size of area receiving more than the given radiant exposure		
	18 kt	0.91 Mt	9.1 Mt
250 kJ/m²			
Diameter (km)	5.5	35.4	96.6
Area (ha)	2 350	98 500	732 000
500 kJ/m²			
Diameter (km)	3·9	25.1	67.6
Area (ha)	1 170	49 500	359 000
750 kJ/m²			
Diameter (km)	3.2	20.6	54.7
Area (ha)	781	33 300	235 000
1 000 kJ/m²			
Diameter (km)	2.8	17.7	48.3
Area (ha)	602	24 600	183 000

Notes:

(a) For an explanation of bomb size designations, see note 2.

(b) The data are derived from those of Glasstone (1964: 333).

(c) The data presented would obtain on an unusually clear day, visibility 80 km. A reduction in visibility from 80 km to 16 km, the situation on a moderately clear day, would reduce the radiant exposures presented above to roughly 81 per cent of the values given (Glasstone, 1964: 319–320), and thus the diameters to roughly 81 per cent and the areas to 65 per cent. (For somewhat different reduction values, see the Defense Civil Preparedness Agency (1973: III: 4).)

(d) The explosions are so-called typical air bursts.[5] Comparable data for surface bursts would have diameters roughly 80 per cent and areas 64 per cent of those presented (Glasstone, 1964: 632).

(e) A given pulse of radiant exposure from a 0.91 Mt bomb is about 64 per cent as potent as one from an 18 kt bomb; the pulse of radiant exposure from a 9.1 Mt bomb is about 77 per cent as potent as one from a 0.91 Mt bomb (cf. tables 1.5 and 1.6). Thus 500 kJ/m² from an 18 kt bomb, 750 kJ/m² from a 0.91 Mt bomb and 1 000 kJ/m² from a 9.1 Mt are all roughly comparable in their ability to do damage.

Beyond the immediate fires that result from a nuclear detonation, there is likely to be a higher incidence of subsequent fires. This is so because, over a period of time, there will be a zone of vegetation killed by nuclear radiation that will provide an excellent source of fuel. The ecological consequences of large-scale wildfires are examined in Chapter 3.

Another effect of the exceedingly high temperatures momentarily produced by a nuclear detonation is to transform a certain fraction of the air into such oxides of nitrogen as nitric oxide (NO) and nitrogen dioxide (NO_2) (Bauer and Gilmore, 1975; Foley and Ruderman, 1973; Goldsmith *et al.*, 1973; Johnston *et al.*, 1973). Actually, the thermal energy that drives these reactions derives not only from the pulse of thermal radiation, but also from shock heating and bombardment by nuclear radiation. An air burst of an 18 kt bomb produces about 100×10^3 kg of these oxides of nitrogen, a 0.91 Mt bomb about 5×10^6 kg and a 9.1 Mt bomb about 50×10^6 kg. Much of this material finds its way into the lower stratosphere, where it reacts catalytically with the ozone (O_3), degrading it to oxygen gas (O_2). The implications of this effect are discussed in section III.

Nuclear radiation

Nuclear radiation represents only about 15 per cent of the total energy release of a nuclear fission bomb, and perhaps half that amount for a fission/fusion bomb (Table 1.1). About one third of the nuclear radiation released is dissipated during the first minute following detonation (Table 1.8) and thus over a relatively restricted area. Following this initial burst, the residual nuclear radiation is dissipated ever more slowly and widely. For an air burst, the radioactive contamination that occurs during the first minute (the so-called initial radiation) is the portion of substantial ecological concern. For a surface burst, this contamination is spread during roughly the first 24 hours (the so-called early radiation) owing to

Table 1.8. Dissipation of nuclear radiation from a nuclear bomb explosion

		Energy dissipated		
		(10^{12} J)	(10^{12} J)	(10^{15} J)
	Bomb size:	18 kt	0.91 Mt	9.1 Mt
First minute (60 s)		4.2	105	1.05
First hour (3600 s)		8.8	220	2.20
First day (86.4 ks)		10.9	272	2.72
First week (605 ks)		11.6	291	2.91
First month (2.63 Ms)		12.1	301	3.01
First year (31.6 Ms)		12.4	310	3.10
Total (infinity dose)		**12.6**	**314**	**3.14**

Notes:
   (a) For an explanation of bomb size designations, see note 2.
   (b) The data are derived from those of Glasstone (1964: 424).
   (c) The 18 kt bomb is a fission bomb whereas the 0.91 Mt and 9.1 Mt bombs are half fission and half fusion.
   (d) The first minute of nuclear radiation is usually referred to as the initial radiation, and what comes after that as the residual radiation. The first day of nuclear radiation is usually referred to as the early radiation.

the fall-out of surface materials made radioactive by neutron bombardment and injected into the atmosphere by the blast.

The sources, forms and amounts of nuclear radiation can differ remarkably depending upon bomb type (for example, fission versus fission/fusion; 'clean' versus 'dirty'), bomb size and where detonated (for example, air versus surface versus sub-surface) (Glasstone, 1964: VIII–IX).

The discussion here is based largely upon the biological impact of gamma radiation and, moreover, of gamma radiation whose source is external to the affected organisms. The estimates of impact must therefore be recognized as being somewhat conservative. Within the past several years, the significance of the less penetrating beta radiation (electrons) has come to be understood as an additional insult to the environment (Kantz, 1971; Murphy and McCormick, 1971; Rhoads and Platt, 1971; Rhoads et al., 1971), and inclusion of the beta radiation might increase total dose levels by as much as a factor or two. Moreover, particularly with wildlife, an additional source of radioactive exposure comes from ingested radionuclides such as ^{89}Sr, ^{90}Sr, ^{131}I, ^{137}Cs and perhaps ^{239}Pu. Although such internal exposures would, depending upon feeding habits and other factors, add only 1 per cent to 10 per cent to total exposure, their biological effect can be magnified if the radioactive substance concentrates at a particular location within the body. Strontium and plutonium, for example, tend to concentrate near the bone marrow, iodine in the thyroid gland and caesium in the blood.

The lethal dose levels from nuclear radiation have been summarized for many plants (Sparrow et al., 1971; Sparrow and Sparrow, 1965), for some mammals (Spalding and Holland, 1971) and for various other organisms (Wurtz, 1963). The lethal level for most of the mammals tested (that is, the dose that kills 50 per cent of exposed organisms, or LD_{50}) falls between 0.3 kR and 0.8 kR; the level for man seems to fall between 0.4 kR and 0.5 kR. Birds are killed by dose levels comparable to those that kill mammals. For amphibians and reptiles, the lethal dose appears to be about three times that for mammals.

The lethal dose levels for the higher plants spans the mammalian and reptilian ranges. Many conifers are at the sensitive end of this spectrum and some of the grasses are at the resistant end. All of the higher plants are more resistant to radioactive damage during their dormant periods. Insects for the most part are about a hundred times as resistant as mammals. However, social insects such as honey bees (*Apis mellifera*: Apidae) (important as pollinators) are destroyed by 5 kR (Auerbach, 1968; Goolsby, 1968). Many bacteria, algae and fungi can withstand doses a thousand times greater than those that kill mammals.

The effect of nuclear radiation on the survival of the higher plants can be predicted fairly well, since their chromosome volume (and thus also their degree of polyploidy) turns out to be well correlated with their radio-resistance (Sparrow *et al.*, 1971; Sparrow and Sparrow, 1965). Although this relationship may also hold for insects, it does not appear to hold for mammals (Comroy *et al.*, 1971). Those plants better able to cope with nature's more routine adversities, such as low temperature, drought or wind, are often the more radio-resistant ones (Woodwell, 1967). For both flora and fauna, age and season can influence radio-sensitivity. Moreover, root systems, soil micro-organisms and burrowing animals receive partial shielding by the earth, thereby avoiding some nuclear (as well as thermal) radiation damage (Blumenfeld, 1966).

Table 1.9. Initial nuclear radiation from a nuclear bomb exploded in the troposphere

Nuclear radiation during first 60 s		Size of area receiving more than the given radiation		
	Bomb size:	18 kt	0.91 Mt	9.1 Mt
0.5 kR				
Diameter (km)		2.6	4.4	5.5
Area (ha)		545	1 510	2 380
2 kR				
Diameter (km)		2.0	3.7	4.8
Area (ha)		318	1 080	1 840
10 kR				
Diameter (km)		1.3	2.9	4.0
Area (ha)		129	648	1 250
20 kR				
Diameter (km)		1.0	2.6	3.7
Area (ha)		79	523	1 060
70 kR				
Diameter (km)		0.5	2.0	3.1
Area (ha)		18	312	759

Notes:
   (*a*) For an explanation of bomb size designations, see note 2.
   (*b*) The data are derived from those of Glasstone (1964: 380).
   (*c*) The 18 kt bomb is a fission bomb whereas the 0.91 Mt and 9.1 Mt bombs are half fission and half fusion.
   (*d*) The initial (first 60 s) nuclear radiation provided in the table represents about 33 per cent of the ultimate total (table 1.8).
   (*e*) The explosions are so-called typical air bursts.[5] Comparable data for surface bursts would have diameters roughly 67 per cent and areas 44 per cent of those presented (Glasstone, 1964: 379).
   (*f*) The data presented in this table can also be used as a rough approximation of the contamination patterns for the ultimate total nuclear radiation of an air burst inasmuch as the residual radiation would be dispersed over a vast area (Glasstone, 1964: 415).

12

The impact of massive nuclear radiation on entire ecosystems has been considered in terms of the damage sustained by the dominant vegetation. The dominant vegetation accounts not only for a substantial fraction of the ecosystem's primary production, but also provides shelter for many of the animals in the system. To destroy a coniferous forest (that is, to kill essentially 100 per cent of the dominant vegetation) requires a total dose of about 2 kR; to destroy a temperate dicotyledonous forest requires 10 kR; to destroy grassland (prairie) requires 20 kR; and to destroy a biotype dominated by herbaceous non-grasses (forbs) requires about 70 kR (note 7).

In order to be able to relate all of the above information on lethal levels of nuclear radiation to the ecological impact of a bomb, it is, of

Table 1.10. Early nuclear radiation from a nuclear bomb exploded at the surface

Nuclear radiation during first 24 h		Size of area receiving more than the given radiation		
	Bomb size:	18 kt	0.91 Mt	9.1 Mt
0.5 kR				
Elliptical axes (km)		2.3 × 15.8	14.5 × 83	27.3 × 189
Area (ha)		2 850	94 500	405 000
2 kR				
Elliptical axes (km)		1.1 × 7.8	10.3 × 45	18.8 × 120
Area (ha)		674	36 400	177 000
10 kR				
Elliptical axes (km)		0.7 × 2.7	7.1 × 23	12.7 × 64
Area (ha)		148	12 800	63 800
20 kR				
Elliptical axes (km)		0.6 × 1.6	5.8 × 16	10.6 × 47
Area (ha)		75	7 290	39 100
70 kR				
Elliptical axes (km)		0.5 × 1.1	4.0 × 9	7.0 × 22
Area (ha)		43	2 830	12 100

Notes:

(a) For an explanation of bomb size designations, see note 2.

(b) The data are derived from those of Glasstone (1964: 457, 450, 429).

(c) The 18 kt bomb is a fission bomb, whereas the 0.91 Mt and 9.1 Mt bombs are half fission and half fusion.

(d) The early (first 24 h) nuclear radiation provided in the table represents about 87 per cent of the ultimate total (table 1.8). A uniform wind direction and speed throughout the lower atmosphere of 6.7 m/s as well as no rain are postulated for the entire 24 h period.

(e) Comparable data for a so-called typical air burst[5] would be roughly equivalent to those presented in table 1.9 inasmuch as those presented in the present table are based for the most part on radioactive fallout particles produced from surface materials incorporated into the fireball at the time of detonation.

course, necessary to know how large an area is subjected to such levels. Thus, a 0.91 Mt bomb would destroy coniferous forests over an area of about 1 100 ha if an air burst (Table 1.9), but over perhaps 36×10^3 ha if a surface burst (Table 1.10). Such a bomb would destroy boreal or temperate forest of any sort on about 650 ha if an air burst, or on about 13×10^3 ha if a surface burst. Similarly, grasslands would be destroyed on about 520 ha if an air burst, or on about 7 300 ha if a surface burst.

The same 0.91 Mt bomb would kill most mammals over an area of about 1 500 ha if an air burst, or on about 94×10^3 ha if a surface burst. Such a bomb would destroy most vertebrates on about 1 100 ha if an air burst, or on 36×10^3 ha if a surface burst.

These areas of radioactive contamination for surface bursts (Table 1.10) may be compared with some information released by the USA on one of its large Pacific test explosions. This is the notorious 'Bravo' shot of 1 March 1954 at Bikini (Glasstone, 1964: 460–464; Conard *et al.*, 1975; Lapp, 1958). Considering the differences in yield and so forth, the data do, in fact, coincide rather well (Table 1.11). It is fortunate that the immense zone of lethality created by this trial was able to spend itself over a trackless ocean expanse, at least for the most part.

Table 1.11. Nuclear radiation from the nuclear bomb exploded at the surface at Namu Island, Bikini Atoll, 1 March 1954

Nuclear radiation during first 96 h	Size of area receiving more than the given radiation
0.5 kR	
Elliptical axes (km)	62×326
Area (ha)	1 590 000
2 kR	
Elliptical axes (km)	30×210
Area (ha)	495 000
10 kR	
Elliptical axes (km)	15×100
Area (ha)	118 000

Notes:

(*a*) The bomb was one designated as 13.6 Mt; for an explanation of this designation (Glasstone, 1964: 673), see note 2.

(*b*) The data are derived from those of Glasstone (1964: 462).

(*c*) The bomb (code-named 'Bravo') was about half fission and half fusion (US Atomic Energy Commission, priv. comm., 9 Jan. 1974).

(*d*) The 96 h nuclear radiation provided in the table represents about 92 per cent of the ultimate total (table 1.8). There was no rain during this 96 h period. Based on arrival time, the average wind speed during the first 20 h was 7.4 m/s (Glasstone, 1964: 462).

The discussion in the present section has largely dwelt upon nuclear radiation in terms of lethal levels. There are a number of more subtle long-term effects that can be expected to occur in those organisms exposed to a sublethal dose. These include reduced fertility, shortened life span, higher incidence of neoplasms and increased mutational frequency. Such effects, of deep concern with respect to human populations, seem to have only modest direct significance with respect to the plant and animal populations within an ecosystem. Moreover, following a nuclear detonation, one can expect a slight worldwide increase in the so-called background radiation that will last for years (Kulp, 1965; Nier *et al.*, 1975). The stress imposed by this increase is apparently equivalent to the stresses from other pollutants (Woodwell, 1970) and thus, although almost insignificant by itself, adds to the others.

III. Ecological consequences

General

Once the dust has settled, so to speak, a terrestrial nuclear attack will have left a region devastated by the several intense forms of energy dissipation described in the previous sections. The present section is devoted to the ecological ramifications of such devastation.[8]

In what follows, the environmental impact of nuclear attack is described in three categories: the earth itself or geosphere; the atmosphere overlying this geosphere; and the living things, or biosphere, that live upon and within the geosphere and atmosphere. But first it is necessary to indicate the geographical extent of the devastation being dealt with. The various forms of destruction previously described occur in concert, overlapping and reinforcing each other. A nuclear detonation will desolate several hundred hectares and will have a variety of serious effects that diminish outward over an area of several thousand hectares (Tables 1.12 and 1.13). The area of mortality to living things from nuclear radiation is an extensive one for either air or surface bursts, but is particularly impressive for the latter case. Thus, the nuclear radiation from a 0.91 Mt surface burst will kill most trees over an area of 13×10^3 ha and most vertebrates on 36×10^3 ha (Table 1.13). Another major environmental threat from a nuclear detonation, especially in the less wet regions and seasons, results from the thermal radiation. Under appropriate weather and site conditions, a 0.91 Mt air burst will initiate

Table 1.12. Damage to biota from a nuclear bomb exploded in the troposphere

Type of damage	Area suffering the given type of damage (ha)		
Bomb size:	18 kt	0.91 Mt	9.1 Mt
Craterization by the blast wave	0	0	0
Trees blown down by the blast wave	565	14 100	82 000
Trees killed by nuclear radiation	129	648	1 250
All vegetation killed by nuclear radiation	18	312	759
Dry vegetation ignited by thermal radiation	1 170	33 300	183 000
Vertebrates killed by the blast wave	43	591	2 740
Vertebrates killed by nuclear radiation	318	1 080	1 840
Vertebrates killed by thermal radiation	1 570	42 000	235 000

Notes:

(a) For an explanation of bomb size designations, see note 2.

(b) Craterization by the blast wave is from Table 1.4. Trees blown down by the blast wave are from Table 1.2, using the 90 per cent blowdown data. Tree mortality by nuclear radiation is from Table 1.9, using the 10 kR data. All-vegetation mortality by nuclear radiation is from Table 1.9, using the 70 kR data. Dry vegetation ignitions by thermal radiation is from Table 1.7, using the 500 kJ/m² datum for the 18 kt bomb, the 750 kJ/m² datum for the 0.91 Mt bomb, and the 1 000 kJ/m² datum for the 9.1 Mt bomb (cf. Table 1.5). Vertebrate mortality by the blast wave is from Table 1.3, using the lethal-to-50 per cent data. Vertebrate mortality by nuclear radiation is from Table 1.9, using the 2 kR data. Vertebrate mortality by thermal radiation is from Table 1.6, using the lethal-to-50 per cent data for interpolation in Table 1.7.

(c) The 18 kt bomb is a fission bomb, whereas the 0.91 Mt and 9.1 Mt bombs are half fission and half fusion.

(d) The explosions are so-called typical air bursts.[5] Comparable data for surface bursts are presented in Table 1.13.

wildfires over perhaps 33×10^3 ha and burn to death most vertebrates on 42×10^3 (Table 1.12). Hypothetical scenarios of a nuclear attack against the conterminous United States, with its 783×10^6 ha of land, often suggest a total expenditure of between 5×10^3 Mt and 10×10^3 Mt, divided half and half between air and surface bursts and with the shots centred upon urban, industrial and military targets.

Geosphere

A matter of major concern is the site degradation that will occur over

Table 1.13. Damage to biota from a nuclear bomb exploded at the surface

Type of damage	Area suffering the given type of damage (ha)		
Bomb size:	18 kt	0.91 Mt	9.1 Mt
Craterization by the blast wave	1	12	57
Trees blown down by the blast wave	362	9 040	52 500
Trees killed by nuclear radiation	148	12 800	63 800
All vegetation killed by nuclear radiation	43	2 830	12 100
Dry vegetation ignited by thermal radiation	749	21 300	117 000
Vertebrates killed by the blast wave	24	332	1 540
Vertebrates killed by nuclear radiation	674	36 400	177 000
Vertebrates killed by thermal radiation	1 000	26 900	150 000

Notes:

(a) For an explanation of bomb size designations, see note 2.

(b) Craterization by the blast wave is from Table 1.4. Trees blown down by the blast wave is from Table 1.2, using the 90 per cent blowdown data reduced to 64 per cent of the given values to convert to surface burst. Tree mortality by nuclear radiation is from Table 1.10, using the 10 kR data. All-vegetation mortality by nuclear radiation is from Table 1.10, using the 70 kR data. Dry vegetation ignitions by thermal radiation is from Table 1.7, using the 500 kJ/m^2 datum for the 18 kt bomb, the 750 kJ/m^2 datum for the 0.91 Mt bomb, and the 1 000 kJ/m^2 datum for the 9.1 Mt bomb (cf. Table 1.5), all reduced to 64 per cent of the given values to convert to surface burst. Vertebrate mortality by the blast wave is from Table 1.3, using the lethal-to-50 per cent data reduced to 56 per cent of the given values to convert to surface burst. Vertebrate mortality by nuclear radiation is from Table 1.10, using the 2 kR data. Vertebrate mortality by thermal radiation is from Table 1.6, using the lethal-to-50 per cent data for interpolation in Table 1.7, then reduced to 64 per cent of the values obtained to convert to surface burst.

(c) The 18 kt bomb is a fission bomb, whereas the 0.91 Mt and 9.1 Mt bombs are half fission and half fusion.

(d) Comparable data for so-called typical air bursts[5] are presented in Table 1.12.

the entire area of a nuclear attack as a result of greatly accelerated wind and water erosion (Craft, 1964; Katz, 1966). A related concern is the accelerated loss to the area of minerals in solution, that is, of nutrient dumping. These insults to the geomass of an ecosystem will be especially pronounced while the region in question remains barren or sparsely vegetated. Moreover, the fires associated with the nuclear attack would aggravate these situations. Severe and extensive site degradation of these sorts could extend the time required for ecological recovery by many years or decades beyond what might be expected on the basis of past experience.

The damage to the geosphere just alluded to refers to its terrestrial fraction, sometimes called the lithosphere. The aquatic fraction, or hydrosphere, would also be subjected to some abuse. Unless it is a direct target (Glasstone, 1964: VI), the damage is, however, at a more modest level and is not further discussed here (see Nier *et al.*, 1975: 102–161).

Atmosphere

The question arises as to how a nuclear attack will alter the atmospheric conditions and thereby the weather.[9] It appears that the two most likely sources of ecological disturbance of the atmosphere would arise from the injection into the stratosphere[4] of dust particles (particulate aerosol) on the one hand, and of oxides of nitrogen (for example, NO, NO_2) on the other.

Surface bursts blast out huge craters. Some of the displaced material – perhaps 0.5 per cent of it (Nier *et al.*, 1975: 54) – is injected into the stratosphere as a fine dust. For a 0.91 Mt bomb, this would thus amount to perhaps 19×10^3 m^3 (50×10^6 kg) of material (Table 1.4). The stratospheric residence time of this dust would be up to several years. Such aerosol supplies condensation nuclei for cloud formation. It also acts as a partial barrier to radiation to and from the earth, both in its own right and as a result of the clouds formed.

One of the major volcanic eruptions within the past century occurred at Krakatoa Island, Indonesia (latitude 6° S), in August 1883. This event has been calculated to have introduced a dust veil into the stratosphere consisting of about 30×10^6 m^3 (80×10^9 kg) of fine tephra.[10] This stratospheric particulate aerosol contamination is claimed to have resulted in the lowering of temperatures in the mid latitudes of the southern hemisphere by possibly as much as 0.5°C, and in the mid latitudes of the northern by possibly as much as 0.2°C, these depressions diminishing to zero during a period of about 38 months (Lamb, 1970: 475, 519; Budyko, 1971: 444; see also Pollack *et al.*, 1976). A modest change in temperature can, of course, have some ecological ramifications.[11] The dust veil also had other modest atmospheric effects on a global scale that persisted for at least five years after the event (Ingersoll, 1963: II; 1964–1965; Meinel and Meinel, 1967).

About 1 600 0.91 Mt nuclear bombs detonated as surface bursts would introduce approximately as much fine particulate matter into the stratosphere as did Krakatoa. (Sub-surface bursts could reduce this number to about 130 (Table 1.4: note *e*).)

Aerial bursts generate immense amounts of several odd oxides of nitrogen. Some fraction of these chemical species finds its way into the lower stratosphere where it catalytically degrades the ozone (O_3) to ordinary oxygen gas (O_2). Such a depletion of the ozone layer permits, among other things, a greater fraction of the solar ultra-violet radiation to reach the earth, especially that biologically active portion in the wavelength range of approximately 280 nm to 315 nm (so-called UV-B) (Cutchis, 1974; Johnson, 1973).

It has been suggested that to destroy 50 per cent of the ozone layer of either the northern or the southern hemisphere would require the detonation of some 10^4 0.91 Mt bombs in the troposphere of that hemisphere, with recovery progressing at about 8 per cent per year (Bauer and Gilmore, 1975; Johnston et al., 1973; Nier et al., 1975: 42; Whitten and Borucki, 1975). If the bombs were detonated in the upper atmosphere, then a considerably lower number might be required to achieve the same level of effect (Hampson, 1974). A 50 per cent depletion in the ozone layer would increase the amount of ultra-violet radiation reaching the ground by a factor of three or more (Cutchis, 1974; Reid et al., 1976: 179). Under normal circumstances in the mid latitudes (and at any elevation below about 2 000 m), a similar increase in ultra-violet radiation would be achieved by shifting toward the equator by about 16° of latitude (ca. 1 800 km) (Cutchis, 1974). As to distance above sea level, there is virtually no effect on ultra-violet exposure in the biologically active range between 280 nm and 315 nm up to 1 500 m or so; above that elevation, exposure can be taken to increase by roughly 1 per cent per 100 m for at least the next 3 000 m (Caldwell, 1968).

Ultra-violet radiation (especially at wavelengths shorter than about 300 nm) has the ability to damage various macro-molecules such as deoxyribonucleic acid (DNA) and proteins, and thereby the cells and thus the organisms of which they are a part (Giese, 1964–1973; Urbach, 1969). Small organisms, especially micro-organisms are, by virtue of their surface-to-volume ratio, *potentially* more vulnerable to such damage than large ones. Moreover, fauna active in the open and during daytime are, by virtue of these habits, *potentially* more vulnerable than secretive and nocturnal ones. On the other hand, the small and the more exposed organisms for various other reasons are likely to be less prone to ultra-violet damage.

The ecological significance of ultra-violet enrichment of the environment has been considered, at least superficially, by a number of authors (Eigner, 1975; Hampson, 1974; Johnston, 1974 a, b; Nier et al., 1975; Reid et al., 1976; Ruderman, 1974). The impact would, of course, depend upon the level and duration of enrichment. On the basis of the largely hypothetical information currently available, it seems that tropospheric bursts totalling the 9×10^3 Mt discussed above would exert only a marginal influence on natural ecosystems via the transient ultra-violet enrichment of the environment that would result. This supposition finds some support in the researches of Caldwell (1968) with plants growing in the field under a modest diversity of ultra-violet regimes; and also in the reviews by Caldwell (1971) and Levitt (1972: 453–459). The possible impact of ambient ultra-violet enhancement on humans is noted below.

Biosphere

Ecological recovery of both the barren and partially destroyed areas resulting from a nuclear attack can be expected to soon begin. Indeed, some pertinent observations on such recolonization and subsequent succession are available from actual nuclear test sites. One of these is situated in the Mohave (Great Basin) Desert in Nevada (Allred *et al.*, 1965; Schultz, 1966). In addition to more than a dozen underground tests, this site was subjected over an eight-year period to at least 89 small above-ground detonations (the majority of them air bursts[5] averaging 10.1 kg each, and with the largest being 67.1 kg (Glasstone, 1964: 439, 671 ff). One is indebted to Shields and her colleagues for the following information (Rickard and Shields, 1963; Shields and Rickard, 1961; Shields and Wells, 1962; 1963; Shields *et al.*, 1963).

Initially each of the detonations had totally cleaned an area of all life, an area that ranged in size between 73 ha and 204 ha. Depending upon local site conditions (and presumably also on type of device, yield and type of burst), the original zone of complete or severe vegetational damage per detonation was roughly 400 ha to 1 375 ha in size. No evidence was detected of initial vegetational damage at any explosion site beyond an area of approximately 3 255 ha. The denuded central areas were invaded by pioneer species over a period of three to four years and the adjacent zones of severe damage also began their slow process of ecological recovery. So far as could be recognized, the subsequent pattern of succession was of the sort and rate to be expected in this desert region following any severe disturbance of the habitat, a process spanning many decades.

Biologists have also studied nuclear test sites in the tropical Pacific area (Berrill, 1966; Hines, 1962). As reported by Palumbo (1962) and Held (1960) for Eniwetok Island and by Fosberg (1959 a, b) for several islands in Rongelap Atoll and elsewhere, vegetational recovery from nuclear devastation seems to take its normal, here relatively rapid, successional course. In a study of the effect of radionuclides with particular reference to the omnivorous land crab *Coenobita perlatus* (Coenobitidae), Held (1960) noted that the population of this crab soon returned to normal following the nuclear testing on Eniwetok. Two years after testing, moreover, ^{90}Sr, ^{137}Cs and ^{144}Ce seemed to have established themselves permanently in the biogeochemical cycling involving *Coenobita*. Also on Eniwetok, Jackson (1969) was able to attribute the local extinction of the Polynesian rat (*Rattus exulans*; Muridae) to the nuclear testing there.

It seems from the above evidence that biotic recovery can be expected to more or less follow the normal patterns of ecological succession for the region in question. Unfortunately, the above picture may not be the whole story. For one thing, vegetational recovery will be hindered to the extent that seed sources are no longer available in a region, a function of the severity and geographical extent of the attack. Another serious concern is the question of ecosystem stability. The numerous plants and animals in a region differ widely in their relative radio-sensitivities as well as to the other insults of a nuclear attack. As a result, many subtle and some not so subtle imbalances could be created in the predator/prey, host/parasite, and endless other species interactions that form the very basis of an ecosystem. In particular, troubles might arise as a result of the relative radio-resistances exhibited by certain taxa such as the insects, bacteria and fungi – all of which are capable of causing mischief, both to man and nature.

It is rather difficult to prognosticate on the particulars of ecosystem stability following an attack, or rather on the lack of it. First of all, one is dealing with a system of pioneer communities, with their limited species diversity and notorious instability. Secondly, the considerations of relative radio- and other sensitivities mentioned earlier will be complicated by the different relative reproductive potentials of the species. Thirdly, animals have different feeding habits, and lie at different positions in the food web. The tendency for some radionuclides to become more concentrated as they work their way up this ladder will provide a disproportionate stress on the carnivores (including man) at the top. Thus, to generalize, one might expect the populations of the more specialized animals (specialized with respect to either their food or physical site requirements) to be most seriously affected initially and to recover their former status most slowly through the years.

The simplified, early-successional ecosystems that can be expected to establish themselves in a region subjected to nuclear attack will not only be relatively unstable for the reasons suggested, but will also be inferior because of their considerably reduced biomass. The biomass will be even lower than that predicted on the basis of experience with ecological recovery from disruption by non-nuclear means. Trees are in general more radio-sensitive than shrubs, high shrubs more than low shrubs, woody plants more than herbaceous plants, and angiosperms more than mosses and lichens (Sparrow *et al.*, 1971; Sparrow and Sparrow, 1965; Whicker and Fraley, 1974; Woodwell, 1967; Woodwell and Holt, 1971). A reduced biomass results in reduced ecosystem productivity, reduced, for example, by as much as 80 per cent in a change from forest to grassland.

Finally, it has been suggested that a nuclear attack involving about 9×10^3 Mt might depress global temperatures by several tenths of a degree Celsius, with recovery occurring over a period of several years (Nier *et al.*, 1975). There might thus also be some modest concomitant alteration in the amount of precipitation. This suggestion seems to be an exaggeration although, if true, a change in the weather of this magnitude could depress agricultural productivity, at least for some crops, by perhaps 1 per cent (note 12).

IV. Conclusion

Uncertainty may exist about the future likelihood of nuclear war. On the other hand, there is no doubt that nuclear weapons should be eliminated from the military arsenals of the world. Even the most modest and restrained nuclear initiative by one belligerent could well be countered in kind, this in turn perhaps leading to an escalating exchange. The USA and the USSR are said each to possess sufficient nuclear might to destroy not only each other, but all human life on earth. England, France, China, India and perhaps other nations possess more modest nuclear arsenals. Despite desultory negotiations in the face of the already existing overkill, the arms race between the USA and the USSR continues for ever more and better bombs, ever more and better delivery systems and ever more though largely illusory countermeasures (SIPRI, 1975 d; Scoville and Osborn, 1970; Epstein, 1976; SIPRI, 1974 b; York, 1970).

Even the very limited nuclear attacks by the United States during World War II had a profound impact on man, his artifacts and his social systems. The immediate social consequences of such attack, largely beyond the scope of this book, have been well captured by a number of eyewitnesses and other authors.[13] A word is in order, however, on the long-term effects on human health.

The subtle effects of nuclear war are of long duration, as the very thorough, continuing studies of the survivors of Hiroshima and Nagasaki have demonstrated (Miller, 1974; Blot and Miller, 1973; Wood *et al.*, 1967; Lifton, 1967; Okada *et al.*, 1975). The more important disorders that have been noted among those survivors include increased incidence of leukaemia, thyroid tumours, lenticular opacities and chromosomal aberrations in the peripheral blood lymphocytes. For the survivors who were infants at the time of the blasts, this list must be extended to include modest impairment in growth and development. For the survivors who were *in utero* at the time, it must be extended once again, this time to include microcephaly and mental retardation.

The Hiroshima and Nagasaki findings have found independent confirmation from the also very detailed and long-term studies of the survivors of the test detonation of the 13.6 Mt fission/fusion device of 1 March 1954 at Bikini that was described earlier. This event continues to take its human toll among the accidentally exposed group (Conard *et al.*, 1975). More than 100 persons unfortunately were within about 185 km of the detonation (23 on a fishing vessel and 89 on Rongelap Atoll) and were as a result exposed to roughly 0.2 kR of nuclear radiation from the early fall-out. Several deaths as well as a substantial number of tumours, some of them malignant, are attributable to this exposure. Included is an especially high frequency of thyroid tumours among those who were children or *in utero* at the time – and the number of these cases continues to rise.

US testing ended at Bikini and Eniwetok in 1958. In August 1975 the US Energy Research and Development Administration (successor to the US Atomic Energy Commission) found Bikini not yet habitable owing to the continued radioactive contamination of the drinking water and vegetation (Nordheimer, 1975). Two decades has, however, sufficed for Eniwetok (now Enewetak) to attain a presumably safe level (Wilford, 1977).

There has been some recent speculation on the effects on human health that a major nuclear exchange might have via atmospheric alterations of a widespread nature (Ahmed, 1975). One concern involves the increase in skin cancers that would result from ultra-violet enrichment of the environment owing to depletion of the stratospheric ozone layer. On the assumption that the geographical differences in non-melanoma skin cancer frequency reported by Scotto *et al.* (1974) are attributable to the normal latitudinal differences in ultra-violet intensity and on the basis of the correlation reported by Cutchis (1974) between the amount of stratospheric ozone and the intensity of ultra-violet radiation reaching the earth, Nier *et al.* (1975: 185–200) calculated that nuclear bursts in the troposphere of the northern hemisphere totalling 9×10^3 Mt would (assuming no avoidance behaviour) increase the normal frequency of skin cancers in that hemisphere by about 10 per cent, a value that would diminish to zero over the subsequent nine decades.[14]

The nuclear arms race is a danger even without war. Not only are natural resources squandered in the production of a nuclear arsenal, but the earth is subsequently polluted with worrisome amounts of radioactive isotopes during the manufacture and especially the testing of the weapons. Moreover, McPhee (1973) and Willrich and Taylor (1974), among others, have recently publicized the potential threat of nuclear weapons falling into the hands of irresponsible subnational groups or even individuals.

In closing, it must be reiterated that a major nuclear exchange must be avoided at all costs for it would have prohibitive consequences for both man and nature.

Notes to Chapter 1

1. There is a voluminous literature dealing with nuclear weapons and nuclear war. It runs the gamut from descriptive to theoretical, from scientific to polemical, from simple to complex and from accessible to unavailable. Glasstone (1964) provides the single most useful source for the technical aspects of nuclear weapons and their effects (another revision is in progress). See also the report by the Defense Civil Preparedness Agency (1973). For an excellent over-all summary of the effects of nuclear weapons and on the implications of their employment, see Vellodi et al. (1968). Other brief summaries are also available (ACDA, n.d., 1975?; Health, Education and Welfare, 1959 c; Brode, 1968). See also the bibliography by O'Callaghan (1973).

   Descriptions of the ecological impact of nuclear weapons and war are cited in note 8 and of the social impact in note 13.

2. Nuclear bombs are categorized according to their size, that is, energy yield, in terms of the yield of an equivalent weight of 2,4,6-trinitrotoluene (TNT). The energy yield (or 'heat of explosion') of TNT by definition is taken to be 4.615×10^6 J/kg (Kinney, 1962: 2). The kilotonne (kt) used here as a measure of nuclear bomb size thus designates an energy yield from 10^6 kg of 'defined' TNT or 4.615×10^{12} J; similarly, one megatonne (Mt) is in this context the equivalent of 10^9 kg of TNT releasing 4.615×10^{15} J. The S.I. prefixes 'k-' and 'M-' are employed here with 'tonne' in the context of nuclear weapons despite the inappropriateness of this procedure, owing to common usage.

   Unfortunately, the term 'kiloton' as used by the US Department of Defense and other US agencies is the equivalent of 0.907×10^6 kg of TNT (4.187×10^{12} J) and its 'megaton' of 0.907×10^9 kg of TNT (4.187×10^{15} J).

   Two basic categories of nuclear bombs exist: (1) the atomic bomb, which relies on the complete fission of about 64.8 g/kt of ^{235}U and/or ^{239}Pu; and (2) the hydrogen bomb, which relies on fission to trigger the fusion of H isotopes (for purposes of approximation, the yield of this latter bomb being considered to be half from fission and half from fusion). A bomb relying on the fission of ^{235}U is about 5 per cent efficient and thus contains about 1.30 kg/kt of fission yield whereas one relying on ^{239}Pu is about 15 per cent efficient and thus contains about 432 g/kt of fission yield (Vellodi et al., 1968: 54–55). The atomic bombs are usually in the kilotonne range, whereas the hydrogen bombs are usually in the megatonne but can also be in the kilotonne range. About 50 per cent of the energy yield of atomic bombs is released in the form of a blast (shock) wave, about 35 per cent as thermal radiation and the remaining 15 per cent as nuclear radiation (Table 1.1). The comparable values for hydrogen bombs are about 54.5 per cent, 38 per cent and 7.5 per cent, respectively.

The fission reaction of a nuclear bomb produces about 320×10^{21} fission fragments per kilotonne of fission yield (UNSCEAR, 1972: 57) weighing about 62.5 g (Glasstone, 1964: 417), these two values, it is assumed, referring to the situation 1 h after the detonation. On the basis of Avogadro's number (602×10^{21} particles/mol), the fission products per kilotonne of fission bomb after 1 h thus represent the equivalent of 531 mmol of a conglomerate of radioactive isotopes having an average mass number of 118. This mixture (the result of both fission and neutron activation) contains some 200 isotopes of about three dozen elements.

The fusion reaction of a hydrogen bomb results in an excess of between 10^{23} and 10^{24} atoms of ^3H per kilotonne of fusion yield (UNSCEAR, 1972: 57). Using the geometric mean of these two extremes, that is, 316×10^{21} and dividing this value by Avogadro's number as well as by the mass number (that is, 3), one arrives at 175 mg of ^3H per kilotonne of fusion yield.

To recapitulate, a 1 kt atomic (fission) bomb produces about 62.5 g of mixed fission products (that is, as determined 1 h after detonation). A 1 Mt hydrogen bomb ($\frac{1}{2}$ fission, $\frac{1}{2}$ fusion) produces about 31.25 kg of mixed fission products plus about 87.4 g of ^3H.

The numerous fission products of a nuclear bomb decay at greatly different rates. One hour after the detonation of an atomic (fission) bomb there are said to be 440 MCi/kt of fission yield (Shapiro, 1974: 6), that is, 7 055 MCi/kg of mixed fission products. The ^3H disseminated by a fusion reaction (with its half-life of 12.26 years) has a decay rate of 10.12 MCi/kg. Thus, 1 h after the detonation of a hydrogen bomb ($\frac{1}{2}$ fission, $\frac{1}{2}$ fusion) there would be 220 500 MCi/Mt from the mixed fission products plus about 976 kCi/Mt from the ^3H.

Most of the fission products are extremely short-lived. Their combined decay rate during the initial half year approximates a log/log linear curve having a slope of -1.2; thereafter the over-all decay rate becomes even more rapid, following a new log/log linear curve of slope -2.3 (Glasstone, 1964: 420). In other words, 50 per cent of the fission products present at 1 h after detonation have disappeared about 1.78 h after detonation, 90 per cent about 6.81 h after detonation, 99 per cent about 46.4 h after detonation and 99.9 per cent about 316 h (13.2 d) after detonation. About 42.6 parts per million (ppm) remain after half a year and about 8.66 ppm after one year. One hundred days after detonation is sometimes used as a reference point. If what remains at 100 d (that is, 87.85 ppm of the 1 h value) is taken as 100 per cent, then 48.5 per cent remains half a year after detonation and 9.86 per cent remains one year after detonation.

These decay parameters can also be expressed more directly in relation to the nuclear bombs themselves. For a fission bomb, the 440 MCi/kt that obtains at 1 h has decayed to 38.7 kCi/kt after 100 d and to 3.81 kCi/kt after one year. (Thus, at 100 d there are 620 kCi/kg of original fission products.) For a hydrogen bomb, the 220 500

MCi/Mt of mixed fission products obtaining at 1 h have decayed to 19.4 MCi/Mt after 100 d and to 1.91 MCi/Mt after one year. The latter bomb's 976 kCi/Mt of ^{3}H present at 1 h decays to 960 kCi/Mt after 100 d and to 922 kCi/Mt after one year. On the other hand, a small but biologically important group of fission products is rather long-lived (that is, with half-lives measurable in years), including ^{90}Sr and ^{137}Cs.

Three bomb sizes are often used in the present text for purposes of illustration: 18 kt $(88.736 \times 10^{12}$ J$)$, 0.91 Mt $(4.187 \times 10^{15}$ J$)$ and 9.1 Mt $(41.868 \times 10^{15}$ J$)$. These are equivalent to 20 'kilotons', 1 'megaton' and 10 'megatons', respectively, in common US terminology. The 18 kt bomb used is a fission bomb whereas the 0.91 Mt and 9.1 Mt bombs are half fission and half fusion. When air bursts are given, these refer to so-called typical air bursts[5].

3. Of the 14.3×10^9 kg of conventional munitions expended by the USA during the Second Indochina War, it can be estimated that 74 per cent contained high explosives; for this fraction an explosive content of 35 per cent is estimated. One can thus calculate an explosive energy yield[2] for that war of approximately 3.7 Mt. Expenditures by the other side would add an insignificant amount to this value, of the order of 0.01 Mt.

4. The earth's atmosphere extends upward very roughly 150 km. It is divided into the lower atmosphere, which represents more than 99 per cent of the atmospheric mass, and the upper atmosphere with less than 1 per cent of the mass. In the concentric atmospheric spheres given below the paranthetically noted altitudinal bands can only be given as rough approximations since the values vary appreciably with both latitude and season.

The lower atmosphere (ca. 0–55 km) is divided into the troposphere (ca. 0–12 km), which represents more than 87 per cent of the atmospheric mass, and the stratosphere (ca. 12–55 km), about 12 per cent of the mass. The stratosphere, in turn, can be divided into the lower stratosphere (ca. 12–30 km) and the upper stratosphere (ca. 30–55 km).

Some ozone is found throughout the atmosphere, its over-all average concentration being 635 μg/kg (820 μg/m^3). Thus, at 0°C and 101 kPa, i.e., at 'standard' temperature and pressure (STP), the atmospheric ozone would constitute a band with an average thickness of about 3.1 mm. The atmospheric ozone is not distributed evenly, but is found largely in the lower stratosphere, indeed, largely within a so-called ozone layer (ca. 20–30 km) in which the atmospheric concentration of ozone is up to a hundred times the over-all average.

The upper atmosphere (ca. 55–150 km) is divided into the mesosphere (ca. 55–80 km) and the ionosphere (= thermosphere) (ca. 80–150 km).

The charged high-energy particles comprising the Van Allen belt (= magnetosphere) (ca. 250–25 000 km) are well above the atmosphere.

5. The explosion of a nuclear bomb is classed as an air burst when it occurs within the lower atmosphere (see note 4), but at an altitude sufficiently high that its fireball does not touch the earth's surface. For an 18 kt bomb, this minimum altitude is 186 m, for a 0.91 Mt bomb it is 853 m and for a 9.1 Mt bomb it is 2 195 m (Glasstone, 1964: 79).

The optimal height for an air burst – a so-called typical air burst – is within the troposphere,[4] varying with bomb size. A 'typical' air burst of an 18 kt bomb is at an altitude of 564 m, for a 0·91 Mt bomb it is at 2 077 m and for a 9·1 Mt bomb it is at 4 476 m (Glasstone, 1964: 114, 127, 638). Air bursts in the present text are these 'typical' ones.

6. The likelihood, extent and consequences of fires brought about by nuclear attack have been dealt with by Glasstone (1964: VII), Broido (1960; 1963), Chandler *et al.*

(1963), Craft (1964), Defense Civil Preparedness Agency (1973: III), Hill (1961), Huschke (1966), Ayres (1965: Vol. I:II) and others. See also Chapter 3.

7. The data presented have been estimated by Woodwell and Sparrow (1963). Seemingly comparable measurements by Platt (1963) for similar ecosystems have yielded values up to twice as high. However, the data used here have more recently been confirmed by Woodwell and Holt (1971). They also find support in related data provided by Sparrow *et al.* (1971). The coniferous forest value is supported by OKunewick (1966). Whicker and Fraley (1974) agree with the coniferous and temperate dicotyledonous values presented, but suggest that the grassland value should be 100 kR. They add that to destroy tropical rain forest would require 40 kR; and to destroy a moss–lichen community would require 500 kR.

8. The ecological impact of nuclear weapons or war has been reviewed by Ayres (1965), Eberhardt (1967), Glass (1962), Hollister and Eberhardt (1965), Mitchell (1961), Nier *et al.* (1975), Osburn (1968), Platt (1963), Stonier (1964: XI–XII), Wolfe (1959), Woodwell (1963), Woodwell and Holt (1971), Woodwell and Sparrow (1963), Wurtz (1963) and others (see also Parker and Healy, 1955; Whicker and Fraley, 1974).

   For the relationship of nuclear weapons or war to fire, see note 6; for the relationship to weather, see note 9.

9. The impact of nuclear weapons on the weather has been discussed by Ayres (1965: Vol. I: III), Batten (1966), Mason (1955), Nier *et al.* (1975: 24–63), Stonier (1964: XII) and others. See also the bibliography by O'Callaghan (1973). The manipulation of rainfall for hostile purposes is described in Chapter 3.

10. The amount of fine tephra (particulate aerosol ejecta) that in August 1883 was introduced by Krakatoa into the atmosphere or, more to the point here, into the stratosphere[4] is not known with any degree of accuracy. The very few more-or-less independent modern estimates follow. A number of other values have been published in the last several years, but these all seem to be either derivations or misderivations of one or more of those noted here. A density of 2 650 kg/m^3 is assumed (Lutz and Chandler, 1946: 236; Daly *et al.*, 1966).

    To begin with, Lamb (1970: 475, 519; priv. comm., 26 Feb. 1976) estimates that the total amount of fine tephra injected into the *atmosphere* as a whole was about 6×10^9 m (16×10^{12} kg). Mitchell (1970: 146; priv. comm., 27 Feb. 1976) estimates that the amount injected into the *stratosphere* alone was 19×10^6 m^3 (50×10^9 kg). And Deirmendjian (1973: 293; priv. comm., 8 Mar. 1976) estimates the stratospheric injection as having been 30×10^6 m^3 (80×10^9 kg). Deirmendjian's value is adopted here as the most reliable one currently available.

11. Some idea of the ecological impact of *sustained* temperature differentials can be obtained by comparing natural ecosystems along extended north–south transects; or, alternatively, at different altitudes without change in latitude. Air temperature drops more or less uniformly with increasing altitude within the troposphere at a rate that averages 6.4°C/km (Strahler, 1975: 105). By way of comparison, the mean July temperature in the northern hemisphere decreases as one travels northward by roughly 0·58°C per degree of north latitude (or 5.3°C per 1 000 km) (after *Times*, 1968: Plate 5). In order words, a rise in altitude of about 91 m provides a decrease in average summer air temperature comparable to a northward move of 1° of latitude (that is, a rise in altitude of about 820 m is in this respect the equivalent of a northward shift of 1 000 km).

    The following additional data are derived from those of Spurr and Barnes (1973: 96–97) and find support in those of Lutz and Chandler (1946: 267–268). In the eastern USA, a 1°C change in average annual air temperature is achieved by shifting due north or south by 00° 54' of latitude, that is, by 100 km. The same change can be achieved by shifting up or down by 183 m of elevation. In the western USA, a 1°C change in average annual air temperature is achieved by shifting due north or south by 01° 17' of latitude, that is, by 143 km. The same change can be achieved by shifting up or down by 157 m of elevation.

For information on the extent to which modest changes in temperature (and of precipitation) influence agricultural productivity, see note 12.

12. The impact of changes in normal weather (precipitation and temperature) on agricultural productivity has been investigated in some detail. For a recent description of the subject, see Thompson (1975), who has been among those in the forefront of this field (Thompson, 1969 a, b; 1970). McQuigg (1975) has prepared a well annotated bibliography on the subject. Three mid-latitude examples will suggest the magnitudes of change to be expected in agricultural productivity as a result of modest and transitory changes in the weather. More drastic effects could be expected locally, especially at the limits of a crop's range or under otherwise marginal conditions.

In the central United States, a 10 mm drop in July rainfall will decrease the yield of corn (*Zea mays*; Gramineae) by about 95 kg/ha (Thompson, 1969 a; see also Runge, 1969–1970). At a yield of 5 375 kg/ha (the US corn belt average for 1967), this represents a decline of 1.8 per cent. A 1°C decrease from the optimal temperature during any month of the growing season will result in essentially no change in yield (unless it occurs during the first month). On the other hand, a similar increase will decrease yield between 100 kg/ha and 200 kg/ha, depending upon the month, that is, by 1.9 to 3.7 per cent.

In the central United States, a 10 mm drop in either July or August rainfall will decrease the yield of soybeans (*Glycine max*; Leguminosae) by about 35 kg/ha (Thompson, 1970). At a yield of 1 800 kg/ha (the approximate central states average for 1967) this represents a decline of 1.9 per cent. A 1°C decrease from the optimal temperature during July will decrease yield by about 45 kg/ha, that is, by 2.5 per cent. A similar increase of 1°C will decrease the yield even more, by about 80 kg/ha, that is, by 4.4 per cent.

The carrying capacity of range lands (grasslands) is also affected by precipitation. The following data are derived from those of Chapline and Cooperrider (1941) for the western United States. From about 200 mm to 600 mm of annual precipitation (normal for grasslands), every additional 44 mm of annual precipitation provides forage for one additional cow (*Bos taurus*; Bovidae) per 100 ha. At an annual precipitation of 400 mm, these range lands can support 6.37 cows/100 ha. A 10 mm decrease in the annual precipitation reduces this value by 0.225 cow/100 ha, that is, by 3.5 per cent.

Modest changes in the weather can also influence the incidence of diseases and insect attack of crops, forest trees, and other plants (Foister, 1935; Graham, 1956: 262–265; Hepting, 1963; Valli, 1966), of livestock and other animals (Smith, 1970), and of humans (Sargent and Tromp, 1964). See also Chapter 3.

For information on how the temperature changes with latitude or altitude, see note 11.

13. The social or human impact of nuclear weapons or war has been reviewed many times. The damage caused by the 13 kt and 21 kt nuclear-fission air bursts over Hiroshima and Nagasaki, respectively has been well captured by Siemes (1946–1947), Hersey (1946), Hachiya (1955), Nagai (1951), Liebow (1965–1966) and D'Olier et al. (1946), among others. Vellodi et al. (1968) have prepared a succinct summary of these World War II data. They also describe the probable impact of a 1 Mt ground burst on a real (though unnamed) city of 1.2×10^6 inhabitants and go on to outline the probable

effects of other, more extensive attacks. The postulated short-term consequences of 18 Mt ground or air bursts in the middle of New York City have been vividly described – in brief by the Scientists' Committee for Radiation Information (1962) and at some length by Stonier (1963). Ervin *et al.* (1962) have provided a similar discussion for Boston from a somewhat different perspective. Holifield (1959) gathered much information on what might result from a 3 580 Mt attack on the USA and its overseas bases (with all of the bombs detonated at ground level; each half fission and half fusion). Commoner (1966: V) speculates briefly on the impact of nuclear war. Stonier (1964) provides an extended scenario as a follow-up of his earlier article (Stonier, 1963). York (1975) explains the ease with which Europe would be destroyed by a nuclear exchange between the NATO and Warsaw Pact nations. And a detailed description of what a nuclear attack would do to West Germany has been compiled (Weizsäcker, 1971).

The single most useful source of technical information is by Glasstone (1964). Recovery after an attack has been covered by a number of authors (Wigner *et al.*, 1969; Health, Education and Welfare, 1959 c; Defense Civil Preparedness Agency, 1973) and a number of partially relevant bibliographies exist (Popper and Lybrand, 1960; Rayner, 1957–1958; Quarantelli, 1970).

Post-attack problems of an immediate nature are examined by Aronow *et al.* (1963). The likelihood of plague epidemics following nuclear attack is assessed by Mitchell (1966). Various long-range problems of human health following nuclear war, especially those deriving from nuclear radiation, have been examined numerous times (Edvarson, 1975; Ervin *et al.*, 1962; Glass, 1962; Glasstone, 1964: VIII–XII; Nier *et al.*, 1975: 162–212; Schubert and Lapp, 1957; Arena, 1971; UNSCEAR, 1972; Vellodi *et al.*, 1968; Wood *et al.*, 1967; Miller, 1974; Conard *et al.*, 1975; Okada *et al.*, 1975).

Effects on agriculture and questions of post-attack recovery have been brought together in greatest detail by Bensen and Sparrow (1971). A number of additional sources of such information also exist (Ayres, 1965: Vol. II; Fowler, 1965; Katz, 1966; National Academy of Sciences *et al.*, 1968; Nier *et al.*, 1975: 80–101; Slater *et al.*, 1960; Sparrow *et al.*, 1971).

Finally, attention should be drawn to the very powerful film *The War Game* by Watkins (1966) which depicts the presumed results of a nuclear attack on an industrial city. Moreover, and its shortcomings notwithstanding (Inglis, 1968; Shapiro, 1974), one can further recommend the fictional account by Shute (1957) of what might well be the aftermath of some major nuclear exchange of the future, especially one employing 'dirty' bombs and techniques.

14. Scotto *et al.* (1974) seem to provide the best published data that permit an analysis of the probable relationship between the incidence of human skin cancer and level of ultra-violet radiation exposure as the latter relates to latitude. Their data on non-melanoma skin cancer frequency among US Caucasians are presented in the table below.

A first-order equation least-squares regression analysis can be performed correlating the logarithm of the annual number of cases with the secant of the latitude. The log transformation is done on the basis of Cutchis (1974) and Reid *et al.* (1976: 179). The secant transformation is done on the basis of the ultra-violet shielding effect of the atmospheric ozone (Cutchis, 1974). No correction is made for altitude on the basis of Caldwell (1968: 251). Although the correlation is weak ($r^2 = 0.70$), the data suggest that there is an average increase of 168 cases per 10^6 year per degree shift toward the equator (that is, 1.51 cases/km) in the latitudinal range of 45° to 30°.

Recently, Scotto *et al.* (1976: 6) have published data on the annual accumulation

Table 1.14. Frequencies of non-melanoma skin cancer among US Caucasians

Location	Latitude	Average altitude (m)	Cases per 10^6 per year
Dallas–Fort Worth Texas	32° 46′ N	170	3790
San Francisco–Oakland California	37° 47′ N	200	1840
[Des Moines] Iowa	41° 35′ N	290	1240
Minneapolis–Saint Paul Minnesota	44° 58′ N	260	1510

Note:
The cancer data are from Scotto *et al.* (1974).

of ultra-violet radiation reportedly in the wavelength range causing erythaema (sunburn), and thus presumably also cancer, for essentially the above four locations. Their data follow (given in units of which about four are said to produce erythaema of typical Caucasian skin): Fort Worth, 16 059; Oakland, 15 086; Des Moines, 12 516; and Minneapolis, 10 650. Unfortunately, a regression analysis comparable to the one done above, in this instance of log of number of cases versus annual ultra-violet exposure, does not show as good a relationship ($r^2 = 0.60$), and this despite a very close correlation between ultra-violet level and secant of latitude ($r^2 = 0.97$).

Thus, although these data suggest a relationship between skin cancer and ultra-violet exposure, they are not by themselves fully convincing.

2. Chemical and biological weapons

Superior numerals, thus [5], refer to notes on pages 46–48.

I. Introduction

Chemical warfare refers to the military use of chemical agents for hostile purposes; biological warfare refers to the use of living organisms, usually micro-organisms, for such purposes. The utility of these agents as weapons depends upon their toxicity, pathogenicity or deteriorating abilities.[1] Chemical or biological agents can be directed against enemy personnel, against their livestock or crops, against their natural eco-systems or even against their *matériel*.

In the present chapter are presented a brief history of chemical and biological warfare, descriptions of the agents involved in such warfare and discussions of the ecological consequences of their use. Chemical anti-plant agents are dealt with at length elsewhere (SIPRI, 1976 a) and are therefore not covered here. Nor is the use of larger animals, such as various insects (Ambrose, 1973, 1974; Beck, 1937) and cetaceans (Wallace, 1973), which have been considered for military purposes, since the environmental ramifications are relatively minor.

II. Description

History

Throughout military history, there are numerous minor examples of chemical warfare and even some of biological warfare.[1] However, chemical weapons were not employed on a grand scale until World War I (note 2), and then not again massively until the Second Indochina War. The former instance is outlined below, the latter elsewhere (SIPRI, 1976 a). Fortunately, there has so far been no large-scale use of biological weapons.

During World War I, large quantities of chemical agents of a wide diversity were employed by the several belligerents. No less than 45 agents have been listed: 18 lethal ones (of which 14 were lung agents and

31

4 were dermal agents) and 27 classed as harassing agents (SIPRI, 1971 a: I). The combined World War I expenditure of these chemicals was well over 100×10^6 kg, with dose rates in some localities that eventually must have exceeded 100 kg/ha.

Among the most heavily used chemicals during World War I were four harassing agents (xylyl bromide, benzyl bromide, bromoacetone and ethyl iodoacetate), four lethal lung agents (chlorine, phosgene, trichloromethyl chloroformate and chloropicrin), and one lethal dermal agent (mustard gas or bis[2-chloroethyl]sulphide). Many of these agents are today obsolete.

There appear to be no studies or even observations of the impact that the World War I chemicals had on the animals or plants of Europe or, indeed, on any of the involved ecosystems. However, their impact on the enmeshed fauna (at least its mammalian component) must have been great, to judge from the enormous human toll taken by these chemicals, despite the evasive and protective measures taken by the combatants. Chemical warfare during World War I is known to have produced 1.3×10^6 casualties, of which 10^5 were fatal. Epstein *et al.* (1969: 71) mention that the regions in question were half a century later in normal and fully productive use. However, only a most detailed examination would reveal any subtle, long-term ecosystem debilitation that might have occurred so long after the fact.

Anti-personnel agents

A wide array of chemical and biological weapons could exist in the military repertoires of at least the major powers (Army and Air Force, 1965, 1967; SIPRI, 1973 b). The anti-personnel agents are covered in the present section, whereas those other than anti-personnel are left to the next one.

The chemical anti-personnel agents are usually separated according to their approximate level of toxicity into 'harassing', 'incapacitating' and 'lethal'. However, the actual level of danger of any particular agent depends upon its manner of application, the concentration employed and the nature or condition of the recipient. The lethal-agent category is usually further divided on the basis of primary physiological action. Thus there are the 'nerve' agents that attack the nervous system, the 'blood' agents that poison the blood, the 'lung' or 'respiratory' agents that asphyxiate, and the 'dermal' or 'cutaneous' agents that blister the skin. The chemical agents of biotic origin (as opposed to those that are synthesized in the laboratory) are generally classed by themselves irrespective of their mode of action.

The biological anti-personnel agents of potential utility are meant for dissemination as live organisms and are most often divided according to their taxonomic position rather than to their degree of toxicity or mode of action. Thus there are assumed to exist a variety of viral, rickettsial, bacterial, fungal and even protozoan agents.

Various factors influence the military usefulness of chemical and biological weapons. Whether or not any one of these factors is considered strategically or tactically favourable depends upon the military and political situations and perhaps also upon one's individual perspective. First of all, despite the wide diversity of known or suspected chemical and biological agents, it appears that most can be formulated for delivery as a gas or else as an aerosol (that is, as a suspension in air of ultra-fine liquid or solid particles). Secondly, overt delivery can be via projectile (grenade, shell, bomb, missile or the like) or via spray equipment (mounted on vehicles, ships or aircraft). Covert delivery by saboteur can take a variety of forms.

It is well within present military capabilities to attack an area hundreds if not thousands of hectares in size. Moreover, the production of at least some of the agents is inexpensive in comparison with alternative weapons of comparable impact. Chemical and biological munitions also weigh less than their conventional counterparts, a factor of some logistical importance. For at least some of the agents, the extent of their production and stockpiling and even of their testing can be kept secret with relative ease.

Among the possible chemical and biological agents there are some for which neither an effective warning system nor an effective system of defence seems feasible. Thus, in addition to their physiological impact, these agents could instill terror in an enemy. Still another attribute to consider is that the action of a number of agents is delayed for hours or even days. Finally, the effectiveness of their delivery and of their potency depend in some instances rather heavily on the prevailing meteorological conditions.

Agents other than anti-personnel

A variety of chemical and biological anti-animal, anti-plant and anti-*matériel* agents can be imagined, and some may have been used. Livestock or other animals could be attacked with a number of presumably available agents.[3] Many of the chemical agents categorized as anti-personnel agents could be employed for this purpose. Even a biological attack on livestock might involve an anti-personnel agent, for example,

Bacillus anthracis (Bacillaceae), discussed below. However, Epstein *et al.* (1969: 46) enumerate 16 biological agents that seem especially suited for use against domestic animals, nine of them viral, two rickettsial, three bacterial and two fungal.

Attacks on an enemy's crops or other vegetation of use to him have, of course, become a matter of recent military history.[4] Biological attacks on crop plants are also feasible. Indeed, Epstein *et al.* (1969: 47) list 13 likely candidates, five viral, three bacterial and five fungal. Their tabulation includes serious diseases of rice (*Oryza sativa;* Gramineae), corn (*Zea mays;* Gramineae), wheat (*Triticum vulgare;* Gramineae) and potato (*Solanum tuberosum;* Solanaceae). Moreover, there appears to be no reason why such economic crops as cotton (*Gossypium hirsutum;* Malvaceae), coffee (*Coffea arabica;* Rubiaceae), rubber (*Hevea brasiliensis;* Euphorbiaceae) or sugar cane (*Saccharum officinarum;* Gramineae) might not also be similarly singled out for destruction.

Although most chemical and biological agents leave an enemy's *matériel* unscathed, some do not. Chemical agents are said to exist that have the purpose of destroying equipment and other artifacts of use to the enemy. Thomas and Thomas (1970: 16) suggest the existence of anti-lubricant agents that would cause equipment to break down (see also Gravel *et al.*, 1971–1972: I: 579). Moreover, during the Second Indochina War, the USA is alleged to have disseminated chemicals over North Vietnam for the purpose of fouling up ('attenuating') the radars the enemy used for aiming its defensive surface-to-air missiles (Hersh, 1972). Furthermore, the USA recently admitted to having considered during that war the dropping of emulsifying agents onto unpaved Laotian roads in order to make them impassable (Pell, 1974: 123).

III. Ecological consequences

General

The ecological consequences of chemical or biological warfare can run the gamut from inconsequential to disastrous. Five more or less arbitrarily chosen possibilities are explored below. The first of these cases involves chemical harassing agents and uses 'CS' (*o*-chlorobenzalmalononitrile) as an example, leaning especially upon experience from the Second Indochina War. The remaining four cases are more speculative, since these agents apparently have not yet been employed for hostile military purposes: 'VX' (*S*-(2-diisopropylaminoethyl) *O*-ethyl methyl phosphonothiolate) as an example of lethal synthetics; botulinal toxin as an example of naturally occurring lethal chemicals; the bacterium causing anthrax as an example of micro-organisms as biological agents; and the virus causing yellow fever as an example of viruses as biological agents.

In these examples, a whole host of esoteric chemical and bizarre biological possibilities is ignored as well as the synergistic impact that might be achieved from the simultaneous applications of different agents. However, the general nature of the impact of this class of weapons will be suggested by the cases outlined.

Chemical harassing agents

A number of non-lethal, harassing agents are to be found today in the military (and police) arsenals of the world, among them 'CN' or 'mace' (ω-chloroacetophenone), 'DM' or 'adamsite' (10-chloro-5,10-dihydrophenarsazine), and 'CS' (*o*-chlorobenzalmalononitrile) (Army and Air Force, 1967). CS in one form or another appears to be the harassing agent of current military preference.[5] It results in militarily significant harassment of unprotected personnel at a particulate aerosol concentration in the atmosphere somewhat above 1 mg/m^3. Used at this level, CS induces intense lacrimation (crying), sternutation (sneezing) and irritation of the upper respiratory tract.

A tactical innovation of the Second Indochina War was the employment by the USA of CS1 (a finely pulverized form of CS) for protracted area denial (Blumenfeld and Meselson, 1971). An especially non-degradable form – CS2 – was developed in 1968 for this use. Whereas the application of CS1 can render an area inhospitable for perhaps 15 days (Army, 1969: 16), that of CS2 will do so for 30 to 45 days (Cannon, 1971: 146). Precise durations depend, of course, on such factors as initial level of application and subsequent rainfall.

Although the US Department of Defense has released no information on US expenditures of CS in Indochina, one can at least gain an indication of their magnitude from the procurement figures available for the war years (Table 2.1). The total quantity of CS overtly procured by the US Department of Defense during this time amounted to about 9×10^6 kg, about four fifths of this in bulk form and the remainder directly incorporated into munitions. About 30 per cent of the total was in the more persistent CS2 form.

Table 2.1. US procurement of CS gas during the Second Indochina War period: a breakdown by type and year

Fiscal year	Quantity of CS procured (10^3 kg)					
	CS in bulk	CS1 in bulk	CS2 in bulk	CS in munitions	CS1 in munitions	Total
1961–62	?	?	0	?	?	?
1962–63	?	?	0	?	?	?
1963–64	102	64	0	106	?	272
1964–65	42	83	0	42	?	167
1965–66	171	552	0	0	4	727
1966–67	198	349	0	797	26	1 371
1967–68	324	1 474	131	350	6	2 284
1968–69	915	73	1 762	351	26	3 127
1969–70	0	161	830	58	13	1 062
1970–71	0	0	0	33	8	41
1971–72	?	?	?	?	?	?
1972–73	?	?	?	?	?	?
Total	**1 753**	**2 755**	**2 723**	**1 737**	**83**	**9 052**

Notes:

(a) As far as possible, the above data are derived from those of Fulbright (1972: 307); values not obtainable from this source are derived to the extent possible from those of Mahon (1969: 124); values not obtainable from either of these sources are derived from those of McCarthy (1969 a: 15765). Amounts of CS contained in the munitions are from the Army (1969: II); amounts not obtainable from this source are derived to the extent possible from the Army (1967); amounts not obtainable from either of these sources are from the US Army (priv. comm., 17 Jun. 1974).

(b) Missing procurement data have not been released by the US Department of Defense.

(c) Information on CS expenditures in Indochina has never been released by the US Department of Defense.

(d) 'CS' is the code name for *o*-chlorobenzalmalononitrile. 'CS1' refers to a finely pulverized (micronized) form of CS, whereas 'CS2' is a powder that has been treated to make it water-repellent and thus less rapidly degradable under field conditions.

The level of CS application considered necessary by the military to achieve satisfactory area interdiction appears to have fallen somewhere between 1 kg/ha and 10 kg/ha. The quantity procured was therefore sufficient to interdict at one time or another during the course of the war between 1×10^6 ha and 9×10^6 ha of Indochina. Although at least some CS was employed against each of the four Indochinese countries, most of it was expended against South Vietnam, an area of 17×10^6 ha.

It appears reasonable to assume that the CS so liberally applied to the South Vietnamese environment had no major ecological effects inasmuch as none has been reported in the literature. More subtle effects could, of course, have escaped attention. These would hinge upon the toxicity of CS to the various biota exposed to it during the several weeks of the chemical's existence following its field application; and on this subject, a certain amount of information is available. To begin with, it appears that CS harasses and is toxic to the warm-blooded vertebrates at roughly the same levels as for man. For example, Punte *et al.* (1962) found that rats (*Rattus rattus;* Muridae), mice (*Mus musculus;* Muridae) and pigeons (*Columba livia;* Columbidae) were only slightly more resistant than man to CS via inhalation, whereas guinea-pigs (*Cavia porcellus;* Caviidae) and rabbits (*Oryctolagus cuniculus;* Leporidae) were somewhat more sensitive. Chickens (*Gallus gallus;* Phasianidae) are somewhat less irritated by a given level of CS aerosol exposure than are humans. At least the mammalian toxicity of CS is partially attributable to its conversion *in vivo* to cyanide (Frankenberg and Sörbo, 1973).

With respect to CS contamination of the aquatic habitat, Ward (1973) has reported that the common killifish (*Fundulus heteroclitus;* Cyprinodontidae) is killed by 4 g/m^3 in the ambient water (50 per cent mortality within 96 h, i.e., 96 h LC_{50}), and that the duckweed *Wolffia papulifera* (Lemnaceae) is injured by concentrations of 5 g/m^3 and killed by 100 g/m^3, concentrations not likely to be achieved in the field.

CS also appears to be somewhat toxic to terrestrial vegetation, injury to trees having been reported following their exposure during a civil riot-control operation (Cockrell, 1971). Various different compounds chemically related to CS have been reported to have herbicidal, fungicidal, insecticidal or nematocidal properties (Jones, 1972), and these attributes may well be shared to a greater or lesser extent by CS.

There is little doubt that CS causes at least mild and transient ecological perturbation. It is therefore entirely feasible that such ecological debilitation could become a serious concern of the future if chemical area denial were carried out with agents more toxic or more persistent than CS2.

Lethal synthetics

Among the highly poisonous substances that are assumed to be synthesized and stockpiled for use as agents of chemical warfare are phosgene (carbonyl chloride), hydrogen cyanide, mustard gas (bis[2-chloroethyl]-sulphide), 'GB' or 'sarin' (isopropyl methylphosphonofluoridate) and 'VX' (S-(2-diisopropylaminoethyl) O-ethyl methyl phosphonothiolate). The last is one of a family of extraordinarily lethal organophosphorus compounds – the so-called V agents – stumbled upon by chemists during the mid 1950s in their search for better insecticides (and whose chemical structure has recently been made public (Sidell and Groff, 1974)).[6]

The V agents are singled out for brief discussion since they, and especially VX, are often considered the most important of the lethal synthetic chemical warfare agents. Kaplan et al. (1970) have calculated that, depending upon method of dispersal and weather conditions, an area of 400 ha to 4 000 ha could be subjected to a human lethal dose of VX by the 4×10^3 kg payload of a single aircraft. Epstein et al. (1969) discuss the possibility of similar chemical attacks covering 5 000 ha or more. Marriott (1969) claims that a single tactical US 'sergeant' missile with a 726 kg payload of VX will produce at least a 33 per cent casualty rate over a target area of 200 ha.

VX and its relatives are said to be essentially colourless, odourless and non-volatile liquids that lend themselves well to military aerosol dispersion. Entry of organophosphorus compounds of this sort is especially hazardous via inhalation (Hartwell and Hayes, 1965), but is also possible and highly dangerous via the skin (Fredricksson, 1961), making protective action most difficult to carry out. Indeed, a dermal application of less than 10 mg of VX is said to be lethal (Kaplan et al., 1970: 40). The primary mode of toxic action of the V agents is the rapid inhibition of the enzyme acetylcholinesterase, essential for the transmission of nerve impulses.

Although very little direct information is available on the V agents, their ecological impact might be similar to that of the organophosphorus insecticides with which they share anti-cholinesterase activity (Fest and Schmidt, 1973). The most important of the commercial organophosphorus insecticides is 'parathion' (O,O-diethyl O-p-nitrophenyl phosphorothioate). Great precautions must be taken in applying parathion and its relatives in order to avoid medical disasters (Barnes et al., 1957). Indeed, there is much controversy over their routine use in agriculture.

Information available on the organophosphorus insecticides[6] makes it clear that if the nerve agents were used in an attack at levels lethal to personnel, they would simultaneously destroy the other exposed non-human vertebrates. They would also kill many of the invertebrates, particularly various of the arthropods. On the other hand, the exposed vegetation, although it would absorb the agents, would largely be spared, it seems. However, exposed plants would for a time provide a secondary source of contamination for the herbivores feeding on them (Mulla et al., 1966). In fact, it has been reported that vegetation accidentally contaminated with VX continued to be a danger to sheep (Ovis aries; Bovidae) for at least three weeks (Boffey, 1968).

Based on what is known from investigations involving parathion and similar organophosphorus insecticides, neither environmental persistence nor ecological (food chain) concentration would be expected to be particular problems with the V agents, particularly in terrestrial ecosystems. Keith (1969), however, suggests that the avian insectivores, at least, would secondarily ingest lethal levels of such agents by preferentially feeding on the readily available dead and weakened arthropods. He is convinced that there is a high incidence of generally unrecognized organophosphorus poisoning of wildlife associated with the use of parathion and similar insecticides. Moreover, the danger to contaminated aquatic habitats might be somewhat higher than to terrestrial ones (Mulla *et al.*, 1966).

It is clear that an attack with V agents, while it probably will not have a long-term residual effect, would result in an immediate zoological catastrophe. This can become a matter of serious concern if the attack extends over hundreds or even thousands of hectares, as well as it might.

Natural toxins

A number of naturally occurring substances are proposed from time to time as candidates for development as agents of chemical warfare. Most of these are antigenic proteins, and they can range in toxicity from temporarily incapacitating to highly lethal.[7]

Botulinal toxin appears to head the list of natural poisons. However, the list also includes the enterotoxins obtained from *Staphylococcus* spp. (Micrococcaceae), ricin (found in castor beans, the fruit of *Ricinus communis* (Euphorbiaceae)), abrin (found in the seeds of the Indian licorice or jequirity bean (*Abrus precatorius*; Fabaceae)), cicutoxin (found in the roots of the European water hemlock (*Cicuta virosa*; Umbelliferae)) and phallin (from the death cup, the basidiomycete *Amanita phalloides* (Agaricaceae)). The toxins or venoms to be obtained from certain snakes (Ophidia), lizards (Sauria), frogs (Ranidae), ticks (Acarida), fish (Pisces) and coelenterates (Cnidaria) (e.g., jelly fish (Schyphozoa) and sea anemones (Actiniaria)) provide additional possibilities. Some of these would seem to lend themselves to biological mass production, while others might have to await means of synthesis before becoming militarily useful. The possible military use of botulinal toxin is briefly elaborated upon below.

Botulinal toxin is well known as the extraordinarily poisonous product of the anaerobic bacterium *Clostridium botulinum* (Bacillaceae), responsible for the acute food poisoning known as botulism.[7] It appears that this neurotoxin (of which at least half a dozen different antigenic groups exist) can be readily produced in large quantities and can be disseminated as an aerosol. Botulinal toxin can gain effective entry not only via the normal oral route, but also through inhalation and subsequent absorption through any mucous membrane. The lethal dose for humans varies with the route of entry, but is of the order of 1 μg or less (some reports suggesting much less).

Botulinal toxin functions by interfering with the release of acetylcholine at the neuromuscular junction, thereby preventing the subsequent contraction of the muscles and thus leading to flaccid paralysis. Without protection or treatment, the mortality rate when the toxin is ingested (that is, from botulinal food poisoning) can be expected to reach 65 per cent; when it is inhaled the mortality rate is likely to be higher. If the toxin is properly stabilized for military dispersion, the area of lethal coverage with a botulinal toxin attack has been estimated by Kaplan *et al.* (1970) to be 1 200 ha per aircraft.

The ecological consequences of a widespread attack with botulinal toxin can only be guessed at from the fragments of available information. The toxin is highly toxic to a number of animals, but man appears to be the most sensitive. From the veterinary literature it becomes clear that botulism is a serious potential problem among chickens (*Gallus gallus;* Phasianidae), game-farm pheasants (*Phasianus colchicus;* Phasianidae) and mink (*Mustela vison;* Mustelidae) raised for their pelts. It is somewhat less of a problem for horses (*Equus caballus;* Equidae), cattle (*Bos taurus;* Bovidae) and sheep (*Ovis aries;* Bovidae); and it is a rare occurrence in swine (*Sus scrofa;* Suidae), dogs (*Canis familiaris;* Canidae) and cats (*Felis catus;* Felidae). In the wild, the birds appear to be particularly susceptible to botulinal mortality, at least 72 avian species being known to succumb to the toxin (Rosen, 1971). One exception, however, is the vulture (*Cathartes aura;* Cathartidae) (M. N. Rosen, Cal. Dept. Fish and Game, priv. comm., 5 Feb. 1974). The most sensitive birds are found among the water fowl and shore birds. Botulism (under the name of limberneck) can be responsible for the death of many thousands of wild ducks (Anatidae) at a time. Finally it is important to mention that botulinal toxin can remain stable in the environment and be a continuing source of danger for as long as a week, particularly under cool, anaerobic conditions such as occur in non-moving water (Army and Air Force, 1967).

Thus on the face of it, it would seem that a widespread botulinal toxin attack might well wreak havoc within the bird population of the region in question. It would, moreover, selectively remove from it some of the mammals and perhaps other animals, depending upon their innate susceptibility, their feeding habits and other factors. Of course, the impact of such an attack might be even more devastating than has just been suggested. The available literature is based primarily upon the entry of the toxin (in conjunction with the bacterium) via the oral route where, depending upon the species, a greater or lesser amount of digestive detoxication occurs. It is quite conceivable that the virulence of the toxin becomes greatly enhanced for some species – perhaps by more than an order of magnitude – if entry should be gained via the respiratory route (Lamanna, 1961).

Micro-organisms

Various micro-organisms appear to be suitable for use as agents of biological warfare.[8] In addition to the bacteria discussed in the present section and the viruses of the next one, these include such rickettsia as *Rickettsia prowazekii* (Rickettsiaceae) (the cause of typhus) and *Coxiella burnetii* (Rickettsiaceae) (the cause of Q fever), such fungi as *Coccidioides immitis* (Moniliaceae) (the cause of desert fever or coccidioidomycosis) and such protozoa as *Toxoplasma gondii* (Haplosporida) (the cause of toxoplasmosis).

Of the bacteria, up to about a dozen highly virulent species appear to be eminently suitable for biological warfare. The list includes *Pasteurella pestis* (Brucellaceae?) (the cause of plague), *Francisella tularensis* (Brucellaceae?) (the cause of tularemia), *Brucella abortus* (Brucellaceae?) (a cause of undulant fever or brucellosis), *Salmonella typhi* (Enterobacteriaceae) (the cause of typhoid fever) and *Bacillus anthracis* (Bacillaceae) (the cause of anthrax).

The use of *Pasteurella pestis* as an agent of biological warfare may date back to the mid 14th century (Derbes, 1966). Feodosiya (then Kaffa, an important Black Sea port) had been able to withstand a three-year siege, but fell in 1346 shortly after plague-infected cadavers were catapulted over its walls to initiate a decimating plague within.

The highly virulent bacterium *Bacillus anthracis* is the causative agent of the febrile and septicaemic (blood poisoning) disease known as anthrax. This exceedingly infectious disease of most mammals and a variety of other animals is often fatal if left to run its own course (Choquette, 1970). Among the groups that have been experimentally demonstrated to contract the disease are a variety of mammals, birds, amphibians and fish (L. P. E. Choquette, Can. Dept. Environ., priv. comm., 22 Feb. 1974). Normal dissemination is via the bacterial spores, which are transmitted and gain entry in a multiplicity of ways. The pulmonary form of the disease, contracted by spore inhalation, is nearly always rapidly fatal.

The spores of *Bacillus anthracis* are easy to mass-produce, are extraordinarily resistant to the vicissitudes of the environment and lend themselves well to military aerosol dispersion. The inhalation of less than 1 μg of spores provides a lethal dose to humans. Moreover, it is apparently possible to produce mutant forms of *B. anthracis* that do not respond to presently available antibiotic therapy. Calculations by Kaplan *et al.* (1970) suggest that a single aircraft would easily be able to deliver a dose of spores initially lethal to 75 per cent of the humans over an area of perhaps 4 000 ha; Hedén (1967) and Epstein *et al.* (1969) suggest significantly larger areas.

A large-scale attack with *Bacillus anthracis* spores would debilitate if not destroy many of the populations of mammals throughout the attacked region. Moreover, it would have a greater or lesser impact on numerous other animal taxa as well.

Bacillus anthracis appears capable of establishing itself in a wide range of climates. Thus in many parts of the world a biological attack with these bacteria would establish them in the local ecosystems, thereby providing permanent reservoirs of the disease. Occasional outbreaks could be expected to occur from then on. Even in regions not conducive to permanent naturalization, spores in the soil can remain viable and a continuing focus of infection for many years. In fact, Wilson and Russell (1964) found that *B. anthracis* spores can remain alive in soil for at least 60 years (cf. also SIPRI, 1973 b: 131). Even if man were to attempt to undo the results of such an assault on the environment he would find, to quote one authority, that 'the control of anthrax in free-living animals presents many problems, some of them seemingly insurmountable' (Choquette, 1970: 262).

It becomes evident that bacterial warfare could result in significant ecosystem debilitation of indefinite duration.

Viruses

More than a dozen viruses are possible agents of biological warfare.[9] In fact, a virus was employed in one of the few more-or-less well documented instances of biological warfare. During one of the French and Indian wars in the American colonies, the British in 1763 had the admitted intent to spread smallpox virus insidiously among their Indian enemies for the express purpose of debilitating them, and then, so it seems, carried out this scheme (Stearn and Stearn, 1945: 44–45).

Among the less exotic viruses that seem eminently suitable for use as biological agents are those causing yellow fever, dengue fever, Rift

Valley fever and one dangerous disease or another referred to as encephalitis. The different possible viruses range in toxicity from temporarily incapacitating to lethal. Several can be transmitted as an aerosol, whereas others may require military dissemination via an infected vector organism such as a mosquito (Culicidae) or tick (Acarida). The virus that causes yellow fever is singled out for discussion here.

The yellow fever virus (*Flavovirus febricis*) (an arthropod-borne arbovirus in antigenic group B) normally lives and multiplies within certain mosquitoes, most important among them *Aëdes aegypti* (Culicidae) and *Haemogogus* spp. (Culicidae). It is transmitted to man, some other primates and perhaps several further species of warm-blooded vertebrates by these insects when they feed on the blood of their prey. On the other hand, this virus appears to be without effect on reptiles or amphibians (Bugher, 1951: 361, 379–380), nor does it appear to cause any harm to birds (Bugher, 1951: 360–361) or arthropods (R. W. Chamberlain, US Public Health Serv., priv. comm., 9 Apr. 1974).

Yellow fever has been a scourge of mankind for centuries, with occasional epidemics occurring to this day (Burnet and White, 1972: XIX). One such epidemic during 1960 to 1962 killed more than 15×10^3 Ethiopians (Sérié *et al.*, 1964). The yellow fever fatality rate for unprotected humans is often between 30 and 40 per cent, but goes as high as 85 per cent when the disease is introduced into a virgin area, as it did in the Ethiopian epidemic just mentioned.

The yellow fever virus would seem to make a fine biological warfare agent because of the ease with which large quantities could be prepared in the laboratory, and because it can be disseminated directly to humans as an aerosol, bypassing the militarily cumbersome mosquito (Culicidae) vector. Kaplan *et al.* (1970) estimate that the initial zone of lethal contamination from a yellow fever virus attack would cover an area of 600 ha per aircraft.

A large-scale attack with yellow fever virus in the warmer portions of the world might well establish a permanent new reservoir of the disease. The introduction of this virus into a tropical forest ecosystem would presumably have a significantly adverse effect on the subhuman primates into the indefinite future. Establishing it in Asia via intentional introduction would be a particular tragedy since it has not as yet become established in that part of the world. According to Karstad (1970: 63), once the yellow fever virus has established itself in a tropical forest, it becomes impossible to control either the arthropod vectors or the mammalian host reservoirs.

It seems safe to conclude that the introduction of a virus into a new habitat could have substantial long-term consequences. For example, the spectacular myxomatosis epizootics of recent years that have laid waste rabbit (*Oryctolagus cuniculus*; Leporidae) populations in various parts of the world provide us with a vivid demonstration of how readily and uncontrollably an introduced virus can spread (Fenner and Ratcliffe, 1965).

IV. Conclusion

Chemical and biological weapons have been employed from antiquity to the present and – international agreements and unilateral renunciations notwithstanding – their employment could be repeated in the future. A number of the agents are relatively inexpensive and easy to manufacture, lend themselves to a variety of overt and covert means of delivery and are militarily effective in the sense that they directly or indirectly render an enemy *hors de combat*. Some would claim that there is a sufficiently widespread public revulsion against chemical and biological weapons to prevent the use of the lethal ones, at least. However, Brown (1968) has argued on the basis of an analysis of the World War II experience that this may be a rather ineffectual deterrent (see also SIPRI, 1971 b).

The massive use by the USA of anti-personnel chemicals as well as anti-plant chemicals during the Second Indochina War suggests that these and similar agents would be used in at least the counter-insurgency wars of the future. In fact, a number of laudatory statements were made about these weapons by military authors writing about that war.

Chemical or biological weapons could find a place in other types of future war as well. Some nations may consider them their substitute for nuclear weaponry, perhaps as weapons of aggression, perhaps only for use *in extremis*, when the nation's very existence is at stake. Other nations may use certain of the available weapons because they do not destroy *matériel*, or perhaps in the belief that they are more humane than the conventional alternatives. Larson (1970), a human geneticist, considers it possible that chemical weapons will be developed in the future that possess ethnic or racial specificity (see also SIPRI, 1973 b: 317–319). No suitable biochemical divergences have as yet been discovered, to judge from the open literature (Chern and Beutler, 1975). However, it seems likely that some nation might be tempted to employ such weapons under certain adversary conditions, should they become available.

Some would suggest that the drawbacks of chemical and biological weapons, especially of the latter, outweigh their military attractions (Hjertonsson, 1973; Miettinen, 1974). Thus it is often argued that the more lethal of the agents are simply too inhumane for man to employ against his fellow man. The use of the various non-lethal harassing and temporarily incapacitating agents are decried because, on the one hand, even these can be lethal under various readily visualized circumstances and, on the other, because of the high likelihood of an escalation to the unambiguously lethal agents.

Another potent argument against the use of chemical or biological agents is the relatively uncontrollable and indiscriminate nature of these weapons. Their impact – presumably contrary to desire – is as likely to be felt by the civil as military sectors of the recipient nation. In fact, the vagaries of wind and water currents and of bird and other animal migrations lead to the possibility that their effect would be felt by some neutral third party, or even by the originating power.

The argument against even stockpiling chemical or biological weapons – to provide, for example, a deterrent in kind – is that their availability will eventually lead to their use. Their manufacture, testing and stockpiling have also been opposed on the grounds that accidental releases are possible during these and related operations. Indeed, a number of serious accidents are already on record. These include the so-called Bari incident in 1943, where escaped mustard gas (bis[2-chloroethyl]-sulphide) inadvertently killed over 100 people (Infield, 1971; Saunders, 1967) and the one in 1968 at Skull Valley, Utah where escaped VX gas (S-(2-diisopropylaminoethyl) O-ethyl methyl phosphonothiolate) inadvertently killed over 4 000 sheep (*Ovis aries*; Bovidae) (Boffey, 1968; Brodine *et al.*, 1969; Dawson, 1969; Hersh, 1968–1969; Reuss, 1969; VanKampen *et al.*, 1969). The release by the US Army of *Serratia marcescens* (Enterobacteriaceae) in California during 1950, apparently in order to test means of disseminating bacterial agents, appears ultimately to have resulted in more than a dozen innocent civilian fatalities (Mills and Drew, 1976: 33; see also Wheat *et al.*, 1951). Conversely, the current development of the so-called binary chemical agents (which do not gain their potency until two relatively harmless components are combined en route to the target) mitigates somewhat the possibility of accidents (Henahan, 1974; Kanegis, 1970–1971; Norman, 1973; Robinson, 1973; 1975; SIPRI, 1973 b: 306–308).

To all of the above arguments against the employment of chemical or biological weapons must be added the potential long-range effects on man and nature of a massive chemical or microbiological intrusion. Neither the magnitude of the immediate effects nor the severity of the ultimate consequences of chemical or biological warfare can be predicted with any measure of confidence (SIPRI, 1971 c; Mayer, 1948). One is thus forced to make the conservative assumption that warfare of this type could result in significant ecological debilitation and is therefore an unacceptable pursuit for this reason as well.

In conclusion, it seems that chemical or biological agents could be considered a weapon of choice by some belligerents for selected tactical or strategic purposes, either singly, in combinations amongst themselves, or in conjunction with other types of weapon. Indeed, a number of the chemical or biological weapons would appear to hold a particular attraction for use against a guerrilla force or other adversary that has only modest medical resources at its command and that is, moreover, unlikely to be able to retaliate in kind.

Notes to Chapter 2

1. The literature on chemical and biological warfare that is openly available deals for the most part with the historical, political, and legal aspects of the subject, to a lesser extent with the military, chemical and medical aspects, and virtually overlooks the biological and ecological aspects.

    Of the available literature, the most important item is the exhaustive study of 20th century chemical and biological warfare by SIPRI (1971–1975). A number of other recent book-length treatments are available, some by military authorities (Brown, 1968; Rosebury, 1949; Rothschild, 1964) and several that have emanated from the civil sector (Clarke, 1968; Cookson and Nottingham, 1969; Hersh, 1968; McCarthy, 1969 b; Thomas and Thomas, 1970). The latter group could be extended through the addition of a number of collections of articles (Alexander et al., 1971; Baudisch et al., 1971; Bulletin of the Atomic Scientists, 1960; Neilands et al., 1972; Ronneberg et al., 1960; Rose, 1969; Scientist and Citizen, 1967). There are many widely scattered brief treatments of the subject, including several that provide interesting historical information (Batten, 1960; Cook, 1971; Derbes, 1966; Kokatnur, 1948; Miles, 1970; Nordenskiöld, 1918; West, 1919) and a number that are bibliographies (Armed Forces Chemical Journal, 1964; Meeker, 1972; Robinson, 1974; Tarr, 1965; Wasan, 1970; Westing, 1974 a) and some others that are noteworthy for one reason or another (Holmberg, 1975; Langer, 1967; Meselson, 1970; Sidel and Goldwyn, 1966; SIPRI, 1974 a).

    The summary by Epstein et al. (1969) particularly as complemented by Kaplan et al. (1970) must be singled out as clearly the best available brief treatments of chemical and biological warfare, and especially so in the present context.

    For specific references to chemical warfare, see note 6; and to biological warfare, see note 8.

2. Although a number of books dealing with chemical warfare as it was waged during World War I appeared in the years immediately following that conflict, the best source to begin with is the review by SIPRI (1971 a). Cook (1971) provides an excellent brief account of the initiation of the use of chemicals in World War I.

3. The literature touching upon chemical anti-animal agents is scarce (Epstein *et al.*, 1969) so that one must rely for this category upon that of the chemical anti-personnel agents.[6]

Biological anti-animal agents are discussed by Epstein *et al.* (1969), the Agricultural Research Service (1961) and the Army and Air Force (1965: VII). Siegmund *et al.* (1973) provide a number of pertinent veterinary summaries. The effects of some of the pertinent micro-organisms on domestic animals are covered by Bruner and Gillespie (1973), and on warm-blooded wildlife by Davis *et al.* (1971) and Davis *et al.* (1970). For information on biological anti-personnel agents, see note 8.

4. Chemical anti-plant warfare is covered elsewhere (SIPRI, 1976 a). For a bibliography on the subject, see Westing (1974 a).

Biological anti-plant agents are discussed by Epstein *et al.* (1969), the Agricultural Research Service (1961) and the Army and Air Force (1965: VIII). For background information on many of the militarily attractive plant diseases, the reader is referred to Horsfall and Dimond (1959–1960), Smith (1973) and Boyce (1961).

5. For a detailed examination of the chemical and physiological properties of 'CS' (*o*-chlorobenzalmalononitrile) and for an introduction to the pertinent literature, see Jones (1972). See also Sanford (1976), SIPRI (1971 a: 185–209; 1973 b: 45–46, etc.). Chemicals agents in general are covered in note 6.

Neilands (1972 a) provides an extensive review of the use of CS by the USA in Indochina, and there are a number of additional sources for such information (Blumenfeld and Meselson, 1971; Blumenthal, 1969; Hersh, 1968: 167–186; SIPRI, 1971 a: 185–209; Rose and Rose, 1972; Verwey, 1977). Military (tactical) evaluations have been favourable (Miller, 1966; Peterkin, 1972; VanRiper, 1972; *Army Digest*, 1968).

CS is often referred to as a gas although this is not the case. It is in fact a solid that is dispersed as an ultra-fine powder (aerosol). When CS is manufactured in finely pulverized (micronized) form it is referred to as CS1, and when the latter in turn is made water-repellent (and thus less rapidly degradable under field conditions), it is known as CS2.

6. There is a considerable literature devoted to chemical warfare and the agents involved, especially if one includes publications covering both chemical and biological agents.[1]
The chemical-agent literature includes items by the Army and Air Force (1967), Health, Education and Welfare (1959 b), Lohs (1974 a, b), Neilands (1973), SIPRI (1973 a; 1975 a, b) and Watkins *et al.* (1968). For literature on 'CS' (*o*-chlorobenzalmalononitrile), see note 5; for literature on toxins, see note 7.

Both the so-called 'G' and 'V' agents are sufficiently similar to the organophosphorus insecticides to permit one to lean upon the literature dealing with this class of compounds. The basic text on the chemistry of the organophosphorus insecticides is by Fest and Schmidt (1973). Their medical toxicology has been summarized by Hayes (1963) and Schumacher (1970); see also Lisella *et al.* (1975–1976). Their veterinary toxicology is covered by Radeleff (1970: VII). Their levels of toxicity for numerous animals have been compiled by Pimentel (1971), Tucker and Crabtree (1970) and Heath *et al.* (1972). Bibliographies relevant in part have been prepared by Fox (1970), Ingram and Tarzwell (1954), Headley and Erickson (1970) and Thomas *et al.* (1964).

7. Some of the more comprehensive recent publications on natural poisons, venoms and toxins are by Ajl *et al.* (1970–1972), Bücherl *et al.* (1968–1971), Halstead (1965–1970), Purchase (1974), Rǎsková (1971–1972), Simpson and Curtis (1971–1974), and Vries and Kochva (1971–1973). Moreover, SIPRI (1974 a) has speculated upon the utility of some of these toxins for military purposes.

Specifically with respect to botulinal toxin, excellent reviews have been prepared by Lamanna (1959) and Lamanna and Carr (1967). Holvey *et al.* (1972: 711-714) provide a medical summary for botulinal toxin; Siegmund *et al.* (1973: 345-347, 1083-1084) and Bruner and Gillespie (1973: 368-377) provide veterinary summaries. Rosen (1971) reviews botulism in wild birds.

8. In addition to the literature, that deals with both biological and chemical warfare,[1] there exist a considerable number of useful items dealing specifically with biological weapons, including those by the Agricultural Research Service (1961), Barrairon (1973), Federal Civil Defense Administration (1951), Fothergill (1963), Health, Education and Welfare (1959 a), Hedén (1967), Jenkins (1963), Kaplan (1960), Leitenberg (1967), Mayer (1948), Rosebury (1960) and Rosebury and Kabat (1947). For literature dealing with viruses, see note 9.

   For general medical summaries of the diseases caused by many of the potential biological warfare organisms, the reader is referred to Holvey *et al.* (1972); similarly, for veterinary summaries one can turn to Siegmund *et al.* (1973) and Bruner and Gillespie (1973). Davis and Anderson (1971), Davis *et al.* (1971) and Davis *et al.* (1970) have brought together much pertinent information on infectious and parasitic diseases of wild mammals and birds.

   Specifically with respect to anthrax, Holvey *et al.* (1972: 161-163) provide a medical summary, and Siegmund *et al.* (1973: 328-331) a veterinary summary. Bruner and Gillespie (1973: 344-358) discuss the disease with respect to domestic animals, whereas Choquette (1970) performs this function for wild mammals.

9. The use of viruses in biological warfare is discussed by Epstein *et al.* (1969), Kaplan *et al.* (1970) and SIPRI (1973 b). Medical information on many of the pertinent viruses is summarized by Holvey *et al.* (1972), and veterinary information by Siegmund *et al.* (1973) and Bruner and Gillespie (1973). Their relationships to wildlife are covered in part by Davis *et al.* (1971) and Davis *et al.* (1970). Literature dealing with biological warfare in general is covered in note 8.

   Yellow fever is covered thoroughly by Strode (1951). See also Burnet and White (1972: XIX) and Gillett (1972: 208-223).

3. Geophysical and environmental weapons

Superior numerals, thus [5], refer to notes on pages 62-63.

I. Introduction

Increasing attention is being paid to the manipulation of geophysical or environmental forces for hostile purposes. Some categories of this type of warfare, including the instigation of fires and of floods, have been practised since ancient times. Others, such as rain-making, are in their infancy. And still others are only possibilities for the future.[1]

This chapter describes several of these so-called geophysical or environmental weapons as well as the ecological consequences of their employment. Special emphasis is given to the military use of fire, of floods and of rain-making.

II. Description

General

Geophysical warfare can involve hostile manipulations of the atmosphere, of the land and its associated fresh waters, or of the oceans. The present section touches upon a number of the more speculative possibilities involved. A number of hostile modifications of the atmosphere have been suggested as military possibilities for the future. In addition to the rainfall modification covered below, these include various manipulations of the electrical properties of the ionosphere or troposphere. The purpose of this form of attack would be to interfere with enemy radio, radar or other electromagnetic waves, thereby disrupting enemy communication, remote sensing, navigation and missile guidance systems. Indeed, it appears that some primitive attempts have already been made along these lines. It is reported that during the Second Indochina War the USA attempted to disrupt North Vietnamese radars being used for aiming defensive surface-to-air missiles by introducing undisclosed chemical agents into the troposphere (Hersh, 1972).

If techniques were to be devised for initiating hurricanes or cyclones – or even for only redirecting natural ones – this would make available to the military an immensely destructive force. Moreover, if cloud-to-ground lightning could be controlled, those capable of doing so would finally have achieved a power hitherto reserved for Zeus alone (Ritchie, 1959).

The layer of ozone that envelops the earth within the lower stratosphere is considered to be necessary to shield the earth's biota from harmful amounts of ultra-violet radiation, a subject that was touched upon in Chapter 1. It is perhaps already within our capability to open a 'window' in this ozone layer over an enemy's territory by injecting into it a bromine compound via controlled releases from an orbiting satellite (Sullivan, 1975).

Hostile manipulations of the land that have been suggested as military possibilities of the future seem for the most part to be highly dependent for their success on the local site factors. For example, if an enemy region happens to be tectonically unstable it might become possible to trigger an earthquake there. Similarly, quiescent volcanoes situated in enemy territory could perhaps be stimulated into destructive activity. Some local landforms might well be amenable to disruption through the triggering of avalanches or landslides. And for enemy tundra regions it might be feasible during the summer season to destroy the vegetational ground cover. This would result in a lowering of the level of the permafrost which, in turn, would reduce the trafficability of the area and could result in additional forms of military inconvenience. Land disruption via flooding is covered below.

Among the hostile ocean modifications that have been suggested as military possibilities for the future are physical or chemical manipulations that are meant to disrupt acoustic (sonar) or electromagnetic properties of the attacked waters. Again the purpose for such attack would be the disruption of enemy underwater communication, remote sensing, navigation and missile guidance systems. A second possibility involving the ocean habitat is the generation of tsunamis for the purpose of destroying coastal cities and other nearshore facilities. One way that has been suggested for creating a tsunami on demand is to set off a nuclear device in an appropriate underwater locality (Clark, 1961).

Fire

Through past ages fire has been the most destructive agent available to man. It should thus come as no surprise that fire has long been used in warfare.[2] Its primary use in war has always been for the destruction of man's artifacts, that is, as an anti-*matériel* weapon; its second major use has been as an anti-personnel weapon. However, the present discussion dwells upon widespread military burning in rural areas. There the destruction of vegetation by incendiary means can be used to deny an enemy forest cover, food, feed or industrial crops of one sort or another.

Fire has been used in war since ancient times. During the battles between the Israelites and the Philistines around the 12th century B.C., Samson is recorded as once having destroyed the Philistines' agricultural and horticultural fields by letting loose amongst them several hundred foxes (*Vulpes;* Canidae) whose tails had first been set afire (Judges 15: 3–5). During the first century B.C., in what is now Italy, Lucretius (ca. 55 B.C.: 209) described a huge forest fire, noting that '. . . a fierce conflagration, roaring balefully, has devoured a forest down to the roots and roasted the earth with penetrative fire. . . . The blaze may have been started . . . by men who had employed fire to scare their enemies in some woodland war. . . .'.

From those times to the present, numerous instances can be cited of the hostile use of fire, mostly for anti-*matériel* or anti-personnel purposes.[2] Until the 17th century, however, such incendiary warfare was to some extent limited by the very restricted range of catapults and other delivery systems that were available for incendiary devices. Then, with the rise of artillery, a useful long-range delivery system became available and various more-or-less efficient incendiary shells were developed (Manucy, 1949: 69–70; Fisher, 1946: 110–111). So-called carcasses – hollow, vented iron shells filled with pitch and ignited at the time of firing – made their début in 1672 and were much used for setting military fires for more than two centuries. Then, beginning in the late 18th century, 'hot shot' – iron cannon balls brought to red heat before firing – came into vogue as incendiary missiles. The hot shot was prepared in shot furnaces, which were standard equipment for artillery batteries during the 19th century.

World War I saw the introduction not only of more sophisticated incendiary artillery shells, but also of the first air-delivered incendiary bombs. The use of these weapons during World War I, although rather limited, gave the world a hint of today's massive incendiary warfare. Indeed, fire has been used extensively for military purposes in more recent times and a diversity of highly efficient incendiary weapons and delivery systems can be found today in the major arsenals of the world (SIPRI, 1975 c: II).

Clearly the most spectacular military application for fire in recent times has been in the decimation of cities. During World War II, for example, the USA and its allies aerially attacked several dozen German and Japanese cities with the express intent of destroying them by fire. Indeed, several of these attacks have carved out for themselves permanent niches in military history. These include especially the destruction of Hamburg in August 1943 (Caidin, 1960), of Dresden in February 1945 (Irving, 1963) and of Tokyo in March 1945 (Bond, 1946: 165–167; Craven and Cate, 1953: XX). The incendiary attack on Tokyo was the most destructive in both life and property of any aerial attack throughout World War II, either conventional or nuclear (Craven and Cate, 1953: 617). The destruction of Pyongyang by the USA during the Korean War provides still another notorious example (Futrell *et al.*, 1961: 258). All in all, it is generally recognized in military circles today that the annihilation of cities is accomplished more expeditiously, less expensively, with higher casualties and with greater demoralization of enemy civilians by incendiary attack than by any other conventional means (Björnerstedt *et al.*, 1973; D'Olier *et al.*, 1947).

The incendiary destruction of crops has been practised on a small scale in modern times by the armed forces of a number of nations. During the Second Anglo–Boer War (1899–1902), for example, the Boers set the torch to wide areas of the veldt in order to deny forage to the advancing British (Wet, 1902: 181). The British for their part have destroyed crops both in local, counter-insurgency warfare (in Malaya (Kutger, 1960–1961)) and in general, large-scale warfare (against Germany during World War II (Björnerstedt *et al.*, 1973: 46; SIPRI, 1975 c: 82, 112–113)). The USA fire-bombed enemy crops during the Second Indochina War (Howard, 1972) and considers incendiary attack to be one of the recommended procedures for destroying enemy crops, especially in counter-insurgency warfare (Army, 1967–1970: 69; 1969: 50).

Intentional large-scale forest destruction by fire for military purposes seems to have been tried only rarely in modern times. The Japanese during World War II attempted with little success to set wildfires in the western USA, primarily via balloon-delivered incendiary devices.[3] And then there are the US attempts at burning out large forest tracts during the Second Indochina War, described next.

Incendiary weapons were employed during the Second Indochina War in quantities that far exceeded those of any previous war (SIPRI, 1975 c: I). These included magnesium-encased thermit bombs and grenades, white phosphorus bombs and shells, and napalm bombs and canisters. Their use in this war was confined in large part to close-air-support missions. Intentionally set rural wildfires for purposes of area denial or similar widespread harassment, although attempted on several occasions, were forced by natural circumstances to play only a small role in this conflict.

What seems to have been the militarily most successful wide-area incendiary attack of the Second Indochina War was carried out by the USA in the U Minh forest, a stronghold of their enemy in the Delta region (Military Region IV) of South Vietnam. For several weeks in the spring of 1968 the USA was able through repeated heavy incendiary attacks on the U Minh forest to nurture there some fires of uncertain origin (Time, 1968). In another instance, in the spring of 1971, the USA was reported to have dropped enormous quantities of incendiary devices onto the forest lands around a besieged outpost in west central Kontum province (in Military Region II) (Associated Press, 1971). No evaluation of either of these attacks appears to have been made available.

The most noteworthy instances of rural incendiary attack because of their potential for ecological impact were three major attempts by the USA between 1965 and 1967 to initiate massive forest fires over extensive enemy-controlled areas (Hartmann, 1967; McConnell, 1969–1970; Perry, 1968; Randal, 1967; Reinhold, 1972; Shapley, 1972 b). In each of these cases, a large forest area was prepared by herbicide spraying in order to provide an adequate fuel base of dead leaves and twigs. The first of these attempts, 'Operation Sherwood Forest', was carried out during the spring of 1965 for the aim of destroying the almost 3×10^3 ha Boi Loi woods in south-eastern Tay Ninh province (in War Zone C). Then, during 'Operation Hot Tip' in early 1966, an attempt was made to destroy perhaps 7×10^3 ha of forest in the Chu Pong mountains in north central Pleiku province (in Military Region II). And 'Operation Pink Rose' early in 1967 was intended to destroy almost 8×10^3 ha of forest near Xuan Loc in south central Long Khanh province (in War Zone D).

None of these three carefully planned and executed attempts at initiating self-propagating wild fires was successful despite the herbicidal pretreatments, the massive use of incendiary devices and the sundry technical refinements that were added from one operation to the next. The failures can be attributed to the generally wet conditions (high humidity and/or rainfall) that prevail in the region. The finely divided fuels that are necessary to sustain a forest fire take up too much moisture to support combustion when the ambient relative humidity is above 80 per cent, the usual level that obtains throughout much of Indochina. Additionally, not much litter accumulates on the tropical forest floor as a potential source of fuel; and, finally, Mutch (1970) has suggested that tropical rain forests provide a relatively poor grade of fuel even if permitted to become dry (see also Batchelder and Hirt, 1966).

Flooding

Under specialized site conditions, appropriate military actions can bring about flooding of an area. This could be either intentional or unintentional. For example, one of the ramifications of augmenting the rainfall in a region for one military reason or another might be the instigation or enhancement of flooding. Moreover, the likelihood exists of the incidental enhancement of flooding in conjunction with large-scale military land-clearing operations via, for example, chemical anti-plant agents or Rome ploughs (SIPRI, 1976 a).

Where the geography and the season lend themselves to it, the most straightforward means of producing destructive floods is to destroy existing levees, dikes or dams by one means or another. The first two examples given here of such military flooding were, in fact, both self-inflicted. During the Franco–Dutch War of 1672–1678, the Dutch in June 1672 were partially successful in stopping the forces of Louis XIV from overrunning the Netherlands by cutting dikes to create the so-called Holland Water Line (Baxter, 1966: 72–73; Blok, 1907: 380–381). It should be added that this manoeuver was carried out despite the vehement objections of the peasants of the affected region.

The Second Sino–Japanese War of 1937–1945 provides a far more devastating example of intentional military flooding. In order to curtail the Japanese advance, the Chinese in June 1938 dynamited the Huayuan-kow dike of the Yellow River, near Chengchow. This action resulted in the drowning of several thousand Japanese soldiers and stopped their advance along this front. In the process, however, the flood waters also ravaged major portions of Honan, Anhwei and Kiangsu provinces. Indeed, several million hectares of farm lands were inundated in the process, and their crops and topsoil destroyed. The river was not brought back under control until 1947. In terms of more direct human impact, the flooding inundated some eleven cities and more than four thousand villages. At least several hundred thousand Chinese drowned as a result and several million more were left homeless.[5]

During World War II, the Germans in 1944 intentionally flooded with salt water some 200×10^3 ha of agricultural lands in the Netherlands (Aartsen, 1946; Kolko, 1968). This subsequently induced the Dutch to institute a major research programme in order to develop means for rehabiliting these lands (Dorsman, 1947). By way of further example, the USA in August 1943 bombed dikes in an unsuccessful attempt to flood out the Gia Lam airport of Japanese-occupied Hanoi (Craven and Cate, 1950: 527).

During the Korean War, US forces openly attacked irrigation dams in North Korea (Rees, 1964: 381–382). The purpose of these attacks, according to the US Air Force, was two-fold: on the one hand, they were meant to hinder the production by the enemy of its staple food, rice (*Oryza sativa;* Gramineae); and on the other, they were meant as a warning to future Asian enemies of their vulnerability in this regard (Air University Quarterly Review, 1953–1954). Indeed, the destruction of irrigation dams was considered by the USA to be among the most successful of its air operations of the Korean War (Futrell *et al.*, 1961: 627–628, 637).

During the Second Indochina War, the USA again attacked agriculturally important dams, dikes and seawalls with bombing and shelling especially in North Vietnam (Duffett, 1968: 226–235; Lacoste, 1972; Westing, 1973). However, during these hostilities – despite official acceptability of flooding as a means of war (Army, 1962: 36–38) – the USA denied such attacks. It admitted at most that the damage, if any, was inadvertent or 'collateral' (Gliedman, 1972; Porter, 1972).

Rain-making

Military activities presumably can modify meteorological phenomena either inadvertently or by conscious manipulation. One aspect of the latter possibility – rain-making – is the subject of the present section.[6] Apparently eager to test its procedures in the field, or perhaps to show them off, the US Department of Defense has openly attempted (with greater or lesser success) to augment rainfall for civil purposes in such diverse locales as India in 1967, Florida in 1968 and 1970, the Philippines in 1969, Okinawa, Midway and Texas in 1971, and the Azores and California in 1972. Its rain-making and related activities in Indochina, on the other hand, were conducted with great attempts at secrecy.

Beginning in 1963 and continuing at least into 1972, first the US Central Intelligence Agency and then the military carried out extensive attempts to manipulate the rainfall in Indochina. Although all of the countries enmeshed in the Second Indochina War were at one time or another subjected to rain-making attack, it was Laos that bore the brunt of these activities (Table 3.1). The seeding agents employed included silver iodide and lead iodide.

The major reason for the rain-making efforts was reported to be the interdiction of enemy lines of communication, especially the supply routes in south-eastern Laos. Attempts were made each year between

Table 3.1. US cloud seeding operations in the Second Indochina War: a breakdown by year and region

| Year | Seeding cartridges expended | | | | | Total sorties flown |
	South Vietnam	North Vietnam	Cambodia	Laos	**Total**	
1961	0	0	0	0	**0**	0
1962	0	0	0	0	**0**	0
1963	Several	0	0	0	**Several**	Several
1964	?	?	?	?	**?**	?
1965	?	?	?	?	**?**	?
1966	0	0	0	560?	**560?**	56
1967	Several	1 017	0	5 553	**6 570**	591
1968	0	98	0	7 322	**7 420**	734?
1969	0	0	0	9 457	**9 457**	528
1970	0	0	0	8 312	**8 312**	277
1971	0	0	0	11 288	**11 288**	333
1972	1 000?	0	1 000?	2 362?	**4 362**	139
1973	0	0	0	0	**0**	0
Total	**1 000?**	**1 115**	**1 000?**	**44 854?**	**47 969?**	**2 658**

Notes:

(a) The data are from Pell (1974: 92–102) except for the 1963 information, which is from Hersh (1972) and Shapley (1974).

(b) Most of the seeding cartridges used generated either a silver iodide or lead iodide particulate aerosol (Pell, 1974: 91). It appears that the devices used were similar to the commercially available 'Weathercord' (Weather Engineering Corp., Dorval, Quebec), which contains 518 mg of silver iodide (Goyer et al., 1966).

1966 and 1972 to intensify and prolong the annual rainy season in order to make the so-called Ho Chi Minh trail sufficiently muddy to render it impassable, or at least more difficult to use. There were also some unsuccessful attempts (apparently by the Central Intelligence Agency) to achieve a similar result by the aerial application of undisclosed chemical agents with emulsifying action (Pell, 1974: 123). As already mentioned, cloud-seeding in North Vietnam (again with undisclosed chemicals) may have been carried out largely to make inoperable the enemy radars used for aiming defensive surface-to-air missiles (Hersh, 1972). Other reported uses in Indochina included the production of sufficiently bad weather to hamper enemy offensives, the altering of rainfall patterns to aid US bombing missions, the providing of inclement weather to enable the success of covert ground operations, the creation of generally disruptive floods, and the diversion of enemy manpower to undoing the mischief caused by the bad weather instigated.

Although the military seemed satisfied with the level of success of its weather modification operations in Indochina (Gravel *et al.*, 1971–1972: IV:421; Pell, 1974: 103–108), a dispassionate arbiter might be hard pressed to recognize the basis for this satisfaction.

III. Ecological consequences

Fire

Fire has always been a natural factor more or less importantly involved in the shaping of terrestrial ecosystems.[4] Since the beginning of time, there have been innumerable lightning fires. And wherever man has lived, from antiquity to the present, he has continued to set fires, either by accident or design. For a variety of meteorological and other reasons, the frequency and severity of wild fires differ from region to region, running the gamut from common and extensive to virtually non-existent. In the regions of relatively high frequency, fire is in fact the dominant factor determining vegetational (and thus also faunal) composition (Ahlgren and Ahlgren, 1960; Cooper, 1961), irrespective of latitude. Thus, Lutz (1956) has shown that the vegetation characteristic of interior Alaska is determined by the periodic fires that have always been common to that region. Moreover, certain forms of grasslands have become established and perpetuated only through the action of repeated fires, both in temperate zones (Sauer, 1950; Wells, 1965) and in the tropics (Budowski, 1956; Holmes, 1951; Wharton, 1966; 1968).

One might suggest that, as a general rule, the ease with which wild fires can be set and sustained in any particular region is directly correlated with the ability of the natural local ecosystems to survive such assault. The plants indigenous to fire-prone regions have presumably evolved fire survival mechanisms and, in some instances, have even come to depend upon periodic fires in one way or another. Conversely, those plants found in a region rarely subjected to fire are likely to be decimated by a conflagration.

For the many regions throughout the world where natural wildfires are an occasional occurrence, a forest fire is relatively easy to set (at least at certain seasons of the year) and will result in varying amounts of ecological damage. In such a region, a forest fire will injure many of the large trees and kill some of them. The degree of initial damage depends upon the weather conditions at the time of the fire and upon the species of trees involved. The ability of a species to withstand fire damage is, for all but young individuals, to a great extent a function of its bark characteristics, mainly the thickness. Seedlings and saplings are, of course, more highly susceptible to initial damage than larger trees. However, the greatest amount of damage to the trees is caused by the fungi that gain entry via fire wounds (Stickel and Marco, 1936; Hawley and Stickel, 1948: III), and to a lesser extent the insects that do so (Hodges and Pickard, 1971).

Major forest fires can also do a certain amount of harm to the eco-system by damaging the soil. An important source of soil damage is a reduction in the amount of soil litter (that is, of the soil's A_0 horizon). Some litter will burn in the fire (with an associated loss of volatile nitrogen (DeBell and Ralston, 1970; Knight, 1966)), but the greatest ultimate loss is the result of a subsequent diminution of the replenishment of routine losses. Litter with its associated humus is a particularly scarce commodity in the tropics.

With a reduced layer of protective litter, the soil becomes subject to increased erosion and associated problems (Arend, 1941; Lowdermilk, 1930). The loss of nutrients in solution (that is, nutrient dumping) will be a particular problem, perhaps especially the loss of soluble phosphorus (McColl and Grigal, 1975) and soluble potassium (Allen, 1964). Moreover, flood danger will be enhanced.

Fires can also play havoc with the wildlife in an area, both directly and indirectly. However, the degree of damage to any particular species can differ markedly depending upon the season of the year. The direct faunal destruction that is likely to occur as a result of a wild fire has been vividly described by Kipp (1931). Fires are, of course, harmful to animals indirectly via destruction of their food and cover. Moreover, the very different habitat that is likely to develop following a major fire, that is, following vegetational recolonization, will support a new and far less diversified animal community.

Rain-making

One can begin an examination of rain-making with the cloud-seeding agents themselves.[7] Thus, silver iodide and lead iodide (two of the most commonly used agents) can exert at least a minor adverse effect on the ecosystems into which they are introduced (Cooper and Jolly, 1970). Certain aquatic biota such as algae, invertebrates and some fish are the most likely organisms to be harmed by these poisons.

With rainfall augmentation, there is also the possibility of enhanced flood damage. With respect to the Second Indochina War, it remains unknown whether the serious flooding that occurred in North Vietnam in 1971 (Darcourt, 1971; *Vietnam Newsletter*, 1971) can be attributed at least in part to the US attempts at weather manipulation. Indeed, 1971 was the peak year of US cloud-seeding activity (Table 3.1). Even if the seeding was carried out only in Laos, as announced, the prevailing winds during the rainy (cloud-seeding) season are south-westerly, that is, from Laos to North Vietnam. Still another problem associated with increased rainfall would be an enhancement of erosional damage, particularly in hilly terrain and especially when the ground has been previously disrupted by bombing or other hostile activity.

Rainfall manipulation, unless carried out with consistent success over a period of years, would have little obvious effect on most of the plants and animals involved. However, water-dependent insects would be favoured in times of increased rainfall. Since this category of fauna includes a number of important disease vectors, there might be subsequent increases in the incidence of various diseases of wildlife, livestock and humans (Chapter 1, note 12). Indeed, enhanced rainfall could in this and other ways trigger a variety of more-or-less subtle imbalances in the ecosystems being thus tampered with, traceable to the resultant changes in reproductive, growth or mortality rates of some biota. Although such effects are apt to be most pronounced among the lower plants and animals, they are by no means restricted to such forms. For example, the population level of jack-rabbits (*Lepus californicus melanotis*; Leporidae) in Kansas in any particular year is closely correlated with the amount of rainfall during that year (Bronson and Tiemeier, 1959). Moreover, from observations along the coast of Georgia, it is known that a modest shift to an earlier date for the normal autumn rainfall can spell the difference between survival and death for the eggs of the Atlantic loggerhead turtle (*Caretta caretta caretta*; Cheloniidae) (Ragotzkie, 1959).

When rain-making is successful in one area, this may have been at the expense of rainfall diminution in another area, where drought-associated problems could manifest themselves.

Thus, one can safely conclude that seemingly minor changes in precipitation (or in insolation or temperature) could bring about substantial and unexpected changes in the affected ecosystems, both natural and agricultural.

IV. Conclusion

Geophysical or environmental warfare is for the most part still in its infancy. However, its future growth and development appear assured, hinging only upon the continued discovery and refinement of appropriate techniques. As one spokesman for the US Department of Defense admitted in explaining the activities of the Geophysics Group at the US Naval Ordnance Test Station in California, 'Primarily the work is aimed at giving the . . . armed forces . . . the capability of modifying the environment, to their own advantage, or to the disadvantage of an enemy. We regard the weather as a weapon. Anything one can use to get his way is a weapon and the weather is as good a one as any' (Magnuson, 1966: 33).

The human impact of geophysical warfare can range from inconsequential to disastrous, depending upon the techniques employed, the success with which they are employed, the location and duration of their employment and other factors. Moreover, the social impact of hurricanes, earthquakes, lava flows, tidal waves and so forth would be tremendous, should their manipulation become feasible techniques of geophysical warfare.

Rural wildfires initiated by military action could cause a host of severe economic and other social problems, both intentional and unintentional. Even under the best of peaceful conditions, a large rural wildfire can all but overwhelm local efforts to bring it under control, as described in the dramatic account by Holbrook (1943) of some of the major US forest fires of the past and in the gripping fictional, though technically accurate, description by Stewart (1948) of one such fire. In time of war, with the employment of delayed action incendiary devices and scattered anti-personnel mines, the task of fighting a wildfire could become virtually impossible and the fire might have to be left to run its course.

Fires set for hostile purposes can destroy merchantable timber, food crops, rubber plantations and all sorts of other industrial plants, both herbaceous and woody. There can be losses of livestock, buildings and other property. Human lives can be lost as well, even with rural fires. The smoke from the fires contributes to the regional air pollution, with the particulates and some of the hydrocarbons thus generated having both economic and public health ramifications (Hall, 1972; Murphy et al., 1970).

There exists ample civil experience to support the contention that large-scale rural wildfires can be ecologically debilitating and economically devastating. When such fires are of military origin, they are likely to be more damaging than seemingly comparable rural wildfires of non-military origin (even those maliciously set by arsonists). Not only will the military fires be likely to have been initiated and maintained by the massive and repeated applications of highly efficient incendiary devices, but efforts to extinguish them are likely to be hampered by concomitant military actions of various sorts.

The military fires attempted in Indochina were of only minor ecological import owing to the inappropriate regional site conditions. However, if an area not normally subject to natural fires can be ignited by improved incendiary techniques, including appropriate chemical pre-treatment, then the ecological impact could be a very serious one. Indeed, pretreatment of the sort just suggested is a technology already under development (Bentley et al., 1971; Bentley and Graham, 1976; Forman and Longacre, 1969–1970; Philpot and Mutch, 1968).

Napalm and other incendiary weapons can be opposed not only on ecological grounds, but on humanitarian grounds as well (Björner-stedt et al., 1973; Red Cross, 1973; SIPRI, 1972; 1975 c; Wulff et al., 1973).

Flooding for hostile purposes can result in enormous agricultural losses, both immediate and delayed, as was shown so well by the Germans in the Netherlands during World War II and the Chinese during the Second Sino–Japanese War of 1937–1945. That the direct human losses can be staggering was also demonstrated by the latter instance. Enhanced rainfall in areas where malaria is prevalent can lead to immediate increases in the incidence of this disease, owing to the improved habitat conditions for the vector insect (Sargent and Tromp, 1964). A number of other diseases follow a similar course. The health and other effects associated with depletion of the ozone layer in the lower stratosphere were discussed in Chapter 1.

It is thus evident that geophysical or environmental warfare is objectional on several levels. Even with optimistic expectations regarding future refinements in technique, the outcome of geophysical modifications for hostile purposes is likely to be unpredictable in magnitude, spatial confinement, side effects and duration. Thus, the intended effects of such military activities cannot be brought to bear on an enemy without the likelihood of an even greater effect on the regional civil populace, to say nothing of the impact on the regional ecology. A further objection that has been raised on occasion is that some of the techniques of geophysical warfare lend themselves readily to covert application, even during times of ostensible peace. In short, geophysical or environmental manipulations for military purposes might well result in a host of severe ecological and social problems, both immediate and delayed.

Notes to Chapter 3

1. The directions that geophysical and environmental warfare might take in the future have been considered by Barnaby (1975; 1976), Canada (1975), Fedorov (1975), Goldblat (1975), Hecht (1976), Israelyan (1974), Jasani (1975), MacDonald (1968), Schneider (1976), Weiss (1974; 1975) and others. For the special case of military incendiarism, see note 2; and for that of military weather modification, see note 6.

   Weather modification and other geophysical changes associated with nuclear warfare are covered in Chapter 1. For references to weather changes brought about by nuclear war, see Chapter 1, note 9.

2. The thesis that fire was the first great force available to man is reviewed by Stewart (1956). Partington (1960) covers in part the military use of fire in ancient times and Fisher (1946) provides a text on incendiary warfare that includes a brief history of the subject from 60 B.C. to 1945 (Chapter VIII). The use of fire during World War II, primarily for the destruction of cities, has been analysed by D'Olier *et al.* (1947) and by Bond (1946) via a collection of articles. A considerable number of brief accounts of incendiary warfare exist, among them those by Heon (1964), Miller (1958), Lohs (1973) and Sorensen (1948–1949). Certain aspects of incendiary weapon technology have been described by Watkins *et al.* (1968: Pt. II).

   Björnerstedt *et al.* (1973) provide an excellent brief over-all treatment of incendiary warfare. The best single major source of information on the subject is the recent monograph by SIPRI (1975 c). Both Björnerstedt *et al.* and SIPRI emphasize the anti-personnel and anti-*matériel* aspects of incendiary weapons and the social ramifications of their use.

   Incendiary weapons and techniques of the Second Indochina War have been treated by SIPRI (1975 c: 49–63), Shapley (1972 b), Neilands (1970; 1972 b; 1973) and Takman (1967) (with napalm the major focus for the latter two authors). There also exist a number of secret reports on the subject (Forest Service, 1966; 1970; Kusterer, 1966).

   For a discussion of fires associated with nuclear warfare, see Chapter 1: for references to the subject, see Chapter 1, note 6.

3. During World War II the Japanese repeatedly attempted to initiate large-scale forest fires in the western USA as a means of disrupting the US war effort. There was at least one direct fire-bomb air attack against Oregon (Fujita and Harrington, 1961; Goldenson and Danner, 1948; Holbrook, 1944–1945; Webber, 1975: VI–VII). However, the project was carried out primarily via the release of many thousands of large long-range wind-borne balloons carrying incendiary devices (Conley, 1967–1968; Goldenson and Danner, 1948; Mikesh, 1973; Rahm, 1946; Webber, 1975: X–XI; Wilbur, 1950; Winters, 1974: 296).

4. For a comprehensive coverage of wild fires from the standpoint of forestry, see Brown and Davis (1973). The ecological effects of forest and other wild fires have been reviewed by Ahlgren and Ahlgren (1960), Broido (1963), Cooper (1961), Kozlowski and Ahlgren (1974), Lutz (1956), Mobley (1974) and others. A number of relevant bibliographies also exist (Cushwa, 1968; Hare, 1961; Baker, 1975).

5. The various reports on the June 1938 flooding of the Yellow River do not all agree as to the details of the case. The information provided in the text has been pieced together and averaged from the following sources (chosen for their opposing biases): Boyle (1972: 187), Dorn (1974: 177–178), Freeberne (1973: 68–69), Hsu and Chang (1972: 235), Mossdorf (1941: 150–152), Smedley (1943: 221) and Todd (1942: 205, 207, 224).

This destruction of the Huayuankow dike by the Chinese Kuo-min-tang seems to have resulted in more deaths than any other single human action in history. Indeed, some estimates of the total number of resultant drownings approach the million mark (Boyle, 1972: 187; Freeberne, 1973: 69), although the more conservative estimate of 'several hundred thousand' is used in the text. The three closest rivals to this fatality record appear to be the Allied fire bombing of Dresden in February 1945, with an estimated 135×10^3 fatalities (Björnerstedt et al., 1973: 45); the US fire bombing of Tokyo in March 1945, with an estimated 83×10^3 fatalities (Björnerstedt et al., 1973: 46); and the US atomic bombing of Hiroshima in August 1945, with a conservatively estimated 78×10^3 fatalities (Vellodi et al., 1968: 3).

According to H. Bielenstein (Columbia Univ., priv. comm., 16 Jan. 1976), the military destruction in 1938 of the Yellow River containment system was, in fact, a repetition of a similar event that occurred between A.D. 2 and 11. The earlier catastrophe resulted in a great migration of displaced people to the south, as well as in the fall of a dynasty.

6. The literature dealing with intentional weather modification for civil purposes has been compiled in extenso (Grimes, 1972; Taborsky and Thuronyi, 1960; 1962; Thuronyi, 1963; 1964). See also Hess (1974). Weather modification for military purposes has been discussed on several occasions (Kotsch, 1968; Pell, 1972; Studer, 1968–1969; see also note 1).

The best sources of information on military weather manipulation by the USA in Indochina are a series of US Senate documents (Pell, 1972; 1973; 1974). A number of news accounts and articles on the subject have also appeared (Andersson, 1971; Begishev, 1972; Cohn, 1972; Gliedman, 1972: V, etc.; Greenberg, 1972; Hersh, 1972; Horton, 1976; Norman, 1974; Ognibene, 1972; Purrett, 1972; Recherche, 1972; Shapley, 1972 a; 1974), of which those by Granville (1975) and MacDonald (1975–1976) can be singled out.

7. A number of articles explore the ecological consequences of weather modification for civil purposes, among them those by Cooper and Jolly (1969), Livingstone et al. (1966), Sargent (1967), Waggoner (1966) and Whittaker (1967). These reviews deal primarily with the potential ramifications of rainfall manipulation over extended periods of time. All of the authors agree that the potential ecological impact of such activities is likely to be undesirable, despite the good intentions involved.

The influence on ecosystems of sustained minor differences in temperature is covered in Chapter 1, note 11. The influence on agricultural ecosystems of minor changes in temperature or precipitation is covered in Chapter 1, note 12. References to the influence of minor weather changes on the incidence of bacterial, fungal and insect attacks are provided in Chapter 1, note 12 as well.

4. Epilogue

Nuclear or other weapons of mass destruction are today available to numerous nations. The variety and sophistication of these gruesome weapons and their delivery systems continue to increase as do the number of nations to whom they are available. Local wars continue to occur in different regions of the world and the possibility of another global war remains ever present. Given the capability, the belligerents in any war of the future are certain at least to consider using weapons of mass destruction – weapons that have a devastating impact on both man and nature.

On the other hand, it must be recalled that nuclear weapons have not been exploded for hostile purposes for the three decades since World War II, that lethal chemical weapons have not been employed on a large scale for the six decades since World War I, and that biological weapons have never been used on a significant scale. Although chemical harassing agents and chemical anti-plant agents have both been massively employed within the past decade, during the Second Indochina War, their future employment in this fashion has recently been renounced by the USA.

Moreover, there exists a number of multilateral (though far from universal) treaties that include restrictions of one sort or another on the use of weapons of mass destruction.[1] The use or possession of nuclear weapons has been curtailed in several direct of indirect fashions. For example, about 20 Latin American nations (in concert with the USA, the UK, France and China) have agreed to denuclearize approximately 40 per cent of the land area of the Western Hemisphere south of the USA. The World War II peace treaties imposed prohibitions on the possession of nuclear weapons upon most of the defeated nations. Nineteen or more nations (including the USA, the USSR, the UK and France) have agreed to keep Antarctica free of nuclear weapons; at least 62 nations (including the USA, the USSR and the UK) have similarly agreed to keep most of the ocean floor nuclear-free; and about 74 nations (including the USA, the USSR and the UK) have agreed not to station nuclear weapons on the Moon or elsewhere in outer space. Moreover, more than 100 presently non-nuclear nations have agreed to refrain from possessing nuclear weapons. A conglomerate of additional treaties has restricted the ratifying parties in various ways with respect to the testing of nuclear weapons and to their delivery systems.

Some 96 nations have agreed not to use chemical or biological weapons in war. Most of the defeated nations of World War II agreed, in conjunction with their peace treaties, not to possess chemical or biological weapons. And 73 or more nations have agreed not to produce or stockpile either biological weapons or chemical toxin weapons of biological or other origin. Finally, a number of international treaties that would restrict various weapons of mass destruction are currently under negotiation or open for signature.

It can be seen that the desultory international arms control and disarmament negotiations of the past century have resulted in a hodge-podge of fragmentary controls over weapons of mass destruction and that these have gained only partial acceptance. There thus remains an urgent need for a comprehensive and widely accepted ban on the possession and use of nuclear and other weapons of mass destruction. To single out these weapons is to some extent simplistic inasmuch as the achievement of a peaceful and disarmed world represents an enormously complex and multifaceted problem. However, weapons of mass destruction are especially pernicious because their impact simply cannot be confined either to the target area or to the time of attack. In addition to this inability to contain these means of war to either the spatial or temporal boundaries of attack, they are further repulsive because of their partially unpredictable ramifications and because their impact as a rule does not discriminate between combatants and non-combatants. They must as well be condemned because they wreak havoc within the enmeshed ecosystems.

Ecological considerations have not played a dominant rôle in man's past affairs, whether civil or military. To the extent that such considerations did, in fact, intrude upon his decision-making processes, man simply took for granted a position of dominance in the natural global hierarchy. The validity of this supremacy has, however, never been put to an adequate test. To date, even the most severe anthropogenic perturbations of the global ecosystem have been modest and transitory. However, man has finally attained the technological capabilities to do much more than this. It thus remains to be seen whether he will use these capabilities for military purposes, actions that could lead to a Carthaginian peace that is worldwide in scope.

Note to Chapter 4

1. Treaties that place restrictions on weapons of mass destruction have been compiled by the ACDA (1975), Dupuy and Hammerman (1973), Friedman (1972), Kristoferson

(1975), Schindler and Toman (1972) and others. The law of war as it applies to weapons of mass destruction has been analysed by SIPRI (1976 b). See also the briefer treatments by Barnaby (1976), Blix (1974), Goldblat (1975; 1977), Schneider (1976), Thorsson (1975) and Westing (1974 b). Moreover, the section on arms control and disarmament in each of the *SIPRI Yearbooks* is an especially useful source of pertinent information.

References

Aartsen, J. P. van, 1946. Consequences of the war on agriculture in the Netherlands. *Int. Rev. Agric.*, **37**: 5S–34S, 49S–70S, 108S–123S.

ACDA (Arms Control and Disarmament Agency, US), 1975. Arms control and disarmament agreements: texts and history of negotiations. ACDA Publication No. 77, 159 pp.

ACDA (Arms Control and Disarmament Agency, US), [n.d., 1975?]. Worldwide effects of nuclear war: some perspectives. ACDA, 24 pp.

Agricultural Research Service, US, 1961. Leader's guide to agriculture's defense against biological warfare and other outbreaks: a technical presentation. Special Report No. ARS 22-75. 15 pp.

Ahlgren, I. F. and Ahlgren, C. E., 1960. Ecological effects of forest fires. *Botanical Review*, **26**: 483–533.

Ahmed, A. K., 1975. Unshielding the sun: human effects. *Environment*, **17**(3): 6–14.

Air University Quarterly Review, 1953–1954. Attack on the irrigation dams in North Korea. *Air Univ. Quart. Rev.* (now *Air Univ. Rev.*), **6**(4): 40–61.

Ajl, S. J. et al. (eds), 1970–1972. *Microbial Toxins* (Academic Press, New York) 8 vols. [3 821 pp.].

Alexander, A. S. et al., 1971. *Control of Chemical and Biological Weapons.* (Carnegie Endowment for International Peace, New York) 130 pp.

Allen, S. E., 1964. Chemical aspects of heather burning. *J. Applied Ecology*, **1**: 347–367.

Allred, D. M., Beck, D. E. and Jorgensen, C. D., 1965. Summary of the ecological effects of nuclear testing on native animals at the Nevada test site. *Proceedings of the Utah Academy of Sciences, Arts and Letters*, **44**: 252–60.

Ambrose, J. T., 1973. Bees and warfare. *Gleanings in Bee Culture*, **101**(11): 343–345, 364.

Ambrose, J. T., 1974. Insects in warfare. *Army*, **24**(12): 33–38.

Anderson, J., 1971. Air Force turns rainmaker in Laos. *Washington Post* (18 March 1971) p. F7.

Arena, V., 1971. *Ionizing Radiation and Life.* (C. V. Mosby, St. Louis) 543 pp.

Arend, J. L., 1941. Infiltration rates of forest soils in the Missouri Ozarks is affected by woods burning and litter removal. *J. Forestry*, **39**: 726–8.

Armed Forces Chemical Journal, 1964. Chemical warfare bibliography 1957–1963. *Armed Forces Chem. J.* (now *Natl Defense*), **18**(1): 29.

Army, US Dept. of the, 1962. *Barriers and Denial Operations.* US Dept. Army Field Manual No. 31-10, 128 pp.

Army, US Dept. of the, 1967. *Chemical Reference Handbook.* US Dept. Army Field Manual No. 3-8, 132 pp.

Army, US Dept. of the, 1967–1970. *Counterguerrilla Operations.* US Dept. Army Field Manual No. 31-16, 164 + 17 + 18 pp.

Army, U.S. Dept. of the, 1969. *Employment of Riot Control Agents, Flame, Smoke, Antiplant Agents and Personnel Detectors in Counterguerrilla Operations.* US Dept. Army Training Circ. No. 3-16, 85 pp.

Army and Air Force, US Depts of the, 1965. *Military Biology and Biological Agents.* US Dept. Army Technical Manual No. 3-216, 104 + 3 pp.

Army and Air Force, US Depts of the, 1967. *Military Chemistry and Chemical Agents.* US Dept. Army Technical Manual No. 3-215, 101 + 9 + 7 pp. + 2 tables.

Army Digest, 1968. Silent weapons: role of chemicals in lower case warfare. *Army Digest* (now *Soldiers*), **23**(11): 6–11.

Aronow, S., Ervin, F. R. and Sidel, V. W. (eds), 1963. *Fallen Sky: Medical Consequences of Thermonuclear War.* (Hill & Wang, New York), 134 pp.

Associated Press, 1971. Besieged fire base fights off attack by Hanoi commandos. *New York Times* (10 April 1971), p. 7.

Auerbach, S. I., 1968. Postattack insect problems. In National Academy of Sciences *et al.* (eds), *Postattack Recovery from Nuclear War.* (National Academy of Sciences, Washington), 434 pp.: pp. 137–142.

Ayres, R. U., 1965. Environmental effects of nuclear weapons, Rept. No. HI-518-RR. (Hudson Inst, Croton-on-Hudson, N.Y.) 3 Vols. [392 pp.].

Baker, J. O. Jr, 1975. *Selected and Annotated Bibliography for Wilderness Fire Managers.* US Forest Service, 36 pp.

Barnaby, F., 1975. Spread of the capability to do violence: an introduction to environmental warfare. *Ambio*, **4**: 178–85.

Barnaby, F., 1976. Environmental warfare. *Bull. Atomic Scientists*, **32**(5): 36–43.

Barnes, J. M., Hayes, W. J. and Kay, K., 1957. Control of health hazards likely to arise from the use of organo-phosphorus insecticides in vector control. *Bull. World Health Org.*, **16**: 41–61.

Barrairon, P., 1973. [The biological weapon: myth or reality?] *Défense Nationale*, **29**(Aug.–Sep.): 129–142. In French.

Batchelder, R. B. and Hirt, H. F., 1966. *Fire in Tropical Forests and Grasslands.* Rept No. ES-23. US Army Natick Labs, Earth Sciences Div., Natick, Mass., 380 pp.

Batten, E. S., 1966. *Effects of Nuclear War on the Weather and Climate.* Memo. No. RM-4989-TAB. Rand Corp., Santa Monica, Cal., 59 pp.

Batten, J. K., 1960. Chemical warfare in history. *Armed Forces Chem. J.* (now *National Defense*), **14**(2): 16–17, 32.

Baudisch, K., Förster, S., Helbing, H. and Stulz, P. (eds), 1971. *ABC Weapons, Disarmament and the Responsibility of Scientists.* World Federation of Scientific Workers, London, 224 pp.

Bauer, E. and Gilmore, F. R., 1965. Effect of atmospheric nuclear explosions on total ozone. *Reviews of Geophysical and Space Physics*, **13**: 451–8.

Baxter, S. B., 1966. *William III and the Defense of European Liberty 1650–1702.* (Harcourt, Brace & World, New York)., 462 pp. + 8 pl.

Beck, B. F., 1937. Bees as strategists and warriors. *Gleanings in Bee Culture*, **65**: 534–7, 580.

Begishev, V., 1972. Another genocide weapon. *New Times*, **1972**(32): 26–27.

Bensen, D. W. and Sparrow, A. H. (eds), 1971. *Survival of Food Crops and Livestock in the Event of Nuclear War.* Symposium Series No. 24. (US Atomic Energy Commission), 745 pp.

Bentley, J. R., Conrad, C. E. and Schimke, H. E., 1971. *Burning Trials in Shrubby Vegetation Desiccated with Herbicides.* Research Note No. PSW-241. (US Forest Service), 9 pp.

Bentley, J. R. and Graham, C. A., 1976. *Applying Herbicides to Desiccate Manzanita Brushfields before Burning.* Research Note No. PSW-312. (US Forest Service), 8 pp.

Berrill, M., 1966. Stillness on Eniwetok. *Natural History*, **75**(10): 20 5, 70.

Björnerstedt, R. *et al.*, 1973. *Napalm and Other Incendiary Weapons and All Aspects of Their Possible Use.* (United Nations, New York), 63 pp.

Blix, H., 1974. Current efforts to prohibit the use of certain conventional weapons. *Instant Research on Peace and Violence*, **4**: 21–30.

Blok, P. J., 1907. *History of the People of the Netherlands. IV: Frederick Henry, John deWitt, William III.* [translated from the Dutch by O. A. Bierstadt]. (G. P. Putnam's Sons, New York), 566 pp. + 3 maps.

Blot, W. J. and Miller, R. W., 1973. Mental retardation following *in utero* exposure to the atomic bombs of Hiroshima and Nagasaki. *Radiology*, **106**: 617–9.

Blumenfeld, S. and Meselson, M., 1971. Military value and political implications of the use of riot control agents in warfare. In Alexander, A. S. *et al.*, *Control of Chemical and Biological Weapons*. (Carnegie Endowment for International Peace, New York), 130 pp.: pp. 64–93.

Blumenfeld, S. N., 1966. *Nuclear War and Soil Microflora*. Memo. No. RM-4827-TAB. (Rand Corp., Santa Monica, Cal.), 39 pp.

Blumenthal, R., 1969. U.S. now uses tear gas as routine war weapon. *New York Times* (6 December 1969), p. 3.

Boffey, P. M., 1968. Nerve gas: Dugway accident linked to Utah sheep kill. *Science*, **162**: 1460–4.

Bolt, B. A., 1976. *Nuclear Explosions and Earthquakes: the Parted Veil.* (W. H. Freeman, San Francisco), 309 pp.

Bond, H. (ed.), 1946. *Fire and the Air War.* (National Fire Protection Association International, Boston) 260 pp.

Boucher, G., Ryall, A. and Jones, A. E., 1969. Earthquakes associated with underground nuclear explosions. *J. Geophysical Research*, **74**: 3808–20.

Boyce, J. S., 1961. *Forest Pathology.* 3rd Edn (McGraw-Hill, New York), 572 pp.

Boyle, J. H., 1972. *China and Japan at War, 1937–1945: the Politics of Collaboration.* (Stanford University Press, Stanford, Cal.), 430 pp. + 8 pl.

Brode, H. L., 1968. Review of nuclear weapons effects. *Annual Review of Nuclear Science*, **18**: 153–202.

Brodine, V., Gaspar, P. P. and Pallman, A. J. 1969. Wind from Dugway. *Environment*, **11**(1): 2–9, 40–43.

Broido, A., 1960. Mass fires following nuclear attack. *Bull. Atomic Scientists*, **16**: 409–13.

Broido, A., 1963. Effects of fire on major ecosystems. In Woodwell, G. M. (ed.). *Ecological Effects of Nuclear War*. Publ. No. 917. (Brookhaven National Laboratory, Upton, N.Y.), 72 pp.: pp. 11–19.

Bronson, F. H. and Tiemeier, O. W., 1959. Relationship of precipitation and black-tailed jack rabbit populations in Kansas. *Ecology*, **40**: 194–8.

Brown, A. A. and Davis, K. P., 1973. *Forest Fire: Control and Use.* 2nd Edn (McGraw-Hill, New York), 686 pp.

Brown, F. J., 1968. *Chemical Warfare: a Study in Restraints.* (Princeton University Press, Princeton, N.J.), 355 pp.

Bruner, D. W. and Gillespie, J. H., 1973. *Hagan's Infectious Diseases of Domestic Animals.* 6th Edn (Cornell University Press, Ithaca, N.Y.), 1385 pp.

Buchanan, R. E. and Gibbons, N. E. (eds), 1974. *Bergey's Manual of Determinative Bacteriology.* 8th Edn (Williams & Wilkins, Baltimore), 1246 pp.

Bücherl, W., Buckley, E. E. and Deulofeu, V. (eds), 1968–71. *Venomous Animals and Their Venoms. I and II: Venomous Vertebrates. III: Venomous Invertebrates.* (Academic Press, New York) 3 Vols. (707 + 687 + 537 pp.).

Budowski, G., 1956. Tropical savannas, a sequence of forest felling and repeated burnings. *Turrialba*, **6**(1–2): 23–33.

Budyko, M. I., 1971. *Climate and Life* (translated from Russian; Edited by D. H. Miller). (Academic Press, New York, 1974), 508 pp.

Bugher, J. C., 1951. Mammalian host in yellow fever. In Strode, G. K. (ed.), *Yellow Fever.* (McGraw-Hill, New York), 710 pp.: pp. 299–384.

Bulletin of the Atomic Scientists (ed.) 1960. Biological and chemical warfare: an international symposium. *Bull. Atomic Scientists*, **16**: 226–56.

Burnet, M. and White, D. O., 1972. *Natural History of Infectious Disease.* 4th Edn (Cambridge University Press, Cambridge, England), 278 pp.

Caidin, M., 1960. *The Night Hamburg Died.* (Ballantine, New York), 158 pp.

Caldwell, M. M., 1968. Solar ultraviolet radiation as an ecological factor for alpine plants. *Ecological Monographs*, **38**: 243–68.

Caldwell, M. M., 1971. Solar UV irradiation and the growth and development of higher plants. In Giese, A. C. (ed.), *Photophysiology: Current Topics in Photobiology and Photochemistry.* Vol. 6 (Academic Press, New York), 388 pp.: pp. 131–77.

Canada, 1975. *Suggested Preliminary Approach to Considering the Possibility of Concluding a Convention on the Prohibition of Environmental Modification for Military or Other Hostile Purposes.* Document No. CCD/463. Conference of the Committee on Disarmament, Geneva, 21 + 3 pp.

Cannon, H. W. (ed.), 1971. *Investigation into Electronic Battlefield Program.* US Senate Committee on Armed Services, 221 pp.

Chandler, C. C., Storey, T. G. and Tangren, C. D., 1963. *Prediction of Fire Spread Following Nuclear Explosions.* Research Paper No. PSW-5 (US Forest Service), 110 pp.

Chapline, W. R. and Cooperrider, C. K., 1941. Climate and grazing. In *US Dept. Agriculture Yearbook 1941*, pp. 459–76.

Chern, C. J. and Beutler, E., 1975. Pyridoxal kinase: decreased activity in red blood cells of Afro-americans. *Science*, **187**: 1084–86.

Choquette, L. P. E., 1970. Anthrax. In Davis, J. W., Karstad, L. H. and Trainer, D. O. (eds), *Infectious Diseases of Wild Mammals.* (Iowa State University Press, Ames, Ia.), 421 pp.: pp. 256–66.

Clark, W. H., 1961. Chemical and thermonuclear explosives. *Bull. Atomic Scientists*, **17**: 356–60.

Clarke, R., 1968. *Silent Weapons.* (David McKay, New York), 270 pp.

Cockrell, R. A., 1971. Side effect of tear gas. *BioScience*, **21**: 778.

Cohn, V., 1972. Weather war: a gathering storm. *Washington Post* (2 July 1972), pp. C1–C2.

Commoner, B., 1966. *Science and Survival.* (Viking, New York), 150 pp.

Comroy, H. L., Levy, R., Broce, A. B. and Goldman, L. J., 1971. Prediction of species radiosensitivity. In Bensen, D. W. and Sparrow, A. H. (eds), *Survival of Food Crops and Livestock in the Event of Nuclear War.* Symposium Series No. 24. (US Atomic Energy Commission), 745 pp.: pp. 419–33.

Conard, R. A. *et al.*, 1975. *Twenty-year Review of Medical Findings in a Marshallese Population Accidentally Exposed to Radioactive Fallout.* Publication No. BNL50424. (Brookhaven National Laboratory, Upton, N.Y.), 154 pp.

Conley, C. W., 1967–1968. Great Japanese balloon offensive. *Air Univ. Review*, **19**(2): 68–83.

Cook, R. E., 1971. Mist that rolled into the trenches: chemical escalation in World War I. *Bull. Atomic Scientists*, **27**(1): 34–38.

Cookson, J. and Nottingham, J., 1969. *Survey of Chemical and Biological Warfare.* (Sheed & Ward, London), 376 pp. + 10 pl.

Cooper, C. F., 1961. Ecology of fire. *Scientific American*, **204**(4): 150–6, 158, 160, 207.

Cooper, C. F. and Jolly, W. C., 1969. *Ecological Effects of Weather Modification: A Problem Analysis*. University of Michigan Dept. of Resource Planning and Conservation, Ann Arbor, Mich., 160 pp.

Cooper, C. F. and Jolly, W. C., 1970. Ecological effects of silver iodide and other weather modification agents: a review. *Water Resources Research*, **6**: 88–98.

Craft, T. F., 1964. Effects of nuclear explosions on watersheds. *Amer. Water Works Assn. J.*, **56**: 846–52.

Craven, W. F. and Cate, J. L. (eds), 1950. *The Pacific: Guadalcanal to Saipan, August 1942 to July 1944*, Vol. IV in *Army Air Forces in World War II*. (University of Chicago Press, Chicago), 825 pp. + pl.

Craven, W. F. and Cate, J. L. (eds), 1953. The Pacific: Matterhorn to Nagasaki, June 1944 to August 1945, Vol. V in *Army Air Forces in World War II*. (University of Chicago), 878 pp. + pl.

Cushwa, C. T., 1968. *Fire: a Summary of Literature in the United States from the mid-1920's to 1966*. (US Forest Service SE Forest Experiment Sta.; Asheville, N. Car.), 117 pp.

Cutchis, P., 1974. Stratospheric ozone depletion and solar ultraviolet radiation on earth. *Science*, **184**: 13–19.

Daly, R. A., Manger, G. E. and Clark, S. P. Jr, 1966. Density of rocks. In Clark, S. P. Jr (ed.). *Handbook of Physical Constants*. Rev. Edn Memoir No. 97. (Geological Soc. Amer., New York), 587 pp.: pp. 19–26.

Darcourt, P., 1971. When floods and typhoons hit North Vietnam. *US News and World Report*, **71**(20): 46.

Davis, J. W. and Anderson, R. C. (eds), 1971. *Parasitic Diseases of Wild Mammals*. (Iowa State University Press, Ames, Ia.), 364 pp.

Davis, J. W., Anderson, R. C., Karstad, L. and Trainer, D. O. (eds), 1971. *Infectious and Parasitic Diseases of Wild Birds*. (Iowa State University Press, Ames, Ia.), 344 pp.

Davis, J. W., Karstad, L. H. and Trainer, D. O. (eds), 1970. *Infectious Diseases of Wild Mammals*. (Iowa State University Press, Ames, Ia.), 421 pp.

Dawson, W. L. (ed), 1969. *Environmental Dangers of Open-air Testing of Lethal Chemicals*. Report No. 10. US House of Representatives Committee on Government Operations, 62 pp.

DeBell, D. S. and Ralston, C. W., 1970. Release of nitrogen by burning light forest fuels. *Soil Science Soc. Amer. Proc.*, **34**: 936–8.

Defense Civil Preparedness Agency, US, 1973. *DCPA Attack Environment Manual*. Publ. No. CPG 2-1A1-1A9. US Dept. Defense, 9 chaps [530 pp.].

Deirmendjian, D., 1973. On volcanic and other particulate turbidity anomalies. *Adv. Geophysics*, **16**: 267–296.

Derbes, V. J., 1966. DeMussis and the great plague of 1348: a forgotten episode of bacteriological warfare. *J. Amer. Medical Assn*, **196**: 59–62.

D'Olier, F. et al., 1946. *Effects of Atomic Bombs on Hiroshima and Nagasaki*. Pacific War Report No. 3. US Strategic Bombing Survey, 47 pp. + 2 maps.

D'Olier, F. et al., 1947. *Fire Raids on German Cities*. 2nd Edn European War Report No. 193. US Strategic Bombing Survey, 49 pp. + 17 figs.

Dorn, F., 1974. *Sino–Japanese War, 1937–41: from Marco Polo Bridge to Pearl Harbor*. (Macmillan, New York), 477 pp. + pl.

Dorsman, C., 1947. [Damage to horticultural crops from inundation with seawater.] *Tijdschrift over Plantenziekten*, **53**(3): 65–86, In Dutch.

Duffett, J. (ed.), 1968. *Against the Crime of Silence*, Proceedings of the Russell International

War Crimes Tribunal, Stockholm, Copenhagen. (O'Hare Books, Flanders, N.J.), 662 pp.

Dupuy, T. N. and Hammerman, G. M. (eds), 1973. *Documentary History of Arms Control and Disarmament*. (R. R. Bowker, New York), 629 pp.

Eberhardt, L. L., 1967. *Some Ecological Aspects of Nuclear War*. Report No. TID-23939, US Atomic Energy Commission, 29 pp.

Edvarson, K., 1975. Radioecological aspects of nuclear warfare. *Ambio*, **4**: 209–10.

Eigner, J., 1975. Unshielding the sun: environmental effects. *Environment*, **17**(3): 15–18.

Epstein, W., 1976. *Last Chance: Nuclear Proliferation and Arms Control*. (Free Press, N.Y.), 341 pp.

Epstein, W. *et al.*, 1969. *Chemical and Bacteriological (Biological) Weapons and the Effects of Their Possible Use*. (United Nations, New York), 100 pp.

Ervin, F. R., Glazier, J. B., Aronow, S., Nathan, D., Coleman, R., Avery, N., Shohet, S. and Leeman, C., 1962. Medical consequences of thermonuclear war. I. Human and ecologic effects in Massachusetts of an assumed thermonuclear attack on the United States. *New England J. Medicine*, **266**: 1127–37.

Federal Civil Defense Administration, U.S., 1951. *What You Should Know about Biological Warfare: the Official US Government Booklet*. Publication No. PA-2. US Federal Civil Defense Administration, 32 pp.

Fedorov, E. K., 1975. Disarmament in the field of geophysical weapons. *Scientific World*, **19**(3–4): 49–54.

Fenner, F. and Ratcliffe, F. N., 1965. *Myxomatosis*. (Cambridge University Press, Cambridge, England), 379 pp. + 15 pl. + 1 map + 1 tbl.

Fest, C. and Schmidt, K.-J., 1973. *Chemistry of Organophosphorus Pesticides: Reactivity, Synthesis, Mode of Action, Toxicology*. (Springer, New York), 339 pp.

Fisher, G. J. B., 1946. *Incendiary Warfare*. (McGraw-Hill, New York), 125 pp.

Foister, C. E., 1935. Relation of weather to fungous and bacterial diseases. *Botanical Review*, **1**: 497–516.

Foley, H. M. and Ruderman, M. A., 1973. Stratospheric NO production from past nuclear explosions. *J. Geophysical Research*, **78**: 4441–50.

Fons, W. L., Sauer, F. M. and Pong, W. Y., 1957. *Blast Effects on Forest Stands by Nuclear Weapons*. Techn. Rept No. AFSWP-971. US Forest Service, Div. Fire Research, 104 pp.

Forest Service, US, 1966. *Forest Fire Research: Final Report*, phase I, vol. I. (US Forest Service, Washington). ARPA Order No. 818.

Forest Service, US, 1970. *Forest Fire as a Military Weapon*. (US Forest Service, Washington).

Forman, O. L. and Longacre, D. W., 1969–1970. Fire potential increased by weed killers. *Fire Control Notes*, **31**(3): 11–12.

Fosberg, F. R., 1959 a. Long-term effects of radioactive fallout on plants? *Atoll Research Bull.*, **1959**(61), 11 pp.

Fosberg, F. R., 1959 b. Plants and fall-out. *Nature*, **183**: 1448.

Fothergill, L. D., 1963. Some ecological and epidemiological concepts in antipersonnel biological warfare. *Military Medicine*, **128**: 132–4.

Fowler, E. B. (ed), 1965. *Radioactive Fallout, Soils, Plants, Foods, Man*. (Elsevier, New York), 317 pp.

Fox, G. W., 1970. *Pesticides and Ecosystems*. Literature Search No. 70-39. US National Library of Medicine, 24 pp.

Frankenberg, L. and Sörbo, B., 1973. Formation of cyanide from o-chlorobenzylidene malononitrile and its toxicological significance. *Archiv. für Toxikologie*, **31**: 99–108.

Fredriksson, T., 1961. Percutaneous absorption of parathion and paraoxon. IV: Decontamination of human skin from parathion. *Archives Environmental Health*, 3: 185–8.

Freeberne, M., 1973. The land and its people. In Heren, L. *et al. China's Three Thousand Years: the Story of a Great Civilisation*. (Times Newspapers, London), 252 pp. + pl.: pp. 63–102.

Friedman, L. (ed.), 1972. *Law of War: a Documentary History*. (Random House, New York) 2 vols. (1764 pp.).

Fujita, N. and Harrington, J. D., 1961. I bombed the U.S.A. *US Naval Inst. Proc.*, 87(6): 64–9.

Fulbright, J. W. (ed.), 1972. *General Protocol of 1925*. US Senate Committee on Foreign Relations, 439 pp.

Futrell, R. F., Mosely, L. S. and Simpson, A. F., 1961. *United States Air Force in Korea 1950–1953*. (Duell, Sloan & Pearce, New York), 774 pp. + pl.

Giese, A. C. (ed.), 1964–1973. *Photophysiology*. (Academic Press, New York) 8 vols. [2776 pp.].

Gillett, J. D., 1972. *The Mosquito: Its Life, Activities, and Impact on Human Affairs*. (Doubleday, Garden City, N.Y.), 359 pp. + pl.

Glass, B., 1962. Biology of nuclear war. *Amer. Biology Teacher*, 24: 407–25.

Glasstone, S. (ed.), 1964. *Effects of Nuclear Weapons*. Revised edition. US Atomic Energy Commission, 730 pp. + computer.

Gliedman, J., 1972. *Terror from the Sky: North Viet-Nam's Dikes and the U.S. Bombing*. (Vietnam Resource Center, Cambridge, Mass.), 172 pp.

Goldblat, J., 1975. Prohibition of environmental warfare. *Ambio*, 4: 186–90.

Goldblat, J., 1977. Environmental warfare convention: how meaningful is it? *Ambio*, 6: 216–21.

Goldenson, J. and Danner, C. E., 1948. Novel foreign chemical and pyrotechnic munitions. *Chem. and Engin. News*, 26: 1976–78.

Goldsmith, P., Tuck, A. F., Foot, J. S., Simmons, E. L. and Newson, R. L., 1973. Nitrogen oxides, nuclear weapon testing, Concorde and stratospheric ozone. *Nature*, 244: 545–51.

Gooslby, M., 1968. How does nuclear radiation affect honey bees? *Amer. Bee J.*, 108: 352–3.

Goyer, G. G., Grant, L. O. and Henderson, T. J., 1966. Laborarory and field evaluation of Weathercord, a high output cloud seeding device. *J. Applied Meteorology*, 5: 211–6.

Graham, S. A., 1956. Ecology of forest insects. *Annual Rev. Entomology*, 1: 261–280.

Granville; P., 1975 [Perspectives on meteorological and geophysical warfare: a concrete example: the rain-provoking operations in Indochina.] *Défense Nationale*, 31(1): 125–40. In French.

Gravel, M. *et al.* (eds.), 1971–1972. *Pentagon Papers: the Defense Department History of United States Decisionmaking on Vietnam*. (Beacon Press, Boston) 5 vols. (632 + 834 + 746 + 687 + [413] pp.).

Greenberg, D. S., 1972. Vietnam rainmaking: a chronicle of DoD's snowjob. *Science and Govt Rept*, 2(5): 1, 4.

Grimes, A. E., 1972. *Annotated Bibliography on Weather Modification 1960–1969*. Techn. Memo. No. EDS ESIC-1. (US National Oceanic and Atmospheric Administration, Rockville, Md.), 407 pp.

Hachiya, M., 1955. *Hiroshima Diary: the Journal of a Japanese Physician, August 6–September 30, 1945*. Translated from the Japanese and edited by W. Wells. (University of North Carolina Press, Chapel Hill, N. Car.), 238 pp.

Hall, J. A., 1972. *Forest Fuels, prescribed fire, and air quality*. (US Forest Service, Pacific NW Forest and Range Experiment Sta., Portland, Ore.), 44 pp.

Halstead, B. W., 1965–1970. *Poisonous and Venomous Marine Animals of the World. I: Invertebrates. II and III: Vertebrates*. (US Govt Printing Office, Washington) 3 vols. (994 + 1070 + 1006 pp.).

Hampson, J., 1974. Photochemical war on the atmosphere. *Nature*, **250**: 189–91.

Hare, R. C., 1961. Heat effects on living plants. Occasional Paper No. 183. (US Forest Service, S. Forest Experiment Sta., New Orleans), 32 pp.

Hartmann, K., 1967. [Chemical warfare 1966–67.] *Wehrkunde*, **16**: 341–3. In German.

Hartwell, W. V. and Hayes, G. R. Jr, 1965. Respiratory exposure to organic phosphorus insecticides. *Archives Environmental Health*, **11**: 564–8.

Hawley, R. C. and Stickel, P. W., 1948. *Forest Protection*. 2nd Edn (Wiley, New York), 355 pp.

Hayes, W. J. Jr, 1963. *Clinical Handbook on Economic Poisons: Emergency Information for Treating Poisoning*. Publication No. 476. US Public Health Service, 144 pp.

Headley, J. C. and Erickson, E., 1970. *The Pesticide Problem: an Annotated Bibliography*. Research Bull. No. 970. (University of Missouri Agricultural Experiment Sta., Columbia, Mo.), 53 pp.

Health, Education and Welfare, US Dept. of, 1959 a, *Effects of Biological Warfare Agents for use in Readiness Planning*. Emergency Manual Guide No. HEW-2. US Dept. Health, Education and Welfare, 28 pp.

Health, Education and Welfare, US Dept. of, 1959 b. *Effects of Chemical Warfare Agents for use in Readiness Planning*. Emergency Manual Guide No. HEW-3. US Dept. Health, Education and Welfare, 17 pp.

Health, Education and Welfare, US Dept. of, 1959 c. *Effects of Nuclear Weapons for use in Readiness Planning*. Emergency Manual Guide No. HEW-1. US Dept. Health, Education and Welfare, 25 pp.

Heath, R. G., Spann, J. W., Hill, E. F. and Kreitzer, J. F., 1972. *Comparative Dietary Toxicities of Pesticides to Birds*. Special Scientific Report – Wildlife No. 152. US Bureau Sport Fisheries and Wildlife. 57 pp.

Hecht, R., 1976. [Regarding the question of an environmental war.] *Österrechische Militärische Z.*, **14**: 114–115. In German.

Hedén, C.-G., 1967. Defences against biological warfare. *Annual Rev. Microbiology*, **21**: 639–76.

Held, E. E., 1960. Land crabs and fission products at Eniwetok Atoll. *Pacific Science*, **14**: 18–27.

Henahan, J. F., 1974. Nerve-gas controversy: the Army's push for a new chemical weapons system. *Atlantic Monthly*, **234**(3): 52–6.

Heon, N. P., 1964. Flame in war. *Infantry*, **54**(5): 28–32.

Hepting, G. H., 1963. Climate and forest diseases. *Annual Rev. Phytopathology*, **1**: 31–50.

Hersey, J., 1946. *Hiroshima*. (A. A. Knopf, New York), 118 pp.

Hersh, S. M., 1968. *Chemical and Biological Warfare: America's Hidden Arsenal*. (Bobbs–Merrill, Indianapolis), 354 pp.

Hersh, S. [M], 1968–1969. On uncovering the great nerve gas coverup. *Ramparts*, **7**(13): 12–18.

Hersh, S. M., 1972. Rainmaking is used as weapon by U.S. *New York Times* (3 July 1972) 1–2; (4 July) 3; (9 July) E3.

Hess, W. N. (ed.), 1974. *Weather and Climate Modification*. (Wiley, New York), 842 pp.

Hill, J. E., 1961. *Problems of Fire in Nuclear Warfare*. Paper No. P-2414. (Rand Corp., Santa Monica, Cal.), 32 pp.

Hines, N. O., 1962. *Proving Ground: an Account of the Radiobiological Studies in the Pacific, 1946-1961.* (University of Washington Press, Seattle), 366 pp.

Hjertonsson, K., 1973. Study on the prospects of compliance with the Convention on Biological Weapons. *Instant Research on Peace and Violence,* **3**: 211-24.

Hodges, J. D. and Pickard, L. S., 1971. Lightning in the ecology of the southern pine beetle. *Dendroctonus frontalis* (Coleoptera: Scolytidae). *Canadian Entomologist,* **103**: 44-51.

Holbrook, S. H., 1943. *Burning an Empire: the Story of American Forest Fires.* (Macmillan, New York), 229 pp. + 15 pl.

Holbrook, S. [H.], 1944-1945. First bomb. *New Yorker,* **20**(34): 42, 44, 46.

Holifield, C. (ed.), 1959. *Biological and Environmental Effects of Nuclear War. [I.]: Hearings. [II.]: Summary-Analysis.* US Congress Joint Committee on Atomic Energy, 966 + 58 pp. + pl.

Hollister, H. and Eberhardt, L. L., 1965. Problems in estimating the biological consequences of nuclear war (three papers). Report No. TAB-R-5. US Atomic Energy Commission, 40 pp.

Holmberg, B., 1975. Biological aspects of chemical and biological weapons. *Ambio,* **4**: 211-5.

Holmes, C. H., 1951. *Grass, Fern, and Savannah Lands of Ceylon, Their Nature and Ecological Significance.* Paper No. 28. (British Imperial Forestry Institute, Oxford), 95 pp. + 7 pl.

Holvey, D. N. *et al.* (eds), 1972. *Merck Manual of Diagnosis and Therapy.* 12th Edn (Merck, Rahway, N.J.), 1964 pp.

Horsfall, J. G. and Dimond, A. E. (eds), 1959-1960. *Plant Pathology: an Advanced Treatise.* (Academic Press, New York) 3 vols. (674 + 715 + 675 pp.).

Horton, A. M., 1975. Weather modification: a pandora's box. *Air Force Mag.,* **58**(2): 36-40.

Howard, J. D., 1972. *Herbicides in Support of Counterinsurgency Operations: a Cost-Effectiveness Study.* M.S. Thesis. (US Naval Postgrad. School, Monterey, Cal.), 127 pp.

Hsu Long-hsuen and Chang Ming-kai, 1972. *History of the Sino-Japanese War (1937-1945).* 2nd Edn. Translated from the Chinese by Wen Ha-hsiung. (Chung Wu Publ. Co., Taipei), 642 pp. + 16 pl. + 47 maps.

Huschke, R. E., 1966. *Simultaneous Flammability of Wildland Fuels in the United States.* (Memo. No. RM-5073-TAB, Rand Corp., Santa Monica, Cal.), 158 pp.

Infield, G. B., 1971. *Disaster at Bari.* (Macmillan, New York), 301 pp. + 16 pl.

Ingersoll, J. M., 1963. *Historical Examples of Ecological Disaster: Engelmann Spruce Beetle; Krakatau.* Report No. HI-243-RR/A2-3. (Hudson Institute, Croton-on-Hudson, N.Y.), 44 pp.

Ingersoll, J. M., 1964-1965. Volcanoes, nuclear explosions and ecology. *Amer. Scholar,* **34**: 67-77.

Inglis, D., 1968. Nuclear weapons: the outlook for nuclear explosives. In Calder, N. (ed.), *Unless Peace Comes: a Scientific Forecast of New Weapons.* (Viking, New York), 243 pp.: pp. 43-63.

Ingram, W. M. and Tarzwell, C. M., 1954. *Selected Bibliography of Publications Relating to Undesirable Effects Upon Aquatic Life by Algicides, Insecticides, Weedicides.* Publication No. 400. (US Public Health Service), 28 pp.

Irving, D., 1963. *Destruction of Dresden.* (Wm Kimber, London), 255 pp.

Israelyan, V., 1974. New Soviet initiative on disarmament. *International Affairs,* Moscow, **1974**(11): 19-25.

Jackson, W. B., 1969. Survival of rats at Eniwetok Atoll. *Pacific Science*, **23**: 265–75.

Jasani, B. M., 1975. Environmental modifications: new weapons of war? *Ambio*, **4**: 191–8.

Jenkins, D. W., 1963. Defense against insect-disseminated biological warfare agents. *Military Medicine*, **128**: 116–18.

Johnson, F. S., 1973. SSTs, ozone, and skin cancer. *Astronautics and Aeronautics*, **11**(7): 16–21.

Johnston, H. S., 1974 a. Pollution of the stratosphere. *Environmental Conservation*, **1**: 163–76.

Johnston, H. S., 1974 b. Supersonic aircraft and the ozone layer. *Environment and Change*, **2**: 339–50.

Johnston, H. [S.], Whitten, G. and Birks, J., 1973. Effect of nuclear explosions on stratospheric nitric oxide and ozone. *J. Geophysical Research*, **78**: 6107–35.

Jones, G. R. N., 1972. CS and its chemical relatives. *Nature*, **235**: 257–61.

Kanegis, A., 1970–1971. Hidden arsenal: you can't keep a deadly weapon down. *Washington Monthly*, **2**(10): 24–7.

Kantz, A. D., 1971. Measurement of beta dose to vegetation from close-in fallout. In Bensen, D. W. and Sparrow, A. H. (eds), *Survival of Food Crops and Livestock in the Event of Nuclear War*. Symposium Series No. 24. US Atomic Energy Commission, 745 pp.: pp. 56–70.

Kaplan, M. M., 1960. Biological and chemical warfare: communicable diseases and epidemics. *Bull. Atomic Scientists*, **16**: 237–40.

Kaplan, M. [M.], *et al.*, 1970. Health aspects of chemical and biological weapons. (World Health Organization, Geneva), 132 pp.

Karstad, L. H., 1970. Arboviruses. In Davis, J. W., Karstad, L. H. and Trainer, D. O. (eds), *Infectious Diseases of Wild Mammals*. (Iowa State University Press, Ames, Ia.), 421 pp.: pp. 60–7.

Katz, Y. H., 1966. *Nuclear War and Soil Erosion: Some Problems and Prospects*. Memo. No. RM-5203-TAB. (Rand Corp., Santa Monica, Cal.), 87 pp.

Keith, J. O., 1969. [Statement on environmental dangers of organophosphorus insecticides.] In Reuss, H. S. (ed.), *Environmental Dangers of Open-air Testing of Lethal Chemicals*. US House of Representatives Committee on Government Operations, 260 pp.: pp. 99–104.

Kinney, G. F., 1962. *Explosive Shocks in Air*. (Macmillan, New York), 198 pp.

Kipp, D. H., 1931. Wild life in a fire. *Amer. Forests*, **37**: 323–5, 360.

Knight, H., 1966. Loss of nitrogen from the forest floor by burning. *Forestry Chronical*, **42**: 149–52.

Kokatnur, V. R., 1948. Chemical warfare in ancient India. *J. Chemical Education*, **25**: 268–72.

Kolko, G., 1968. Report on the destruction of dikes: Holland 1944–45 and Korea 1953. In Duffett, J. (ed.), *Against the Crime of Silence*. Proceedings of the Russell International War Crimes Tribunal, Stockholm, Copenhagen. (O'Hare Books, Flanders, N.J.), 662 pp.: pp. 224–6.

Kotsch, W. J., 1968. Forecast: change. *U.S. Naval Inst. Proc.*, **94**(1): 69–77.

Kozlowski, T. T. and Ahlgren, C. E. (eds), 1974. *Fire and Ecosystems*. (Academic Press, New York), 542 pp.

Kristoferson, L. (ed.), 1975. Selection of documents . . . pertaining to war and the environment, *Ambio*, **4**: 234–44.

Kudo, R. R., 1966. *Protozoology*. 5th Edn. (C. C. Thomas, Springfield, Ill.), 1174 pp.

Kulp, J. L., 1965. Radionuclides in man from nuclear tests. In Fowler, E. B. (ed.), *Radioactive Fallout, Soils, Plants, Food, Man*. (Elsevier, New York), 317 pp.: pp. 247–84.

Kusterer, D. F., 1966. Application of air-delivered incendiary weapons to limited war in Southeast Asia. Technical Publication No. 4229. (US Naval Ordnance Test Sta., China Lake, Cal.).

Kutger, J. P., 1960–1961. Irregular warfare in transition. *Military Affairs*, **24**: 113–23.

Lacoste, Y., 1972. Bombing the dikes: a geographer's on-the-site analysis. *Nation*, **215**: 298–301.

Lamanna, C., 1959. The most poisonous poison. *Science*, **130**: 763–72.

Lamanna, C., 1961. Immunological aspects of airborne infection: some general considerations of response to inhalation of toxins. *Bacteriological Rev.*, **25**: 323–30.

Lamanna, C. and Carr, C. J., 1967. Botulinal, tetanal, and enterostaphylococcal toxins: a review. *Clinical Pharmacology and Therapeutics*, **8**: 286–332.

Lamb, H. H., 1970. Volcanic dust in the atmosphere: with a chronology and assessment of its meteorological significance. *Phil. Trans. Royal Soc. London*, Ser. A. **266**: 425–533.

Langer, E., 1967. Chemical and biological warfare. I: The research program. II: The weapons and the policies. *Science*, **155**: 174–9, 299–303.

Lapp, R. E., 1958. *Voyage of the Lucky Dragon*. (Harper, New York), 200 pp. + pl.

Larson, C. A., 1970. Ethnic weapons. *Military Rev.*, **50**(11): 3–11.

Lawrence, G. H. M., 1951. *Taxonomy of Vascular Plants*. (Macmillan, New York), 823 pp.

Leitenberg, M., 1967. Biological weapons. *Scientist and Citizen* (now *Environment*), **9**: 153–67.

Levitt, J., 1972. *Responses of Plants to Environmental Stresses*. (Academic Press, New York), 697 pp.

Liebow, A. A., 1965–1966. Encounter with disaster: a medical diary of Hiroshima, 1945. *Yale J. Biology and Medicine*, **38**: 61–239.

Lifton, R. J., 1967. *Death in Life: Survivors of Hiroshima*. (Random House, New York), 594 pp.

Lisella, F. S., Johnson, W. and Lewis, C., 1975–1976. Health aspects of organophosphate insecticide usage. *J. Environmental Health*, **38**: 119–22.

Livingstone, D. A. *et al.*, 1966. Biological aspects of weather modification. *Bull. Ecological Soc. Amer.*, **47**: 39–78.

Lohs, K., 1973. Fire as a means of warfare. *Scientific World*, **17**(1): 18.

Lohs, K.-H., 1974 a. *Chemical Weapons Must be Banned!* (World Federation of Scientific Workers, London), 82 pp.

Lohs, K., 1974 b. [*Synthetic Poisons*]. 4th Edn. Militärverlag der Deutschen Demokratischen Republik, Berlin (DDR) 334 pp. In German.

Lowdermilk, W. C., 1930. Influence of forest litter on run-off, percolation, and erosion. *J. Forestry*, **28**: 474–91.

Lucretius, ca. 55 B.C. On the nature of the universe (translated from the Latin by R. E. Latham, Penguin, Baltimore, 1951), 262 pp.

Lutz, H. J., 1956. *Ecological Effects of Forest Fires in the Interior of Alaska*. Techn. Bull. No. 1133, US Dept. Agriculture, 121 pp.

Lutz, H. J. and Chandler, R. F. Jr, 1946. *Forest Soils*. (Wiley, New York), 514 pp.

MacDonald, G. J. F., 1968. Geophysical warfare: how to wreck the environment. In Calder, N. (ed.), *Unless Peace Comes: a Scientific Forecast of New Weapons*. (Viking Press, New York), 243 pp.; pp. 181–205.

MacDonald, G. J. [F.], 1975–1976. Weather modification as a weapon. *Technology Rev.*, **78**(1–2): 56–63.

Magnuson, W. G. (ed.), 1966. *Weather Modification*. US Senate Comm. on Commerce, 518 pp.

Mahon, G. H. (ed.), 1969. Department of Defense appropriations for 1970, Pt 6, US House of Representatives Comm. on Appropriations, 939 pp.

Manucy, A., 1949. *Artillery Through the Ages: a Short Illustrated History of Cannon, Emphasizing Types Used in America*. History No. 3 of Interpretive Series. US National Park Service, 92 pp.

Marriott, J., 1969. Chemical and biological warfare. *International Defense Review*, 2: 170–4.

Mason, B. J., 1955. Atomic explosions and the weather. *Weather*, 10: 139–41.

Mayer, R. L., 1948. Epidemics and bacteriological warfare. *Scientific Monthly*, 67: 331–7.

McCarthy, R. D., 1969 a. Ban on gas and germ warfare. *US Congressional Record*, 115: 15763–6.

McCarthy, R. D., 1969 b. *Ultimate Folly: War by Pestilence, Asphyxiation, and Defoliation*. (A. A. Knopf, New York), 176 pp.

McColl, J. G. and Grigal, D. F., 1975. Forest fire: effects on phosphorus movement to lakes. *Science*, 188: 1109–11.

McConnell, A. F. Jr, 1969–1970. Mission: ranch hand. *Air Univ. Rev.*, 21(2): 89–94.

McPhee, J., 1973. Curve of binding energy. *New Yorker*, 49(41): 54–145; (42): 50–108; (43): 60–97. Also 1974 (Farrar, Straus & Giroux, New York), 232 pp.

McQuigg, J. D., 1975. *Economic Impacts of Weather Variability*. (Univ. Missouri, Atmospheric Sciences Dept., Columbia, Mo.), 256 pp.

Meeker, T. A., 1972. Chemical/biological warfare. Classroom Study Series 1(2). (Cal. State Univ. Ctr for the Study of Armament and Disarmament, Los Angeles), 27 pp.

Meinel, A. B. and Meinel, M. P., 1967. Volcanic sunset-glow stratum: origin. *Science*, 155: 189.

Meselson, M. S., 1970. Chemical and biological weapons. *Scientific Amer.*, 222(5): 15–25. 148.

Miettinen, J. K., 1974. Chemical arsenal: the time to defuse is now. *Bull. Atomic Scientists*, 30(7): 37–43.

Mikesh, R. C., 1973. *Japan's World War II Balloon Bomb Attacks on North America*. No. 9 in *Annals of Flight*. (Smithsonian Instn, Washington), 85 pp.

Miles, W. D., 1970. Idea of chemical warfare in modern times. *J. History of Ideas*, 31: 297–304.

Miller, L. G., 1966. Use of chemicals in stability operations. *Military Rev.*, 46(12): 43–47.

Miller, R. W., 1974. Late radiation effects: status and needs of epidemiologic research. *Environmental Research*, 8: 221–33.

Miller, W. L. Jr, 1958. Flame for the infantry. *Infantry*, 48(3): 65–72.

Mills, J. and Drew, D., 1976. *Serratia marcescens* endocarditis: a regional illness associated with intravenous drug abuse. *Annals Internal Medicine*, 84: 29–35.

Mitchell, H. H., 1961. *Ecological Problems and Postwar Recuperation: a Preliminary Survey from the Civil Defense Viewpoint*. Research Memo. No. RM-2801-PR. (Rand Corp., Santa Monica, Cal.), 38 pp.

Mitchell, H. H., 1966. Plague in the United States: an assessment of its significance as a problem following a thermonuclear war. Memo. No. RM-4968-TAB. (Rand Corp., Santa Monica, Cal.), 49 pp.

Mitchell, J. M. Jr, 1970. Preliminary evaluation of atmospheric pollution as a cause of the global temperature fluctuation of the past century. In Singer, S. F. (ed.), *Global Effects of Environmental Pollution*. (Springer, New York), 218 pp.: pp. 139–55.

Mobley, H. E., 1974. Fire: its impact on the environment. *J. Forestry*, 72: 414–17.

Mossdorf, O., 1941. [The war in the far east: the Japanese–Chinese conflict.] (W. Conrad, Leipzig), 300 pp. In German.

Mulla, M. S., Keith, J. O. and Gunther, F. A., 1966. Persistence and biological effects of parathion residues in waterfowl habitats. *J. Economic Entomology*, **59**: 1085–90.

Murphy, J. L., Fritschen, L. J. and Cramer, O. P., 1970. Research looks at air quality and forest burning. *J. Forestry*, **68**: 530–5.

Murphy, P. G. and McCormick, J. F., 1971. Ecological effects of acute beta irradiation from simulated-fallout particles on a natural plant community. In Bensen, D. W. and Sparrow, A. H. (eds), *Survival of Food Crops and Livestock in the Event of Nuclear War*. Symposium Series No. 24. (US Atomic Energy Commission), 745 pp.: pp. 454–81.

Mutch, R. W., 1970. Wildland fires and ecosystems: a hypothesis. *Ecology*, **51**: 1046–51.

Nagai, T., 1951. *We of Nagasaki: the Story of Survivors in an Atomic Wasteland*. (Transl. from the Japanese by I. Shirato and H. B. C. Silverman. Duell, Sloan and Pearce, New York), 189 pp.

National Academy of Sciences *et al.* (eds), 1968. *Postattack Recovery from Nuclear War*. (National Academy of Sciences, Washington), 434 pp.

Neilands, J. B., 1970. Vietnam: progress of the chemical war. *Asian Survey*, **10**: 209–29.

Neilands, J. B., 1972 a. Gas warfare in Vietnam in perspective. In Neilands, J. B. *et al.*, *Harvest of Death*. (Free Press, New York), 304 pp.: pp. 3–101.

Neilands, J. B., 1972 b. Napalm survey. In Browning, F. and Forman, D. (eds), *Wasted Nations*. (Harper & Row, New York), 346 pp.: pp. 26–37.

Neilands, J. B., 1973. Survey of chemical and related weapons. *Naturwissenschaften*, **60**: 177–83.

Neilands, J. B., Orians, G. H., Pfeiffer, E. W., Vennema, A. and Westing, A. H., 1972. *Harvest of Death: Chemical Warfare in Vietnam and Cambodia*. (Free Press, New York), 304 pp.

Nier, A. O. C. *et al.*, 1975. *Long-term Worldwide Effects of Multiple Nuclear-weapons Detonations*. (National Academy of Sciences, Washington), 213 pp.

Nordenskiöld, E., 1918. Palisades and "noxious gases" among the South-American Indians. *Ymer Tidskrift*, **38**: 220–43.

Nordheimer, J., 1975. 29 years after U.S. moved them, Bikini natives sue for safe return. *New York Times* 17 October 1975, 70.

Norman, C., 1973. Binary weapons: death in two parts. *Progressive*, **37**(12): 25–7.

Norman, C., 1974. Pentagon admits Vietnam rainmaking. *Nature*, **249**: 402.

O'Callaghan, T. C., 1973. *Bibliography on Geophysical, Geochemical, and Geological Effects of Nuclear Events*. No. 1 in Bibliographies in Science Series. (General Publishing Services, Alexandra, Va.) 48 pp.

Ognibene, P. J., 1972. Making war with the weather. *New Republic*, **167**(12): 12–14.

Okada, S., Hamilton, H. B., Egami, N., Okajima, S., Russell, W. J. and Takeshita, K. (eds), 1975. Review of thirty years study of Hiroshima and Nagasaki atomic bomb survivors. *J. Radiation Research*, Chiba, **16** (supplement): 1–164.

OKunewick, J. P., 1966. *Effects of Acute Doses of γ-radiation on Pine Trees*. Memo. No. RM-4904-TAB. (Rand Corp., Santa Monica, Cal.), 30 pp.

Osburn, W. S. Jr, 1968. Forecasting long-range ecological recovery from nuclear attack. In National Academy of Sciences *et al.* (eds), *Postattack Recovery from Nuclear War*. (National Academy of Sciences, Washington), 434 pp.: pp. 107–35.

Page, C. H. and Vigoureux, P. (eds), 1974. *International System of Units (SI)*. 3rd edn. Special Publication No. 330. US National Bureau of Standards, 43 pp.

Palumbo, R. F., 1962. Recovery of the land plants at Eniwetok Atoll following a nuclear detonation. *Radiation Botany*, 1: 182–9.

Parker, H. M. and Healy, J. W., 1955. Environmental effects of a major reactor disaster. In International Atomic Energy Agency (ed.). *Proceedings of the [First] International Conference on the Peaceful Uses of Atomic Energy*. N.Y.: United Nations Publication No. A/CONF. 8 (United Nations, New York) 17 vols: vol. XIII, pp. 106–9.

Partington, J. R., 1960. *History of Greek Fire and Gunpowder*. (W. Heffer, Cambridge, England), 381 pp. + 3 pl.

Pell, C. (ed.), 1972. *Prohibiting Military Weather Modification*. US Senate Committee on Foreign Relations, 162 pp.

Pell, C., 1973. *Prohibiting Environmental Modification as a Weapon of War*. US Senate Report No. 93–270, 7 pp.

Pell, C. (ed.), 1974. *Weather Modification*. US Senate Committee on Foreign Relations, 123 pp.

Penney, [W. G.], Samuels, D. E. J. and Scorgie, G. C., 1970. Nuclear explosive yields at Hiroshima and Nagasaki. *Phil. Trans. Royal Soc. London*, Series A, 266: 357–424 + 8 pl.

Perry, T. O., 1968. Vietnam: truths of defoliation. *Science*, 160: 601.

Peterkin, F. P., 1972. Chemical warfare: a better alternative. *Marine Corps Gazette*, 56(10): 37–9.

Philpot, C. W. and Mutch, R. W., 1968. *Flammability of Herbicide-treated Guava Foliage*. Research Paper No. INT-54, US Forest Service, 9 pp.

Pimentel, D., 1971. *Ecological Effects of Pesticides on Non-target Species*. (US Office of Science and Technology, Washington), 220 pp.

Platt, R. B., 1963. Ionizing radiation and homeostasis of ecosystems. In Woodwell, G. M. (ed.), *Ecological Effects of Nuclear War*. Publication No. 917 (Brookhaven National Laboratory, Upton, N.Y.), 72 pp.: pp. 39–60.

Pollack, J. B., Toon, O. B., Sagan, C., Summers, A., Baldwin, B. and VanCamp, W., 1976. Volcanic explosions and climatic change: a theoretical assessment. *J. Geophysical Research*, 81: 1071–83.

Popper, R. D. and Lybrand, W. A., 1960. *Inventory of Selected Source Materials Relevant to Integration of Physical and Social Effects of Air Attack*. (Human Sciences Research Publ. No. HSR-RR-60/4-SE, Arlington, Va.).

Porter, D. G., 1972. Bombing the dikes: Nixon's next option. *New Republic*, 166(23): 19–20.

Punte, C. L., Weimer, J. T., Ballard, T. A. and Wilding, J. L., 1962. Toxicological studies on *o*-chlorobenzylidene malononitrile. *Toxicology and Applied Pharmacology*, 4: 656–62.

Purchase, I. F. H. (ed.), 1974. *Mycotoxins*. (Elsevier, Amsterdam), 443 pp.

Purrett, L. A., 1972. Weather modification as a future weapon. *Science News*, 101: 254–5.

Quarantelli, E. L., 1970. Selected annotated bibliography of social science studies on disasters. *American Behavioral Scientist*, 13: 452–6.

Radeleff, R. D., 1970. *Veterinary Toxicology*. 2nd Edn. (Lea & Febiger, Philadelphia), 352 pp.

Ragotzkie, R. A., 1959. Mortality of loggerhead turtle eggs from excessive rainfall. *Ecology*, 40: 303–5.

Rahm, N. M., 1946. Fire fly project. *Fire Control Notes*, 7(2): 4–7.

Randal, J., 1967. Foe's sanctuary hit by fire bombs. *New York Times* (19 January 1967), 1, 3.

Răskovà, H. (ed.), 1971–1972. *Pharmacology and Toxicology of Naturally Occurring Toxins*. (Pergamon, New York) 2 vols. [725 pp. + pl.].

Rayner, J. F., 1957–1958. Studies of disasters and other extreme situations: an annotated selected bibliography. *Human Organization,* **16**(2): 30–40.

Recherche, 1972. [Geophysical warfare makes its discrete debut.] *Recherche,* **3**: 265. In French.

Red Cross, International Committee of the, 1973. *Weapons that May Cause Unnecessary Suffering or Have Indiscriminate Effects.* (International Committee of the Red Cross, Geneva), 72 pp.

Rees, D., 1964. *Korea: the Limited War.* (St. Martin's, New York), 511 pp. + 15 pl.

Reid, G. C., Isaksen, I. S. A., Holzer, T. E. and Crutzen, P. J., 1976. Influence of ancient solar-proton events on the evolution of life. *Nature,* **259**: 177–9.

Reinhold, R., 1972. U.S. attempted to ignite Vietnam forests in '66–67. *New York Times* (21 July 1972), 1–2; (22 July): 5; (23 July): E2.

Reuss, H. S. (ed.), 1969. *Environmental Dangers of Open-air Testing of Lethal Chemicals.* (US House of Representatives Committee on Government Operations), 260 pp.

Rhoads, W. A. and Platt, R. B., 1971. Beta radiation damage to vegetation from close-in fallout from two nuclear detonations. *BioScience,* **21**: 1121–5, 1113.

Rhoads, W. A., Ragsdale, H. L., Platt, R. B. and Romney, E. M., 1971. Radiation doses to vegetation from close-in fallout at Project Schooner. In Bensen, D. W. and Sparrow, A. H. (eds). *Survival of Food Crops and Livestock in the Event of Nuclear War.* Symposium Series No. 24. (US Atomic Energy Commission), 745 pp.: pp. 352–369.

Rickard, W. H. and Shields, L. M., 1963. Early stage in the plant recolonization of a nuclear target area. *Radiation Botany,* **3**: 41–4.

Ritchie, D. J., 1959. Reds may use lightning as weapon. *Missiles and Rockets,* **5**(35): 13–4.

Robinson, J. P., 1973. Binary weapons: a mixed problem. *New Scientist,* **58**: 34–5.

Robinson, J. P., 1974. *Chemical/Biological Warfare: an Introduction and a Bibliography.* Political Issue Series 3(2). (Cal. State Univ. Ctr for the Study of Armament and Disarmament, Los Angeles), 14 + 34 pp.

Robinson, J. P. P., 1975. Special case of chemical and biological weapons. *Bull. Atomic Scientists,* **31**(5): 17–23.

Ronneberg, C. E. *et al.* (eds), 1960. *Nonmilitary Defense: Chemical and Biological Defenses in Perspective.* Advances in Chemistry Series No. 26. (American Chemical Society, Washington), 100 pp.

Rose, H. and Rose, S., 1972. CS gas: an imperialist technology. In Browning, F. and Forman, D. (eds). *Wasted Nations.* (Harper & Row, New York), 346 pp.: pp. 38–49.

Rose, S. (ed), 1969. *CBW: Chemical and Biological Warfare.* (Beacon Press, Boston), 209 pp.

Rosebury, T., 1949. *Peace or Pestilence: Biological Warfare and How to Avoid It.* (McGraw-Hill, New York), 218 pp.

Rosebury, T., 1960. Biological warfare: some historical considerations. *Bull. Atomic Scientists,* **16**: 227–36.

Rosebury, T. and Kabat, E. A., 1947. Bacterial warfare: a critical analysis of the available agents, their possible military applications, and the means for protection against them. *J. Immunology,* **56**: 7–96.

Rosen, M. N., 1971. Botulism. In Davis, J. W., Anderson, R. C., Karstad, L. and Trainer, D. O. (eds). *Infectious and Parasitic Diseases of Wild Birds.* (Iowa State University Press, Ames, Ia), 344 pp.: pp. 100–17.

Rothschild, J. H., 1964. *Tomorrow's Weapons: Chemical and Biological.* (McGraw-Hill, New York), 271 pp.

Ruderman, M. A., 1974. Possible consequences of nearby supernova explosions for atmospheric ozone and terrestrial life. *Science,* **184**: 1079–81.

Runge, E. C. A., 1969–1970. Use weather to predict your corn yields. *Crops and Soil*, **22**(5): 11–13.

Sanford, J. P., 1976. Medical aspects of riot control (harassing) agents. *Ann. Rev. Medicine*, **27**: 421–9.

Sargent, F., II, 1967. Dangerous game: taming the weather. *Scientist and Citizen* (now *Environment*), **9**: 81–8, 96.

Sargent, F., II and Tromp, S. W., 1964. *Survey of Human Biometeorology*. Technical Note No. 65. (World Meteorological Organization, Geneva), 113 pp.

Sauer, C. O., 1950. Grassland climax, fire, and man. *J. Range Mgt*, **3**: 16–21.

Saunders, D. N., 1967. Bari incident. *US Naval Inst. Proc.* **93**(9): 35–9.

Schindler, D. and Toman, J., 1973. *Laws of Armed Conflicts: a Collection of Conventions, Resolutions and Other Documents*. (A. W. Sijthoff, Leiden), 795 pp.

Schneider, M. M., 1976. [Against the military misuse of the environment.] *Deutsche Aussenpolitik*, **21**: 578–601. In German.

Schubert, J. and Lapp, R. E., 1957. *Radiation: What it is and How it Affects You*. (Viking, New York), 314 pp.

Schultz, V., 1966. References on Nevada test site ecological research. *Great Basin Naturalist* **26**(3–4): 79–86.

Schumacher, K., 1970. [Action of chemical warfare agents: symptomatology and therapy.] *Z. f. Ärztliche Fortbildung*, **64**: 97–106. In German.

Scientist and Citizen, (ed.), 1967. Chemical and biological warfare: a special issue. *Scientist and Citizen* (now *Environment*), **9**(7): 111–73.

Scientists' Committee for Radiation Information, 1962. Effects of a 20 megaton bomb. *New Univ. Thought*, **2**(3): 24–33.

Scotto, J., Fears, T. R. and Gori, G. B., 1976. Measurements of ultraviolet radiation in the United States and comparisons with skin cancer data. Publication No. (NIH)76-1029. (US Dept. Health, Education and Welfare), 15 + [202] pp.

Scotto, J., Kopf, A. W. and Urbach, F., 1974. Non-melanoma skin cancer among Caucasians in four areas of the United States. *Cancer*, **34**: 1333–8.

Scoville, H. and Osborn, R., 1970. *Missile Madness*. (Houghton Mifflin, Boston), 77 pp.

Sérié, C., Andral, L., Lindrec, A. and Neri, P., 1964. [Epidemic of yellow fever in Ethiopia (1960–1962): preliminary observations.] *Bull. World Health Org.*, **30**: 299–319. In French.

Shapiro, C. S., 1974. Effects on humans of world-wide stratospheric fall-out in a nuclear war. *Bull. Peace Proposals*, **5**: 186–90.

Shapley, D., 1972 a. Rainmaking: rumored use over Laos alarms arms experts, scientists. *Science*, **176**: 1216–20.

Shapley, D., 1972 b. Technology in Vietnam: fire storm project fizzled out. *Science*, **177**: 239–41.

Shapley, D., 1974. Weather warfare: Pentagon concedes 7-year Vietnam effort. *Science*, **184**: 1059–61.

Shields, L. M. and Rickard, W. H., 1961. Preliminary evaluation of radiation effects at the Nevada test site. In Bailey, D. L. (ed.), *Recent Advances in Botany*. (University of Toronto Press, Toronto), 1766 pp.: pp. 1387–90.

Shields, L. M. and Wells, P. V., 1962. Effects of nuclear testing on desert vegetation. *Science*, **135**: 38–40.

Shields, L. M. and Wells, P. V., 1963. Recovery of vegetation on atomic target areas at the Nevada test site. In Schultz, V. and Klement, A. W. Jr (eds), *Radioecology*. (Reinhold, New York), 746 pp.: pp. 307–10.

Shields, L. M., Wells, P. V. and Rickard, W. H., 1963. Vegetational recovery on atomic target areas in Nevada. *Ecology*, **44**: 697–705.

Shute, N., 1957. *On the Beach*. (Wm Morrow, New York), 320 pp.

Sidel, V. W. and Goldwyn, R. M., 1966. Chemical and biologic weapons: a primer. *New Engl. J. Medicine*, **274**: 21–7.

Sidell, F. R. and Groff, W. A., 1974. Reactivatibility of cholinesterase inhibited by VX and sarin in man. *Toxicology and Applied Pharmacology*, **27**: 241–52.

Siegmund, O. H. *et al.* (eds), 1973. *Merck Veterinary Manual: a Handbook of Diagnosis and Therapy for the Veterinarian*. 4th Edn. (Merck, Rahway, N. J.), 1600 pp.

Siemes, J. B., 1946–1947. *Report from Hiroshima*. Jesuit Missions, **20**: 30–2.

Simpson, L. L. and Curtis, D. R. (eds), 1971–1974. *Neuropoisons: Their Pathophysiological Actions. I: Poisons of Animal Origin. II: Poisons of Plant Origin*. (Plenum, New York) 2 vols. (361 + 306 pp.).

SIPRI (Stockholm International Peace Research Institute), 1971 a. *Problem of Chemical and Biological Warfare. I: Rise of CB Weapons*. (Almqvist & Wiksell, Stockholm), 395 pp.

SIPRI (Stockholm International Peace Research Institute), 1971 b. *Problem of Chemical and Biological Warfare. IV: CB Disarmament Negotiations, 1920–1970*. (Almqvist & Wiksell, Stockholm), 412 pp.

SIPRI (Stockholm International Peace Research Institute), 1971 c. *Problem of Chemical and Biological Warfare. V: Prevention of CBW*. (Almqvist & Wiksell, Stockholm), 287 pp.

SIPRI (Stockholm International Peace Research Institute), 1971–1975. *Problem of Chemical and Biological Warfare*. (Almqvist & Wiksell, Stockholm) 6 vols. (395 + 420 + 194 + 412 + 287 + 308 pp.).

SIPRI (Stockholm International Peace Research Institute), 1972. *Napalm and Incendiary Weapons: Legal and Humanitarian Aspects*. (Stockholm Intl Peace Research Inst., Stockholm), 125 pp.

SIPRI (Stockholm International Peace Research Institute), 1973 a. *Chemical Disarmament: Some Problems of Verification*. (Almqvist & Wiksell, Stockholm), 184 pp.

SIPRI (Stockholm International Peace Research Institute), 1973 b. *Problem of Chemical and Biological Warfare. II: CB Weapons Today*. (Almqvist & Wiksell, Stockholm), 420 pp.

SIPRI (Stockholm International Peace Research Institute), 1974 a. *Effects of Developments in the Biological and Chemical Sciences on CW Disarmament Negotiations*. (Stockholm Intl Peace Research Inst., Stockholm), 54 pp.

SIPRI (Stockholm International Peace Research Institute), 1974 b. *Offensive Missiles*, Paper No. 5. (Stockholm Intl Peace Research Inst., Stockholm), 34 pp.

SIPRI (Stockholm International Peace Research Institute), 1975 a. *Chemical Disarmament: New Weapons for Old*. (Almqvist & Wiksell, Stockholm), 151 pp.

SIPRI (Stockholm International Peace Research Institute), 1975 b. *Delayed Toxic Effects of Chemical Warfare Agents*. (Almqvist & Wiksell, Stockholm), 60 pp.

SIPRI (Stockholm International Peace Research Institute), 1975 c. *Incendiary Weapons*. (Almqvist & Wiksell, Stockholm), 255 pp. + 12 pl.

SIPRI (Stockholm International Peace Research Institute), 1975 d. *Nuclear Age*. (Almqvist & Wiksell, Stockholm), 148 pp.

SIPRI (Stockholm International Peace Research Institute), 1976 a. *Ecological Consequences of the Second Indochina War*. (Almqvist & Wiksell, Stockholm), 119 pp. + 8 pl.

SIPRI (Stockholm International Peace Research Institute), 1976 b. *Law of War and Dubious Weapons*. (Almqvist & Wiksell, Stockholm), 78 pp.

Slater, W. *et al.*, 1960. *Radioactive Materials in Food and Agriculture*. Atomic Energy Series No. 2. (Food and Agriculture Organization, Rome), 123 pp.

Smedley, A., 1943. *Battle Hymn of China*. (A. A. Knopf, New York), 528 + 16 pp. + 8 pl. + 1 map.

Smith, K. M., 1973. *Textbook of Plant Virus Diseases*. 3rd Edn. (Academic Press, New York), 684 pp.

Smith, L. P., 1970. *Weather and Animal Diseases*. Technical Note No. 113. (World Meteorological Organization, Geneva), 49 pp.

Sorensen, H., 1948–1949. History of flame warfare. *Canad. Army J.*, **2**(4): 16–9; (5–6): 15, 31–2; (7–8): 18–23.

Spalding, J. F. and Holland, L. M., 1971. Species recovery from radiation injury. In Bensen, D. W. and Sparrow, A. H. (eds), *Survival of Food Crops and Livestock in the Event of Nuclear War*. Symposium Series No. 24. (US Atomic Energy Commission), 745 pp.: pp. 245–58.

Sparrow, A. H., Schwemmer, S. S. and Bottino, P. J., 1971. Effects of external gamma radiation from radioactive fallout on plants with special reference to crop production. *Radiation Botany*, **11**: 85–118.

Sparrow, R. C. and Sparrow, A. H., 1965. Relative radiosensitivities of woody and herbaceous spermatophytes. *Science*, **147**: 1449–51.

Spurr, S. H. and Barnes, B. V., 1973. *Forest Ecology*. 2nd Edn. (Ronald Press, New York), 571 pp.

Stearn, E. W. and Stearn, A. E., 1945. *Effect of Smallpox on the Destiny of the Amerindian*. (Bruce Humphries, Boston), 153 pp.

Stecher, P. G. *et al.* (eds), 1968. *Merck Index: an Encyclopedia of Chemicals and Drugs*. 8th Edn. (Merck & Co., Rahway, N.J.), 1713 pp.

Stewart, G. R., 1948. *Fire*. (Random House, New York), 336 pp.

Stewart, O. C., 1956. Fire as the first great force employed by man. In Thomas, W. L. Jr (ed.), *Man's Role in Changing the Face of the Earth*. (University of Chicago Press, Chicago), 1193 pp.: pp. 115–33.

Stickel, P. W. and Marco, H. F., 1936. Forest fire damage studies in the northeast. III: Relation between fire injury and fungal infection. *J. Forestry*, **34**: 420–3.

Stonier, T., 1963. Anticipated biological and environmental effects of detonating a twenty-megaton weapon on Columbus Circle in New York City. *Annals N.Y. Acad. Sciences*, **105**: 291–364.

Stonier, T., 1964. *Nuclear Disaster*. (World, Cleveland), 226 pp.

Strahler, A. N., 1975. *Physical Geography*. 4th Edn. (Wiley, New York), 643 + 39 + 17 pp. + pl. + maps.

Strode, G. K. (ed), 1951. *Yellow Fever*. (McGraw-Hill, New York), 710 pp.

Studer, T. A., 1968–1969. Weather modification in support of military operations. *Air Univ. Rev.*, **20**(6): 44–50.

Sullivan, W., 1975. Ozone depletion seen as a war tool. *New York Times* (28 February 1975), 20.

Taborsky, O. and Thuronyi, G., 1960. Annotated bibliography on weather modification. *Meteorological and Geoastrophysical Abstracts*, **11**: 2181–2415.

Taborsky, O. and Thuronyi, G., 1962. Annotated bibliography on weather modification and microphysics of clouds. *Meteorological and Geoastrophysical Abstracts*, **13**: 702–62.

Takman, J. (ed.), 1967. [*Napalm*]. (Rabén & Sjögren, Stockholm), 189 pp. In Swedish.

Tarr, C. W. Jr, 1965. *Selected Bibliography on CBR Warfare, 1961–1964*. Rev. edn. Publication No. UG 447 (US Library Congress, Legislative Reference Service), 4 pp.

Thomas, A. V. W. and Thomas, A. J. Jr, 1970. *Legal Limits on the Use of Chemical and Biological Weapons.* (S. Methodist University Press, Dallas), 332 pp.

Thomas, R. E., Cohen, J. M. and Bendixen, T. W., 1964. *Pesticides in Soil and Water: an Annotated Bibliography.* Publication No. 999-WP-17. (US Public Health Service), 90 pp.

Thompson, L. M., 1969 a. Weather and technology in the production of corn in the U.S. corn belt. *Agronomy J.*, **61**: 453–6.

Thompson, L. M., 1969 b. Weather and technology in the production of wheat in the United States. *J. Soil and Water Conservation*, **24**: 219–24.

Thompson, L. M., 1970. Weather and technology in the production of soybeans in the central United States. *Agronomy J.*, **62**: 232–6.

Thompson, L. M., 1975. Weather variability, climatic change, and grain production. *Science*, **188**: 535–41.

Thorsson, I., 1975. Disarmament negotiations: what are they doing for the environment? *Ambio*, **4**: 199–202.

Thuronyi, G., 1963. Annotated bibliography on weather modification and microphysics of clouds (supplement). *Meteorological and Geoastrophysical Abstracts*, **14**: 144–244.

Thuronyi, G., 1964. Recent literature on weather and climate modification. *Meteorological and Geoastrophysical Abstracts*, **15**: 1518–53.

Time, 1968. Shrinking sanctuary. *Time*, **91**(17): 28.

Times, The, 1968. *Times Atlas of the World.* Comprehensive edition, 2nd edn. (Times Newspapers, London), 272 pp. + 123 pl.

Todd, O. J., 1942. Taming 'flood dragons' along China's Hwang Ho. *National Geographic Mag.*, **81**: 205–34.

Tucker, R. K. and Crabtree, D. G., 1970. *Handbook of Toxicity of Pesticides to Wildlife.* Resource Publication No. 84. (US Fish and Wildlife Service), 131 pp.

UNSCEAR (United Nations Scientific Committee on the Effects of Atomic Radiation), 1972. *Ionizing Radiation: Levels and Effects.* (United Nations, New York) 2 vols., (447 pp.).

Urbach, F. (ed.), 1969. *Biologic Effects of Ultraviolet Radiation: With Emphasis on the Skin.* (Pergamon, New York), 704 pp. + pl.

Valli, V. J., 1966. *Weather and Plant Diseases: a Review.* Technical Note No. 36-AGMET-3. (US Dept. of Commerce), 24 pp.

VanKampen, K. R., James, L. F., Rasmussen, J., Huffaker, R. H. and Fawcett, M. O., 1969. Organic phosphate poisoning of sheep in Skull Valley, Utah. *J. Amer. Veterinary Medical Assn*, **154**: 623–30.

VanRiper, P. K., 1972. Riot control agents in offensive operations. *Marine Corps Gazette*, **56**(4): 18–23.

Vellodi, M. A. *et al.*, 1968. *Effects of the Possible Use of Nuclear Weapons and the Security and Economic Implications for States of the Acquisition and Further Development of these Weapons.* (United Nations, New York), 76 pp.

Verwey, W. D., 1977. *Riot Control Agents and Herbicides in War: Their Humanitarian, Toxicological, Ecological, Polemological, and Legal Aspects.* (A. W. Sijthoff, Leyden), 377 pp.

Vietnam Newsletter, 1971. Worst flood ever. *Vietnam Bull.*, Washington, **6**(9): 7–9.

Vries, A. de and Kochva, E. (eds.), 1971–1973. *Toxins of Animal and Plant Origin.* (Gordon & Breach, New York) 3 vols. (1107 pp.).

Waggoner, P. E., 1966. Weather modification and the living environment. In Darling, F. F. and Milton, J. P. (eds), *Future Environments of North America*. (Natural History Press, Garden City, N.Y.), 770 pp.: pp. 87–98.

Walker, E. P. *et al.*, 1964. *Mammals of the World*. (Johns Hopkins Press, Baltimore) 3 vols. (1500 + 769 pp.).

Wallace, B., 1973. Conscription at sea. *Saturday Rev. Sciences* (now *Saturday Rev.*), 1(2): 44–5.

Ward, F. P., 1973. *Progress in Ecological Research at Edgewood Arsenal, Maryland: Fiscal Years 1971 and 1972*. Special Publication No. 11 00–13. (US Army Edgewood Arsenal, Aberdeen Proving Ground, Md.), 20 pp.

Wasan, R. P., 1970. Chemical and biological warfare: a select bibliography. *Inst. for Defence Studies and Analyses J.*, 2: 365–78.

Watkins, P., 1966. *War Game*. (Brit. Broadcasting Corpn., London) 16 mm B&W sound film, 47 min.

Watkins, T. F., Cackett, J. C. and Hall, R. G., 1968. *Chemical Warfare, Pyrotechnics and the Fireworks Industry*. (Pergamon, Oxford), 114 pp.

Weast, R. C. (ed.), 1974. *Handbook of Chemistry and Physics*. 55th Edn. (CRC Press, Cleveland), [2279 pp.].

Webber, B., 1975. *Retaliation: Japanese Attacks and Allied Countermeasures on the Pacific Coast in World War II*. (Oregon State University Press, Corvallis, Ore.), 178 pp.

Weiss, E. B., 1974. Weather as a weapon. In Russell, R. B. (ed.), *Air, Water, Earth, Fire: the Impact of the Military on World Environmental Order*. (Intl Series No. 2, Sierra Club, San Francisco), 71 pp.: pp. 51–62.

Weiss, E. B., 1975. Weather control: an instrument for war? *Survival*, 16: 64–8.

Weizsäcker, C. F. von (ed.), 1971. [Results of war and prevention of war.] (Carl Hansen, Munich), 699 pp. In German.

Wells, P. V., 1965. Scarp woodland, transported grassland soils, and concept of grassland climate in the Great Plains region. *Science*, 148: 246–9.

West, C. J., 1919. History of poison gases. *Science*, 49: 412–7.

Westing, A. H., 1973. Postwar visit to Hanoi. *Boston Globe* (23 September 1973), A6.

Westing, A. H., 1974 a. *Herbicides as Weapons: a Bibliography*. Political Issues Series 3(1). (Cal. State Univ. Ctr for the Study of Armament and Disarmament, Los Angeles), 36 pp.

Westing, A. H., 1974 b. Proscription of ecocide: arms control and the environment. *Bull. Atomic Scientists*, 30(1): 24–7.

Wet, C. R. de, 1902. *Three Years War (October 1899–June 1902)* (Translated from the Dutch) (Archibald Constable, Westminster, England), 520 pp. + 1 map.

Wharton, C. H., 1966. Man, fire and wild cattle in north Cambodia. *Proc. Tall Timbers Fire Ecology Conf.*, 5: 23–65.

Wharton, C. H., 1968. Man, fire and wild cattle in Southeast Asia. *Proc. Tall Timbers Fire Ecology Conf.*, 7: 107–67.

Wheat, R. P., Zuckerman, A. and Rantz, L. A., 1951. Infection due to chromobacteria: report of eleven cases. *A.M.A. Archives Internal Medicine* (now *Archives Internal Medicine*), 88: 461–6.

Whicker, F. W. and Fraley, L. Jr, 1974. Effects of ionizing radiation on terrestrial plant communities. *Advances Radiation Biology*, 4: 317–66.

Whittaker, R. H., 1967. Ecological implications of weather modification. In Shaw, R. H. (ed.), *Ground Level Climatology*. Publication No. 86. (American Association for the Advancement of Science, Washington), 395 pp.: pp. 367–84.

Whitten, R. C. and Borucki, W. J., 1975. Possible ozone depletions following nuclear explosions. *Nature*, **257**: 38–9.

Wigner, E. P. *et al.*, 1969. *Civil Defense: Little Harbor Report*. Publication No. TID-24690. (US Atomic Energy Commission), 53 pp.

Wilbur, W. H., 1950. Those Japanese balloons. *Reader's Digest*, **57**(340): 23–6.

Wilford, J. N., 1977. U.S. resettles 75 on Pacific atoll evacuated for bomb tests in 40's. *New York Times* (11 April 1977), 1, 8; (12 April) 3.

Willrich, M. and Taylor, T. B., 1974. *Nuclear Theft: Risks and Safeguards*. (Ballinger, Cambridge, Mass.), 252 pp.

Wilson, J. B. and Russell, K. E., 1964. Isolation of *Bacillus anthracis* from soil stored 60 years. *J. Bacteriology*, **87**: 237–8.

Winters, R. K., 1974. *Forest and Man*. (Vantage Press, New York), 393 pp.

Wolfe, J. N., 1959. *Long-time Ecological Effects of Nuclear War*. Report No. TID-5561. (US Atomic Energy Commission), 5 pp.

Wood, J. W., Johnson, K. G., Omori, Y., Kawamoto, S. and Keehn, R. J., 1967. Mental retardation in children exposed in utero to the atomic bombs in Hiroshima and Nagasaki. *Amer. J. Public Health*, **57**: 1381–90.

Woodwell, G. M. (ed.), 1963. *Ecological Effects of Nuclear War*. Publication No. 917. (Brookhaven National Laboratory, Upton, N.Y.), 72 pp.

Woodwell, G. M., 1967. Radiation and the patterns of nature. *Science*, **156**: 461–70.

Woodwell, G. M., 1970. Effects of pollution on the structure and physiology of ecosystems. *Science*, **168**: 429–33.

Woodwell, G. M. and Holt, B. R., 1971. Effect of nuclear war on the structure and function of natural communities: an appraisal based on experiments with gamma radiation. In Bensen, D. W. and Sparrow, A. H. (eds), *Survival of Food Crops and Livestock in the Event of Nuclear War*. Symposium Series No. 24. (US Atomic Energy Commission), 745 pp.: pp. 482–91.

Woodwell, G. M. and Sparrow, A. H., 1963. Effects of ionizing radiation on ecological systems. In Woodwell, G. M. (ed.), *Ecological Effects of Nuclear War*. Publication No. 917. (Brookhaven National Laboratory, Upton, N.Y.), 72 pp., pp. 20–38.

Wulff, T., Janzon, B., Ohlson, L.-O., Petré, T. and Rybeck, B., 1973. *Conventional Weapons, Their Deployment and Effects from a Humanitarian Aspect: Recommendations for the Modernization of International Law*. (Royal Ministry for Foreign Affairs, Stockholm), 182 pp.

Wurtz, R. H., 1963. War and the living environment. *Nuclear Information* (now *Environment*), **5**(10): 1–20.

York, H., 1970. *Race to Oblivion: a Participant's View of the Arms Race*. (Simon & Schuster, New York), 256 pp.

York, H., 1975. Nuclear "balance of terror" in Europe. *Ambio*, **4**: 203–8.

Related SIPRI publications

Listed below is a selection of recent SIPRI monographs related to the subject of the present text. A wealth of relevant materials is also incorporated in the several *SIPRI Yearbooks*.

1. Nuclear weapons

Near-nuclear Countries and the NPT, 1972, 123 pp.

Nuclear Proliferation Problems, 1974, 312 pp.

French Nuclear Tests in the Atmosphere: the Question of Legality, 1974, 38 pp.

Nuclear Age, 1974, 148 pp.

Safeguards Against Nuclear Proliferation, 1975, 114 pp.

Tactical Nuclear Warfare, 1977. In the press.

Postures for Non-proliferation, to appear in 1978.

2. Chemical and biological weapons

Problem of Chemical and Biological Warfare. I. The Rise of CB Weapons, 1971, 395 pp.

Problem of Chemical and Biological Warfare. II. CB Weapons Today, 1973, 420 pp.

Problem of Chemical and Biological Warfare. III. CBW and the Law of War, 1973, 194 pp.

Problem of Chemical and Biological Warfare. IV. CB Disarmament Negotiations, 1920–1970, 1971, 412 pp.

Problem of Chemical and Biological Warfare. V. The Prevention of CBW, 1971, 287 pp.

Problem of Chemical and Biological Warfare. VI. Technical Aspects of Early Warning and Verification, 1975, 308 pp.

Chemical Disarmament: Some Problems of Verification, 1973, 184 pp.

Chemical Disarmament: New Weapons for Old, 1975, 151 pp.

Effects of Developments in the Biological and Chemical Sciences on CW Disarmament Negotiations, 1974, 54 pp.

Delayed Toxic Effects of Chemical Warfare Agents, 1975, 60 pp.

Medical Protection Against Chemical-warfare Agents, 1976, 166 pp.

3. Geophysical and environmental weapons

Incendiary Weapons, 1975, 255 pp + 12 pl.

Ecological Consequences of the Second Indochina War, 1976, 119 pp + 8 pl.

Law of War and Dubious Weapons, 1976, 78 pp.

Environmental Weapons, to appear in 1978.

Warfare and the Human Environment, to appear in 1978.

Index

Strahler, A. N. 27
Stratosphere 18, 23, 26, 50
Strode, G. K. 48
Strontium 11, 21
Sugar cane (*Saccharum officinarum*) 34
Sullivan, W. 50
Swine (*Sus scrofa*) 40

TNT 24
Takman, J. 62
Tay Ninh province 53
Taylor, T. B. 24
Texas 55
Thomas, A. J. (Jr) 34
Thomas, A. V. W. 34
Thompson, L. M. 28
Thyroid gland 11
Ticks (*Acarida*) 39, 43
Tiemeier, O. W. 59
Time (periodical) 53
The Times (newspaper) 27
Tokyo 52, 63
Toxins 39–41, 47, 48
—, literature on 47, 48
Toxoplasma gondii 41
Toxoplasmosis 41
Treaties relating to chemical, biological and nuclear weapons 63, 64
Tromp, S. W. 28, 61
Troposphere 16, 24, 49
Tsunami 50
Tularemia 41
Turtle (Atlantic loggerhead) (*Caretta caretta caretta*) 59
Typhoid fever 41
Typhus 41

UNSCEAR 25, 29
U Minh forest 53
United Kingdom 64
Urbach, F. 19
USA 1, 22, 28–30, 34–36, 44, 47, 49, 52–56, 59, 62–64
US Agricultural Research Service 47
US Air Force 55
US Arms Control and Disarmament Agency 65, 66
US Atomic Energy Commission 2, 14, 23
US Central Intelligence Agency 55, 56

US Defense Civil Preparedness Agency 8, 9, 24, 27, 29
US Department of the Army 35, 36, 52, 55
US Department of Defense 8, 24, 35, 36, 55, 60
US Department of Health, Education and Welfare 29, 47
US Departments of the Army and Air Force 32, 40, 47
US Energy Research and Development Administration 23
US Naval Ordnance Test Station 60
USSR 1, 22, 64

'VX' 35, 37–39, 45
Valli, V. J. 28
VanKampen, K. R. 45
VanRiper, P. K. 47
Vegetation, damage by radiation 13, 14, 16
—, effect of radiation on 11, 12
—, ignition of 7, 16
Vellodi, M. A. 24, 25, 28, 29
Verwey, W. D. 47
Vietnam, North 34, 49, 55, 56, 59
Vietnam, South 36, 53, 56
Viruses 42–44
—, literature on 48

Wallace, B. 31
The War Game (film) 29
Ward, F. P. 37
Warfare, biological 31 ff
—, —, ecological consequences 34 ff
—, —, literature 46–48
—, chemical 31 ff
—, —, ecological consequences 34 ff
—, —, literature 46–48
—, geophysical and environmental 61
—, —, literature on 62
Warsaw Pact Organization 29
Water hemlock (*Cicuta virosa*) 39
Watkins, P. 29
Watkins, T. F. 47, 62
Weapons, chemical and biological 31–48
—, —, literature on 48
—, geophysical and environmental 46 ff
—, incendiary 51–53

94

Routledge Revivals

Industrial Relations: Cost-effective Strategies

The economic recession of the 1980s changed the face of industrial relations in Britain. Originally published in 1985, this book brings together all the major developments from that time and examines organizational strategies in industrial relations from a cost-effectiveness standpoint. Contemporary issues, ever more relevant, such as flexible working patterns, are discussed in relation to the conflicting demands of unions and management. Appropriate courses of action are discussed, with many examples of how new ideas were put into practice.

Industrial Relations: Cost-effective Strategies

Chris Brewster and Stephen Connock

Routledge
Taylor & Francis Group

First published in 1985
by Hutchinson & Co (Publishers) Ltd

This edition first published in 2021 by Routledge
2 Park Square, Milton Park, Abingdon, Oxon, OX14 4RN
and by Routledge
605 Third Avenue, New York, NY 10058

Routledge is an imprint of the Taylor & Francis Group, an informa business

Publisher's Note
The publisher has gone to great lengths to ensure the quality of this reprint but points out that some imperfections in the original copies may be apparent.

Disclaimer
The publisher has made every effort to trace copyright holders and welcomes correspondence from those they have been unable to contact.

ISBN 13: 978-1-032-04312-8 (hbk)
ISBN 13: 978-1-003-19304-3 (ebk)
ISBN 13: 978-1-032-04405-7 (pbk)

DOI: 10.4324/9781003193043

Industrial Relations: Cost-Effective Strategies

Chris Brewster and
Stephen Connock

Hutchinson

London Melbourne Sydney Auckland Johannesburg

Hutchinson & Co. (Publishers) Ltd
An imprint of the Hutchinson Publishing Group

17–21 Conway Street, London W1P 6JD

Hutchinson Publishing Group (Australia) Pty Ltd
16–22 Church Street, Hawthorn, Melbourne, Victoria 3122

Hutchinson Group (NZ) Ltd
32–34 View Road, PO Box 40-086, Glenfield, Auckland 10

Hutchinson Group (SA) (Pty) Ltd
PO Box 337, Bergvlei 2012, South Africa

Brookfield Publishing Company, Inc.
Old Post Road, Brookfield, Vermont 05036 USA

First published 1985

© Chris Brewster and Stephen Connock 1985

Set in VIP Century Schoolbook by
D. P. Media Limited, Hitchin, Hertfordshire

Printed and bound in Great Britain by
Anchor Brendon Ltd, Tiptree, Essex

British Library Cataloguing in Publication Data

Brewster, Chris
    Industrial relations: cost-effective strategies.
    – (Personnel management series)
    I   Industrial relations – Great Britain
    I   Title   II   Connock, Stephen   III   Series
    331'.0941   HD8391

    ISBN 0 09 163081 9

Contents

Acknowledgements

This book has drawn on the experience of many personnel and industrial relations specialists, line managers and trade unionists from all sectors of employment. Their contribution to our thinking deserves our grateful, albeit anonymous, thanks. We would like to thank by name our editor, David Guest, for his encouragement and guidance; and our families, Lynn, Beccle and Tom; Margaret and Adrian, for their forbearance.

CJB
SLC
September 1984

Preface

Managements in all employing organizations are under pressure to devise and implement cost-effective strategies in industrial relations. *Cost-effective* because increasingly fierce competition and financial constraints are dominant in the private and public sectors. *Strategic* because it is through a detailed examination of manpower issues and opportunities that the competition and constraints can be met. That requires organizations to develop well thought out, planned approaches that integrate their industrial relations with overall organizational strategies.

This book has been written with the aim of assisting those involved in, and those studying, industrial relations to understand this new approach. Much industrial relations thinking, and certainly most of the writing, is still dominated by the context in which the Donovan Report was written: powerful, growing unions, double-figure wage settlements, 'fragmented' bargaining arrangements and a reactive and defensive management. Yet the world has changed: managerial control is being reasserted, the unions appear less confident. The climate of industrial relations is markedly different.

In this context managements in both the private and public sector are re-examining their industrial relations, and developing policies and approaches which are relevant to meet their organizational objectives in the future. This involves taking a wider view of industrial relations within the organization than has been traditional, relating it more closely to other managerial policies and objectives as well as to the trade unions and workplace organization and events.[1]

Each organization's management will approach the new industrial relations in a particular way. Those that aim to develop these coherent and relevant policies and approaches are increasingly likely to share certain elements in common. The policies will, for example,

- Have been developed with the aim of improving operational efficiency through maximizing the contribution of employees to organizational objectives.

- Focus on the cost-effectiveness of manpower. As such they will be conscious not only of the need for greater control of labour costs, but also of the need to develop policies which maintain and enhance employee motivation, creativity and commitment.[2] These paradoxical pressures will increase; requiring detailed, well-thought out strategies.

- Absorb very different elements of style (combining, for example, aspects of paternalism, hard-faced pragmatism and open-handed consultation).[3] But they will aim for internal consistency; and consistency with the present and future business strategy of the organization.

At present only a minority vanguard of organizations are developing personnel policies along these lines. This minority however, which has representatives in the public and private sectors, in service industries and manufacturing, is indicative of a growing trend. The issues that we address in this book will be faced by all organizations – sooner rather than later.

In the book we are, to a major extent, looking forward. This is a risky process and we have no expectation that we will have got it totally right. We do believe, however, that the issues we address here and the type of consideration that we give them will become increasingly vital in a rapidly changing and increasingly tough competitive world.

Cost-effective strategies in industrial relations are a central concern for personnel specialists and for line managers. This book will point them towards the crucial issues; help them explore the options and assist them in developing a strategic approach. As such it is intended to be a pragmatic and practical text for managers in employing organizations. Because it covers much that is new in industrial relations, it is also intended to contribute to the increasing attention that teachers and researchers are paying to the management side of industrial relations, and by summarizing and explaining many new developments in the subject it will be particularly useful to students of management and of industrial relations. Too much that is written about industrial relations remains descriptive of institutions and procedures; there is still little of real practical value. In addition, what aims to be practical can often be simply anecdotal, lacking any conceptual framework. This book seeks to redress the balance, to place the emphasis on issues of real concern in the management of industrial relations in the last decades of the twentieth century.

References

1 E. Batstone, A. Ferner and M. Terry, *Consent and Efficiency* (Basil Blackwell, 1984).
   K. E. Thurley and S. Wood (eds), *Industrial Relations and Management Strategy* (Cambridge University Press, 1983).
2 A. Fox, *Beyond Contract: Work, Power and Trust Relations* (Faber, 1974).
   A. W. Gouldner, *Patterns of Industrial Bureaucracy* (Free Press, 1954).
   A. L. Friedman, *Industry and Labour; Class Struggle at Work and Monopoly Capitalism* (Macmillan, 1977).
   C. Littler and G. Salaman, *Class at Work* (Batsford, 1984).

3 A. Fox, *Industrial Sociology and Industrial Relations*, Research Paper 3, Royal Commission on Trade Unions and Employers' Associations, (HMSO, London, 1966).
— 'Industrial Relations: A Social Critique of Pluralist Ideology', in J. Child (ed.), *Man and Organisation* (Allen and Unwin, 1973).
— *Beyond Contract: Work, Power and Trust Relations* (Faber, 1974).
J. Purcell and K. Sisson, 'Management Strategies and Practice', in G. S. Bain (ed.), *Industrial Relations in Britain* (Basil Blackwell, 1983).

Industrial relations in context

Industrial relations in Britain have changed and are continuing to change. Many of the understandings, and hence much of the 'wisdom' of industrial relations, is based on developments in the quarter century following the Second World War. This period was one of full employment, international competition largely from the developed world, growing trade union influence, increasing living standards, an expanding public sector and provision of services, and slowly declining differentials in wealth. The beginning of the 1980s, however, saw a radical change. This book is one of the harbingers of attempts to understand this new situation and the different form of industrial relations involved.

We do not, of course, imply that everything is different. Individuals – managers and employees, personnel specialists and trade union officials and members – can argue correctly that there is still conflict and cooperation, still room to debate the nature of the work effort and how to reward it. Industrial relations too have changed at a different pace in the varying sectors of the British economy. The changes have been incremental, not cataclysmic, although in some sectors, such as coalmining, they have been bitterly fought over. And yet there have been developments of sufficient consistency and magnitude to amount to a qualitative change in the nature of industrial relations.

Where does the difference lie? We explore this issue in detail throughout the book. At this stage we do no more than point to the decline in union membership and influence, a more confident management approach and an increasing segmentation of employment and a wider use of non-union channels of communications at work. Underlying such pointers, however, management is continuing to focus on improving the cost-effectiveness of labour.

In the 1960s and 1970s, good personnel practices involved 'management by agreement', with concerns about job enrichment and other issues associated with the quality of working life, the development of grievance and disciplinary procedures, maintenance of job security and the spread of joint job evaluation schemes. These and similar issues of employee welfare and procedural formalization were accepted industrial relations objectives for many managers. The creation and fostering of good relationships with trade unions and the establishment of industrial peace were seen as

DOI: 10.4324/9781003193043-1

crucial to success. Productivity and competitiveness were also important of course, as the productivity bargaining vogue of the 1960s demonstrates, but if peace required a significant pay increase, the chances were that it was sooner or later conceded. After all, in the economic circumstances of the time, such concessions could often be passed on to the customer.

By the beginning of the 1980s such 'good' personnel practices were being judged more against the criterion of cost-effectiveness. There were very substantial redundancy programmes. It was not just the steel and coalmining industries which halved their workforces; major private sector companies such as ICI also implemented labour force reductions. Managements were more prepared to face industrial action to achieve the new manning or working arrangements which they perceived as critical to organizational success. A survey of industrial relations at the beginning of the 1980s found that the two most frequently mentioned of these managerial objectives were 'lower manpower costs' (76 per cent) and 'more flexible workforce' (64 per cent).[1] The pressure on management to develop policies and address issues in industrial relations that met the crucial criterion of cost-effectiveness has substantially increased. To establish why this pressure has increased we need to explore the context in which organizations operate. This chapter therefore examines many of the key contextual aspects of industrial relations in Britain in the 1980s and 1990s.

Examining the context

As we write we are only a few years into the period, and we do not claim to have a crystal ball which will reveal the future. Our intention is to draw out some of the main threads of the current situation, and the dynamics that we see in it in an attempt to set organizational industrial relations into context. We do so with some diffidence. ACAS pointed out in their 1983 Report that industrial relations is now being conducted 'in the context of an uncertain future and of major and rapid change'.[2] We are conscious that the pace of change is increasing, and that today's forecasts are wrong tomorrow. Within Britain the occupational structure is changing from manufacturing to service, from manual to scientific and technical. The effect of new technology in the factories, at airports, in the high street and in offices is uncertain, but it will be substantial. Furthermore, all these changes are interrelated.

It is thus in an attempt to abstract issues rather than to predict the future that we examine what is happening that has relevance to industrial relations. Understanding contextual changes is the first step towards understanding both changes in industrial relations generally and in the pressures on management to be cost-effective.

We argue that a world economic system and technological change have combined to generate increased international competition; that the British economy has not stood up to that competition well; and that changes within the British economy and governmental action have combined to ensure more stringent pressures on British managers to be cost-effective – but also have provided them with certain opportunities.

The world economic system

Industrial relations in Britain are significantly influenced by events in the international capitalist economic system. Any form of crude ultra-Marxism, which argues that industrial relations is determined in some way by the machinations of that system, is obviously inadequate. Nevertheless, the Marxist commentators on industrial relations are correct in arguing that we must be conscious of, and understand, the influence of international events and economic dynamics if we are to understand British industrial relations. Hyman, for example, writes that 'industrial relations . . . stems from a conflict of industry and society which is closely linked with the operation of contradictory tendencies in the capitalist economic system'.[3]

The world economic system is no longer (if indeed it ever was) simply a conglomeration of individual independent geographical systems which occasionally trade with each other. The world is a cohesive economic system. There are no areas – not the Communist countries, not those vast tracts of territory where millions still live by subsistence agriculture – that remain outside the influence of this global economy.

The influence of this global economy is enormous and continually increasing. National economies, and in particular the 'cash crop' or 'single product' economies of 'the South', are dependent upon this global system. A decrease in the spot price of bauxite, or three-month cocoa beans, means hurried adjustments in financial institutions in the City – and may destroy the economic strategy of a Third World state. Britain, as a complex, multi-product and multi-service economy, is less vulnerable to change in the world economy, but is not immune from it.

Thus it is that established UK industrial relations can be shaken up by events many thousands of miles away. The oil price increases of the early 1970s for example had a major effect on the viability of the British coal industry and on the economic circumstances and confidence of the parties involved. Events in the Middle East had a vital and continuing influence on industrial relations in the British coalfields.

In retrospect it is clear that the dramatic increases in oil prices which occurred in the early 1970s were linked to a downturn in the world economic system and a halt to the previous levels of growth. All of the OECD countries' economies grew more slowly in the period following 1973 than they had done previously.[4] Many of the poorer countries began to build up foreign debts and unemployment rose throughout the world.

Governmental responses varied. There was, in general, a move away from the Keynesian interventionism which, with the Second World War, had pulled the international economic system out of the slump of the

1930s. Many governments opted for policies based on tighter restrictions of money supply and a limited and different form of intervention in their own national economies.

One of the consequences of the recession has been a major attitudinal change amongst employees. The assumption that full employment is a possible, or even rational, goal has been challenged and perhaps no longer exists. Industrial relations now take place, and will continue to take place, in a context of tight competition, unemployment and worry about future employment prospects.

In assessing the world economic system we cannot restrict ourselves to considering only national economies. The activities of multinational corporations (MNCs) are increasingly important. Whilst there are major statistical problems associated with defining the extent of MNC involvement in the world economy it can be safely noted that:

> Multinational corporations, irrespective of their national origins, have grown rapidly in the last decades [and] there is a fair consensus of opinion . . . that multinational corporations will grow in the years ahead. [5]

This is important because 'the present day multinational corporation has an active controlling interest which goes far beyond the capital investment aspect'. [6] The impact of the MNCs on Great Britain is again difficult to quantify, but is manifest. We know that most 'direct company foreign investment appears to be in Western Europe'. [7] Much of this is in the UK. According to the Size Report 23 per cent of the 4000 largest private companies in the UK were owned by overseas interests. [8] We know that there is a substantial number of smaller organizations which are foreign owned; indeed it is a conscious strategy by many overseas investors in the UK to be neither too big nor too prominent. The sources of investment are changing as well. Most foreign owned companies traditionally originated in the United States of America and, to a much lesser extent, in Europe. Over recent years the range has widened to include Arabian and Far Eastern and other investors. This is likely to continue – in June 1984 the Trade and Industry Secretary told the House of Commons: 'Of course there is a justification for particularly attractive terms to bring to this country internationally mobile projects which otherwise might have arrived in, for example, another part of the European Community.' By the early 1980s there were enough Japanese companies in South Wales for a second Japanese school (the first being in London) to be established for the children of expatriate managers.

This is by no means a one-way process. Many apparently 'British' companies are now MNCs based in Britain. They operate internationally, and whilst senior managers will have residual personal commitments to Britain which will be reflected in company statements and some company activities, they will see their field of operations and their markets as world-wide.

The direct impact of MNC activities is on jobs and local economies. The influence of MNCs on employment prospects has been much debated,[9] but with overseas investment by UK institutions running at £4 billion in 1982[10] there can be little doubt that the effect on particular industries is likely to be substantial.

The most obvious manifestation of the international economic system is found in the development of the European Economic Community (EEC). The EEC has major relevance for the MNCs, and for every other employing organization in the UK. It is easy, perhaps, to overestimate the direct effects on Britain's industrial relations of membership of the EEC. There is pressure for industrial democracy and disclosure of information, for job protection and redundancy arrangements, for harmonization of terms and conditions. There are laws about mobility of labour, freedom of association and equal pay for women. These influences are often claimed to be considerable. There is certainly a good deal of concern being expressed by representatives of British industry about the impact of the Transfer of Undertakings Regulations, for example, and requirements on Equal Pay for Work of Equal Value have had a direct effect on UK legislation and in turn on UK organizations. In the practice of employing organizations, however, there is little manifest evidence of these influences. EEC pressures are filtered through national government, through the British managerial culture and then into organizational thinking. Only then do they affect organizational practice. Though some organizations have adapted in response to these influences, for most only a fine mist has come through the filters.

Indirect influences of EEC membership may, by contrast, have been underestimated. These influences include: the effect of increased competition within Europe and the attraction of the UK as a member of the Community to foreign investors. On a different level, regional support policies and financial support for restructuring and redundancies have affected industries such as fishing, coal and steel, agriculture, electronics and aerospace in many different ways.

These indirect influences have been, in part, responsible for significant changes in the structure and strategy of Britain's industries and services. They have encouraged inward investment and they have provided support for specific government programmes. These changes in turn have had an effect on industrial relations: strengthening the embryonic movement for European trade unionism, and changing job structures and traditions in various regions of the country. These indirect influences will continue to be important.

Technological changes
Alongside the increased importance of the world economic system has come technological changes. From the development of the transistor in the late 1940s, technological changes have proceeded with great rapidity.

With hundreds of thousands of electronic components able to be placed on a single chip of silicon, their potential impact becomes enormous. [11]

There has been a massive increase in the power of microelectronic components and a drastic reduction in their price since 1960; and there are now few sectors of the economy without examples of the application of microelectronics.

For example, in engineering, manually controlled machine tools have been increasingly replaced by numerically controlled (NC) machine tools. These in turn have developed into computer numerical controlled (CNC) machine tools, providing for tape control of each machine. There are also significant implications in manufacturing for materials handling where new methods of stock movement, stock control and management information have become possible. Computerization has expanded greatly, especially in the processing of routine information such as that involved in payrolls and sales ledger or purchase ledger systems. Alongside the computer processing of routine information is the development of more sophisticated and comprehensive information processing; such management information systems are only just beginning to be exploited. And in the office environment the increasing use of word processors is having a major impact on work and the way it is organized.

In the services sector there is immense scope for microelectronic applications. For example in banking the automatic cash dispenser is now commonplace and further developments in automation can be expected. If anything the impact of new technology in the service industries, on hotels, airlines, cinemas, public utilities and so on has been underestimated, although there are limits to the process. We still expect a waiter or waitress to bring us a meal in a restaurant or a nurse to care for us in hospital.

For management, significant operational advantages have accrued from the application of new technology. Computerized information systems have enormously reduced the time taken to process information and can provide obvious benefits to customers/users. Manufacturing processes can be more rapid, and the consequent increased volume can reduce unit costs. Productivity can also improve through manning reductions, although this does not always follow from the introduction of new technology. Production and development lead times can be reduced through the use of, for example, computer aided manufacture (CAM) or computer aided design (CAD). Modern computer techniques of 'on line' data processing provide the opportunities for information to be updated by the minute and this means production schedules can be re-planned continuously in the light of changing circumstances. It is this ability which has led to computerized planning and control systems in many manufacturing organizations, with consequent savings on stocks and improvements in lead times and deliveries to customers.

Such technological developments have led to the enormous growth in employment of scientists, technologists and technicians, particularly since 1979.

Such is the importance of software skills that there is a national shortage of suitably qualified software specialists. Aside from software, the increasingly sophisticated equipment in use has created a need for new maintenance skills. The rapid emergence of the 'technician' as a group between the qualified scientists or technologist and the craftsman is linked to developments in technology.

The impact of technological change on industrial relations is considerable. Technological change was historically a precondition for the development of capital surpluses, the move away from the land and the start of the industrial revolution. More recently it has led to the decline of entire industries (ostlery, canals, charcoal making) and the upsurge of new ones (electronics, airlines, telecommunications). It is increasingly making many of the working arrangements in offices and factories irrelevant, and opening up new possibilities.

We return to these issues later in the book. Here we note that one of the factors outside managerial control has been that the combination of new technology and a world economic system has created an unprecedentedly fierce competitive environment.

International competition

Technological change, particularly in communications and transport and in methods of manufacture, enabled a number of Third World countries to use the 1970s to develop conscious strategies of using their cheap labour and rapid industrialization to carve out new markets for themselves. Thus Singapore, Hong Kong, South Korea and Taiwan, to take just some examples from the Pacific, all became major producers of finished products competing in world markets, and – because of high levels of investment and cheap labour, amongst other factors – competing very successfully.

The effect on British industry, and British industrial relations, was swift and immense. Shipbuilding, textiles, electronics, motorbike manufacture and many others found that they could not produce as cheaply. The industrial relations issues changed from pay and conditions to redundancy and survival.

Nor is it just the physical manufacturing process which is internationalized. In the service industry too, whilst some services (such as hotels) have to be provided at certain geographical locations, technological innovations now allow many others (banking, insurance and other financial services are good examples) to be provided over thousands of miles.

The effect on industrial relations was not restricted to a few industries. The impact of Japanese electronics firms on industrial relations thinking in the UK in the early 1980s is well known. It would seem that it is also typical:

for the most part, multinational plants operating in Western European countries have adapted, or had to adapt, to host country labour practices. But while there has been this general absorption or adaptation, there are important exceptions to this process of assimilation as regards a variety of labour practices in every one of the countries studied. So much so, that often the exception and variation introduced in labour practices of multinational subsidiaries seem at least as important to unions as does the general, over-all assimilation of these companies. Furthermore, in a few countries the multinationals' special labour practices have had general influence on national labour practices, and this is especially true in some industries. [12]

For countries like the United Kingdom there are some additional pressures too. In the underdeveloped or developing countries of 'the South',

labour is cheap, hardworking and congenial . . . [and host societies] can offer 'attractive' anti-union legislation; internal work control can be supported by external policing, unionists can be harassed; 'trouble-makers' persecuted; space and safety provisions are frequently much less than can be expected in the West. [13]

Furthermore in these societies

Working conditions . . . compel the labour-force in free production zones and world-market factories in the underdeveloped countries . . . to achieve levels of productivity and intensity of labour, which correspond to the most advanced current levels in the world, and to . . . tolerate wage levels which are not much higher than those which prevailed in Manchester in capitalism's heyday. [14]

The effect has been to cast a harsh competitive light on Britain's economic performance.

The British economy
When put under the spotlight Britain's economic performance in the 1970s was poor. One study concluded 'Britain's problems of macroeconomic performance . . . were similar to those of other industrial countries, only worse.' [15]

The evidence is not just that (except for areas such as unemployment) Britain comes bottom of most tables comparing economic performance in major countries (see Table 1): it is also that Britain has been there for many years. [16] The difference is that through the 1970s the position deteriorated further. This was summarized in 1978 by Bacon and Eltis as follows:

That the British economy has performed comparatively poorly for a very long time is well known. What is less well known is that Britain's economic performance, as measured by the usual statistical yardsticks, has become incredibly worse in the last decade than it was. [17]

The UK has difficulty in meeting international competition, for the following reasons, amongst others:

• Unlike most Third World countries for example, we have a

Table 1   *Economic indicators – GDP growth*

	GDP growth avg. 1975–80 (%)	GDP growth 1980–81 (%)
Austria	3.5	0
Belgium	2.9	−1.25
Denmark	2.6	−0.5
Finland	3.1	1.75
France	3.3	0.5
Italy	3.8	0
Japan	5.1	3.75
Netherlands	2.5	−2.0
Norway	4.6	1.5
Spain	2.2	1.5
Sweden	1.2	0
Switzerland	1.6	1.25
United Kingdom	1.6	−2.0
USA	3.9	1.75
West Germany	3.6	−1.0

Source: OECD. Taken from C. Bratt, *Labor Relations in 17 Countries* (S. A. F. Stockholm, 1982).

comparatively small working population, fewer young people, and an ever increasing number of citizens beyond retirement age to support. Living standards, and employee expectations, are higher than many European and all Third World competitors.

- Our industrial base is long established, and only changed with pain and difficulty. Furthermore, Britain tends to work with older systems and machinery, investing much less than most competitors.[18]

- Our financial system is also long established, and works to short time horizons and operates relatively independently of governments; restricting the options for the financial management of employing organizations and forcing them to adopt short-term views.[19]

- There is, comparatively, a substantial lack of education and training in Britain. West Germany, to take the most quoted comparator, has proportionately twice as many students over the age of 18 in full-time education.[20] In Japan 96 per cent of young people stay at school to 18+; in the USA people who have left school are much more likely to go back for further training later in their careers.[21] Furthermore a National Institute of Economic and Social Research report in 1983 showed that in key areas like numeracy British school children fall well behind their German counterparts. The position is the same in industrial training:

  Inadequacies in training and in the supply of manpower appear . . . a predominant source of Britain's weakness. . . . Not only is 'management' more technically qualified in Germany than in Britain, but the labour force it has to manage has a higher level of technical training.[22]

There were dramatic changes to the British economy as a result.

As a developed capitalist society Britain displays an enormous range and variety of industries. There is still an important and powerful primary sector: farming, mining, forestries. But there is also a complete range of manufacturing and service industries, public sector welfare organizations, transportation companies, charities and strip clubs. To generalize about such polymorphism is dangerous. Inevitably such a diversity within industry means that there will be diversity in industrial relations – an important fact, though one which is often overlooked.

One generalization that can be made safely is that the industrial framework is changing – changing fast. Manufacturing accounted for 33.8 per cent of the UK's GDP activity in 1962; 24.6 per cent in 1980 and is continuing to decline,[23] especially in terms of numbers employed (Figure 1). The service sector by contrast grew and changed: jobs were lost in some areas, gained in others.[24] Up to 1982 the gains were substantially in the public sector.[25] The number of people unemployed rose irregularly

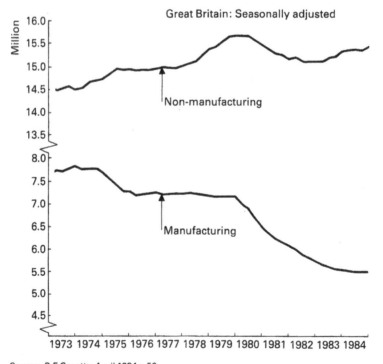

Source: *D E Gazette*, April 1984 p.56

Figure 1   *Manufacturing and non-manufacturing employees in employment*

but inexorably from quarter of a million in 1966 to top three million in 1982. Employment in manual jobs has declined steadily; in 1983 white collar work accounted for more than half the workforce for the first time.[26] Organizational size, in manufacturing at least, increased up to the end of the 1970s, but is now declining.[27] The activity rate of women in the labour force increased rapidly up to 1977 and then stabilized.[28] Part-time employment is far higher in the UK than in most developed countries.[29] And the number of people working outside normal contracts of employment has increased significantly. Nor must we assume that within manufacturing there was little change – even the form of manufacture changes fast (see Figure 2).

The relationship between the changing industrial framework and the international and national base data that we have considered so far is clear. International economic recession has led to a decline in the heavy metal using industries (for example, steel, shipbuilding, etc.). Technological change has led to a growth of the new 'sunrise' industries (for example, computers, electronic offices, international communication). International competition has decimated the textile trade and seriously affected the automobile industry. Changing demographic factors put increasing pressure on social welfare services, and at national level technology, the economy and unemployment are changing the whole way that we live.

The British economy is almost totally interdependent. Each sector, or organization, relies heavily on many others. It is not just the major steel producing plant which sustains a range of maintenance firms, cleaning contractors and steeplejack companies, local law firms, cafes and pubs. Even small offices are linked to public transport, sandwich bars, temporary secretarial agencies and courier services. Many service organizations rely totally on local business; and even private 'independent' engineering firms will be dependent on major purchasers and, often, public sector companies. The economic performance and the industrial relations of each is bound to the others.

Sophisticated modern capitalist economies are not only interdependent, they also comprise a variety of institutions. Britain has public and privately owned businesses, publicly quoted and individually owned shareholdings, cooperatives, charities, partnerships; subsistence agriculture and major government services. Organizations show enormous varieties of size and structure; of purpose; and of success and failure.

For industrial relations two of the most important effects on this varied and interdependent structure of the British economy were unemployment and a changed approach by government. To take unemployment first it is now clear that we are unlikely to reach again the unusual position of the first quarter century after the Second World War when there were more jobs available than people to fill them (Figure 3). Continuing high levels of unemployment are forecast through to, and perhaps beyond, the end of this century.

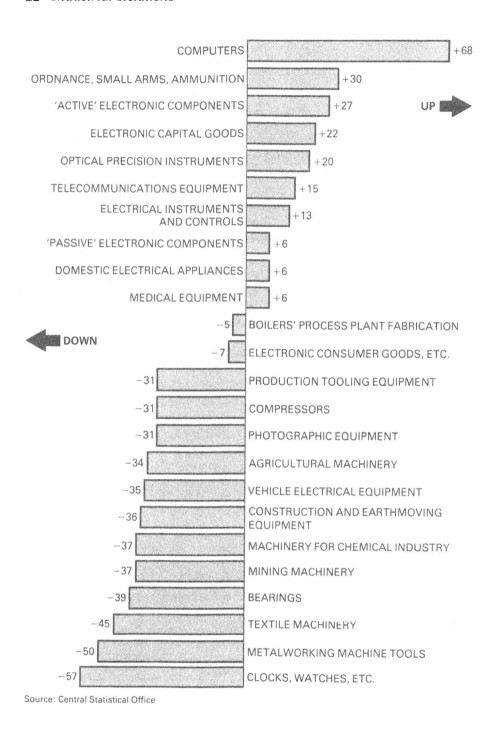

Source: Central Statistical Office

Figure 2 *Percentage changes in UK output, 1979–83*

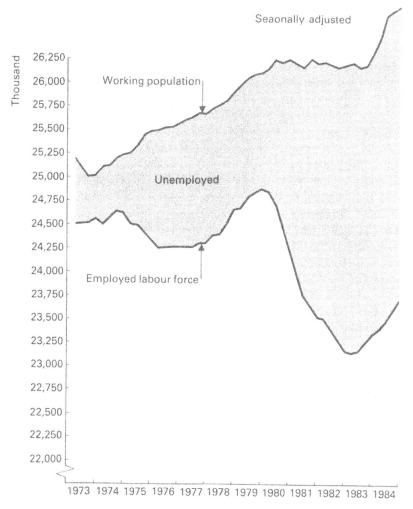

Source: *D E Gazette* April 1984, p.56

Figure 3   *Working population and employed labour force, Great Britain*

Government action

This general national background has immediate effects on industrial relations within organizations – many of them through the actions of government. Industrial relations is a live political issue. The economic strategies of successive Governments, both on a broad and on more specific fronts, are responses to and influences on the national economy and developments within it. In the UK, in contrast to many other countries, there is little political consensus on the way the economy should be run. There are fundamental disagreements between the parties about the main problems to be overcome, the extent of government intervention and public ownership and the levels of unemployment. There is, directly relevant for our purposes here, a debate also about the relationship between economic performance and industrial relations.

In the preface to *Fair Deal at Work*, the Conservative's blueprint for industrial relations reform published in 1968, Prime Minister Heath wrote 'I consider industrial relations to be absolutely crucial to economic progress.'[30] Fifteen years later a Conservative Employment Secretary wrote 'the Government's key objective on industrial relations is to lay the foundations for greater industrial harmony and, thus, prosperity for the country' and 'our success in the '80s and '90s will depend on our success in improving industrial relations'.[31]

Against this view that industrial relations determines economic performance it is argued that it is where the economy is stagnant or under pressure that industrial relations becomes problematic. Whatever the merits of the argument the relationship between the economy and industrial relations is manifest. (R. M. Bell has written an excellent cool assessment of the impact of trade unions at workplace level on the competitiveness of British industry.[32])

As this book is written a 'muscular' form of Conservatism is in the ascendant. In industrial relations the direct effects have been a continuing programme of legislative action and a series of attempts to reduce labour costs. It is possible to exaggerate the long-term effects of both. It has been argued that 'legislative intervention has tended to be increasingly partisan towards the interests of either employers or trade unions since the 1960s, and successive governments have consequently tended to repeal their predecessors' labour laws and institutions' and that despite the fact that the flood of employment law is unlikely to diminish, past experience indicates that

> Two generalizations . . . can be made about the consequences for industrial
> relations of most interventions by government. The first is that their impact is
> greatly influenced by the extent of the employer's initial commitment to collec-
> tive bargaining. The second is that whether intended to inhibit or extend collec-
> tive bargaining, most interventions modify its conduct in unintended ways.[33]

As far as wage costs are concerned labour costs in the UK are below those of many industrialized competitors. Nor is it clear that industrial relations have a simple, unidimensional effect on wage costs, or that union restrictive practices and industrial action, are particularly damaging to the British economy. 'The theoretical analysis of union behaviour by economists is not very satisfactory. . . . Estimates of the effects of unionism on wage costs vary from 8 per cent to 20 per cent.'[34]

More significant may be the change in the government's role as employer. The steady growth in direct state employment, and in subsidiary employment closely related to the state, has been halted. Furthermore there are now pressures to bring employment in the state sector into line with the private sector, rather than as has traditionally been the case to lead in such matters as union recognition, collective bargaining arrangements, pay systems, pensions and associated employment conditions.

The main influence of government, however, may be much more subtle than a catalogue of particular actions reveals. There has been an important change in opinion, both amongst the public at large and amongst those who deal most directly with industrial relations. There has been an unquantifiable, but none the less crucial upsurge in managerial confidence and correspondingly a lessening of confidence in the trade unions. Whether the latter results in more defensive or more compliant unionism will depend largely upon the way that managements develop their approaches to industrial relations.

Pressures and opportunities

So far we have argued that factors such as increasing international competition, including that from the developing countries, and the pace and scope of technological change, have had a major effect on the British economy, leading to significant structural changes in industry. We have identified the reasons why the UK has had difficulties in meeting the challenge of many of these developments. One of the effects has been to put new pressures on managers – but also to open up new opportunities.

The pressures are clear. The private sector is operating under conditions of intense competition. Increases in labour costs, a major cost component for all organizations, cannot be passed readily on to the customer. They have to be both rigorously controlled and matched by productivity improvements. Public sector organizations are operating against ever more rigid objectives set by government – financial, not service, objectives. Managers in this sector are working with reduced budgets, against cash limits.

The result has been to concentrate the minds of managers, on reducing costs and on enhancing cost-effectiveness – focusing on both the cost and the output side of the equation. This has led to many accepted ideas of 'good' personnel practice being re-evaluated. Some have survived, but with a different rationale. Policies covering harmonization of conditions of employment, for example, are now promoted more for creating a framework in which labour can be flexibly deployed than for social or moral reasons. This meets the cost-effectiveness criterion. But others do not; for example, the provision of facilities to union representatives. In the rest of this book we examine these issues in detail against the background of these pressures on management and the criteria that are now being given key prominence.

In the past management have found it extremely difficult to adopt significant measures to improve the cost-effectiveness of labour. Where this has been achieved, it has often been expensive. But the changes in context we have described have affected national opinion, employees and their representatives. In the first four years of the 1980s one pharmaceutical company, investigated by one of the authors, gave pay increases of 4–6 per cent each year and reduced staff by a third; whilst its profits improved by a compounded 25 per cent in each of the four years. This could not have been achieved in the 1970s. Overall, productivity, and hence in some measure competitiveness, has increased significantly in the last few years. This reflects the reduction in employment levels as well as increased investment and improved working practices, but the outcome is shown in the increased profits reported by many organizations in the 1980s. Labour costs in the UK remain relatively low, providing some advantage for, particularly, the UK manufacturing sector, and the British workforce has shown, in certain sectors at least, an immense ability to adapt to a very wide variety of working systems.

The climate of opinion has changed; employees are more prepared to accept the need for significant changes of working practices and demanning. Trade union officials are generally more prepared to cooperate in introducing such changes, whilst their ability to prevent these developments has lessened. The evidence from the beginning of the 1980s is that whilst a few managements have 'ridden' the new opportunities and adopted crude cost-cutting or even anti-union measures, others have taken a more carefully thought out approach. This latter group of vanguard organizations, in the private and public sectors, is challenging traditional approaches to work, assessing innovative ideas, becoming more forward looking and adopting flexible but coherent and consistent policies. It is these approaches and ideas, and in particular these policies, which are the focus of this book; and it is to an overall policy framework that we turn next.

References

1   Urwick Group, *Employee Relations Survey, 1982/3* (Urwick Orr and Partners 1983).
2   *ACAS Annual Report 1983* (HMSO, 1984), p. 1.
3   R. Hyman, *Industrial Relations: a Marxist Introduction* (Macmillan, 1975), p. 3.
4   Organization for Economic Cooperation and Development, *Main Economic Indicators*, various issues.
5   H. Gunter (ed.) *Transnational Industrial Relations* (Macmillan, 1972), p. 17.
6   Gunter, *Transnational Industrial Relations*, p. xii.
7   International Labour Organization, *Multinationals in Western Europe: the industrial relations experience* (ILO, 1976), p. 1.
8   Size Report, *British Companies* (C. and D. Partners, 1979).
9   P. Enderwick, 'Labour and the theory of the multinational corporation', *Industrial Relations Journal*, vol. 13, 2 (1982), pp. 32–43.
10 Central Statistical Office; quoted in *Financial Times*, 26 April 1983.
11 A. Toffler, *Future Shock* (Pan, 1970).
    C. Jenkins and B. Sherman, *The Collapse of Work* (Eyre Methuen, 1979).
    T. Forester (ed.) *The Microelectronics Revolution* (Blackwell, 1980).
12 ILO, *Multinationals in Western Europe*, p. 64.
13 C. Littler and G. Salaman, *Class at Work* (Batsford, 1984), p. 40.
14 F. Frobel, J. Heinrichs and O. Kreye, *The New International Division of Labour* (Cambridge University Press, 1980), p. 36.
15 R. E. Caves and L. B. Krause, *Britain's Economic Performance* (Brookings Institute, 1980).

16 National Economic Development Council, *British Industrial Performance* (NEDC, 1983), p. 14.
17 R. Bacon and W. Eltis, *Britain's Economic Problem: Too Few Producers* (Macmillan, 1978), p. 3.
18 OECD, *Main Economic Indicators*, various issues.
19 L. G. Franko, *The Threat of Japanese Multinationals* (Wiley, 1983).
20 National Economic Development Council, *Competence and Competition: Training and Education in the Federal Republic of Germany, the United States of America and Japan* (NEDC, 1984).
21 Ibid.
22 S. J. Prais, *Productivity and Industrial Structure* (Cambridge University Press, 1981), pp. 263–4.
23 NEDC, *British Industrial Performance*.
24 *Financial Times*, 26 April 1983.
25 Bacon and Eltis, *Britain's Economic Problem*, p. 13.
26 Manpower Services Commission, *Reports*, various.
27 Census of Production, *Reports*, various.
28 Department of Employment, *Gazette* (February 1983).
29 O. Robinson and J. Wallace, 'Growth and Utilisation of Part-time Labour in Great Britain', *Department of Employment Gazette* (Sept. 1984), pp. 391–6.
30 Conservative Central Office, *Fair Deal at Work* (CCO, 1968).
31 N. Tebbitt, 'Industrial relations in the next two decades: government objectives', *Employee Relations*, vol. 5, 1 (1983), pp. 3–6.
32 R. M. Bell, *The Behaviour of Labour, Technical Change and the Competitive Weakness of British Manufacturing* (Technical Change Centre, 1983).
33 W. Brown and K. Sisson, 'Industrial relations in the next decade', *Industrial Relations Journal*, vol. 14.1 (1983), pp. 9–21.
34 A. R. Prest, *The UK Economy* (Weidenfeld and Nicolson, 1984), p. 295.

2
Organizational objectives and industrial relations practice

Having indicated some of the main elements of the context within which industrial relations in Great Britain is located, we now turn to our main theme: the need for organizations to develop forward-looking and proactive industrial relations policies which are integrated with organizational objectives. It is our view that such policies are matters of managerial choice: there is not a 'one right way' which employing organizations should discover. Senior management has a range of possible alternatives on a whole variety of issues. The only prescriptive points we will make are that these issues need to be explored and understood, and that organizations that take definite planning decisions which integrate these issues one with another, and with the overall strategy and structure of the organization, are more likely to enjoy satisfactory industrial relations.

This chapter defines what we mean by an industrial relations policy and how it relates to organizational strategies. We then discuss the aims of industrial relations policies, focusing particularly on the organizational objective of *efficiency*, and some of the issues which will affect those aims. This discussion of the issues forms the agenda for the following chapters.

Industrial relations policies

An industrial relations policy has been defined as: 'A set of proposals and actions which establishes the organization's approach to its employees and acts as a reference point for management.'[1] The constituent parts of this definition indicate, first, that the policy consists of a *set* of factors, that no single management statement or action can be evaluated in isolation. Second, the definition covers *proposals and actions*. Even where an organization does not have a written industrial relations policy, there will nevertheless exist a series of shared expectations about industrial relations. These are developed from the actions of senior management as much as from any statements that they may make. Third, the policy *acts as a reference point for managers*. The overriding objective of an industrial relations policy is to assist management to establish an ordered and consistent approach to non-managerial employees.

Finally, in this definition, this particular policy is about *dealings with employees*. We take a wide definition of industrial relations as being

DOI: 10.4324/9781003193043-2

concerned with all matters – formal and informal – pertaining to contracts of employment and their negotiation and amendment. Many or even most industrial relations policies are not developed deliberately or knowingly, and their creation or amendment is as often influenced by habit or custom as by rational planning.

It is central to our view of these policies that they are seen as a means of coping with the heterogeneity within management rather than a public relations exercise or an attempt to influence the unions or workforce. Management is not a homogeneous whole. There are very significant differences in the roles that different managers play in industrial relations. The distinction between line and staff, operating managers and personnel specialists, is an obvious one; but even within these categories there are differences of function and style which need to be explored. The focus in traditional industrial relations texts on trade unions and particular industries (such as the declining manufacturing sector) has led to insufficient attention being paid to other issues. Many writers refer, in passing as it were, to the words 'company', 'employer' and 'management' as if they were synonymous. Our focus on the management side, and our attempt to cover all industries, makes this casual usage inappropriate for us. The 'employer' is an abstraction. We will use the term sparingly. Control in these organizations is exercised in practice by *management*: those in positions of formal authority under their and their subordinates' contracts of employment. This is the group we will be focusing upon.

We do not, however, make any assumptions that this is a cohesive or unitary group. As the individuals making up this group, *managers* are divided on the basis of level and function as well as personality. So we will on occasion need to refer to managers as well as management.

These are important definitional points, but in a value-laden subject like industrial relations they are also much more. The attempt to treat 'the employer' as a single individual does have the merit of simplifying the issues and clarifying the overall relationship of organizations to the financial and economic system within which they operate. However, we are concerned to examine the more detailed area of the choices and policies open to the managers of the organization. These choices and policies are mediated by individual managers and groups of managers rather than by 'an employer'.

The managers making these choices do so in the light of the industrial relations policy. In saying that, however, we have to make a distinction between what we call 'espoused' industrial relations policies and 'operational' policies.[2] By the espoused policy we mean the general proposals, objectives and standards that top management holds, and/or states that it holds, specifically about the organization's approach to its employees. In that minority of organizations that have written industrial relations policies, it is the espoused industrial relations policy, or elements of it, which are committed to paper.

Organizations have espoused policies in all sorts of areas – marketing, finance, production, customer service. These are often integrated into some form of corporate plan. (Though often the industrial relations policy is omitted.[3]) In practice of course it is not always possible for managers to comply with all these policies. They may conflict; for example – budgetary control (no overtime) v. need for production to meet rush orders (overtime); or need to respond to potential sales (short production runs) v. need for minimum labour and material costs (long production runs). When these policies conflict managers have to make judgements.

In most cases managers try to respond to situations with actions that are likely to bring the results that they perceive their senior managers as wanting most. On an intuitive basis, they establish an ordering of priorities for the various policy demands which is based on their interpretation of top managers' values.

How the managers assess their superiors' priorities will vary with individuals and organizations. Their own experience of the past is often an important factor; and so is their knowledge of the various controls that senior executives apply within the management hierarchy. Indeed, for most line managers the key reference point for their understanding of policy lies in the operation of the control system; in this we include the reward system and the various monitoring processes set up within the organization.

The ordering of priorities by senior management we call the 'operational' policy. This is in practice the policy that managers respond to and try to fulfil. This is the policy that determines how the organization relates to its employees.

Business objectives

How do these policies relate to business objectives? It varies over time. In the 1960s and 1970s *the* issue, as far as industrial relations were concerned, was the need to ensure that output or service was not disrupted by labour disputes. A line of authorities, of which the Donovan Commission[4] was the culmination, stressed that industrial relations (by which they often meant labour disputes) must be seen as a top management responsibility and part of company strategy. At the same time, and perhaps, in hindsight, as a singular occurrence, Britain was experiencing full employment.

The response was that for much of the 1960s and early 1970s the impression was given of industrial relations *driving* the business. A series of colourful and often cynical clichés captured the mood:

'Peace is more important than progress'

'Consensus is more important than change'

'Consistency is more important than costs'

These were the days of high pay settlements and the repeated 'buying-out' of the same restrictive practice. Of course, in some organizations relationships with staff have never been seen as more important than relationships with other groups – customers or suppliers, shareholders, government. This is not to imply that the staff have been seen as unimportant – just that other objectives were given a higher priority. In times of relative boom this may not be obvious – wages and salaries rise fast, working conditions improve. In other circumstances however, financial, production or customer service objectives have been reassessed; in some cases at the expense of personnel policies.

However, in the 1980s the pressures that we outlined in chapter 1 have forced a reappraisal. Companies can no longer afford to maintain industrial peace 'at any price'. All organizations, public and private sector, are under pressure to reduce unit costs, to become more efficient. Managerial responses have taken, broadly, two separate lines. Some organizations have attempted to subordinate industrial relations totally to financial criteria; sometimes at considerable human and social cost; and often without a longer-term consideration. A small but growing vanguard of organizations have adopted the alternative approach, integrating industrial relations into business strategies.

Our argument is that this vanguard has got it right. Industrial relations policies should be ineradicably linked with the other areas of the operation: neither leading, nor subordinate, but part of it.

There have been many examples of the problems that occur otherwise. The other objectives that the organization has will not be achieved if disregarded industrial relations issues go sour. It is more difficult to achieve financial objectives if, for instance, employees are demoralized, withdrawing cooperation or engaging in some form of overt conflict.

Equally, other objectives will be difficult to achieve if wage and salary costs are out of control. Even for the most technologically advanced industries, labour is one of the major operating costs. An unplanned 10 per cent increase in such costs can mean the difference between survival and closure in the private sector, and between the ability to provide a particular service and not in the public sector.

The obtaining, allocation and use of manpower has been a primary managerial task since the Industrial Revolution. In times of recession this task takes on even more importance. When their goods or services are in great demand managements in the private sector can afford to have rather more or less employees than they need, or to be using them inefficiently. As a corollary much of the Civil Service is under less pressure when demands for its services are slack. As recession develops the demands on the health, welfare, education and employment services become greater. And again the less efficient use of manpower that could be tolerated in times of economic boom becomes increasingly inappropriate.

It should already have become clear that we are using the term *efficiency*, to which we shall return continuously throughout the book, to denote the achieving of the organization's narrowly defined objectives with a parsimonious use of the manpower resource. This form of efficiency may well, of course, lead to inefficiency in terms of wider objectives for the organization, or for society as a whole. It might, for example, increase efficiency for the British Steel Corporation if an individual plant is closed; but it could be argued that to throw a large percentage of one town's workforce out of work, to cause the closing of supporting companies and to have many thousands of highly skilled workers on the dole is inefficient for society at large. It might equally increase efficiency in narrowly defined terms for a company providing computer programming services if it can get the same amount of work done with fewer staff. It could be argued, however, that if the company is then unable to respond to a potential large contract because it would take too long to hire and train the programmers to meet that demand, then it is in fact inefficient.

We will be calling 'efficiency' the short-term achievement of company-specific aims through maximizing output (or service) in relation to the minimum costs of producing the output or service. This includes both labour and material and overhead costs. It is the way in which managements, in both the public and the private sector, use the term. In the public service sector such efficiency will be seen as a major contributor to achieving standards of performance in relation to fixed or reducing budgetary constraints. In the public production sector, and in the private sector, such efficiency will be seen as a direct contributor to profit. In either case it is a key objective for all managements.

Improvements in efficiency can be achieved in the manpower area as in others. In manpower, efficiency improvements will be achieved through the dual process of controlling labour costs and improving labour output. Both will to some extent involve decisions in related areas:

- A company in the engineering industry switched its stock control and order processing to a computerized system on line to its major customers. It was able to reduce its headquarters manning to a third of its previous levels. The cost of the new system and staffing was less than a quarter of the previous system; and the service to the customer was better.

- A restaurant in London decided to offer a fast-food service at lunchtime. It quickly found a need to retrain some staff and recruit others. The increased labour costs consumed a great amount of the profits forecast from the operation.

- A travel company launched an advertising programme mid-way through the summer in an attempt to attract last-minute holiday makers to its unfilled holidays. It found that many staff used that period, when normally few people are booking, to take their own holidays. It had to recruit inexperienced, temporary staff to cover the extra business.

In the first case the manpower implications had been taken into account in the actual making of the decision, which had been precipitated by some combination of the cost-savings involved and union pressure. In the two latter cases, with no obvious initial cost element and no trade union representation, these implications had only become apparent after the decisions had been taken.

Problems arise frequently because of the separation in the minds of many managers of industrial relations from other management decisions. Industrial relations specialists and managers in industrial relations departments have in general concentrated upon the trade unions. Academically we have researched and written about and learned more about the trade unions than we have about management.[5]

This has led to 'industrial relations' often being viewed as an implementation problem, to be sorted out (usually, sigh the managers, at great cost and pain) after the more serious management decisions have been taken. We know that it is still only a minority, even of the larger manufacturing organizations, that have personnel directors on the board,[6] although this may be no more than symbolically important. Most companies have now realized the benefit of understanding the manpower constraints as well as the external context in their strategic planning[7] and of having industrial relations issues as an input into all crucial decisions rather than merely dealing with it as a problem afterwards.

The aims of IR policies

A general understanding of the context of industrial relations is important but insufficient in the design of industrial relations policies. The instigators of such policies need a more detailed knowledge of specific issues. We address these issues in the context of a continuing recession where managements are forced to control, to a greater degree, the labour costs of their operation to reduce the ratio of costs to output. The ideas that we consider have to be seen in the light of 'competitive pressure, market pressure, urging each firm constantly and unremittingly to be profitable, never to relax from the threat, real or anticipated of competitive disadvantage'.[8]

It is this threat which ensures that improvements to terms and conditions of employment, for instance, will have to be funded internally. The scope for passing on costs in the form of higher prices will continue to be severely restricted. There is therefore a change of emphasis in the aims of industrial relations policies. The maintenance of procedural and substantive elements in a way which secures a trouble-free industrial relations climate is becoming of necessity less important than achieving business objectives associated, for example, with reducing unit costs through increased productivity. That this is not in turn creating more overt demonstrations of conflict is because of the changes in the balance of power between management and unions characteristic of a recession.

In the light of this changed emphasis in industrial relations policies management will be seeking to promote efficiency, control, stability and predictability. We explore each of these concepts in turn.

Efficiency

Through task flexibility

Efficiency, on the criteria we have set out above, has implications at both the cost and 'benefit' end of industrial relations. The focus in Britain has often been on costs; but it is perhaps on the output side that our industrial relations record is weakest. Although many organizations can point to impressive improvements in efficiency and flexibility, for most managements the maximum benefit from the employment of a given number of employees is reduced by restrictions on the flexibility of labour. Arising from economic necessity and with, perhaps, an increased confidence brought about by the weakening of the trade unions at the beginning of the 1980s, managements are now seeking to remove restrictions on manpower flexibility. Already the issue is being seen as one of the areas in which foreign competition has a distinct advantage. The more formal, often national or industry wide, restrictions have been largely removed; the changing format of apprenticeships in the engineering industry is an instructive example.

The concept of each employee having his or her own job to do is one which was and is supported strongly by the unions as part of their overall approach to job rights. It has also traditionally been supported just as strongly by managements. It is, after all, a logical corollary of the concept of the division of labour: intellectually and practically accepted as 'correct'. The idea of each individual having their own job to do is the foundation of many management techniques such as measurement-by-objectives (MBO) and job evaluation. However, the advance of technology and the straitened economic circumstances of Britain in the 1980s are leading to a re-evaluation. We are beginning to notice that the high growth rate economies of the 1970s were those that had workforces that had flexibility between jobs. We are starting to look more seriously at the ideas of multi-roles and multi-skilling in the context less of job interest, more of organizational efficiency. We are having to re-examine our views on training and re-training. The interface between organizational success (or even survival) and industrial relations is widening.

There are other implications on the output side. Work in an industrial society has always been too complex to rely on 'dumb obedience'. The good soldier Svejk was not alone in realizing that the best way to sabotage a modern organization was simply to follow orders exactly: no more and no less.[9] Management relies on the workforce to use their initiative, skills and creativity beyond the areas which can be overseen. Unless the workforce is motivated to do their jobs in an accurate, timely, and sometimes innovatory manner, the management can fail to meet its objectives.[10]

The UK has in general looked abroad for alternatives – though the establishment of cooperatives, one solution, can fairly be claimed as an indigenous invention (if one that, like so many other British inventions, has been developed abroad). There is renewed interest in such ideas as autonomous work groups, work restructuring and quality circles. These approaches used to be described, in the 1960s for example, as being about improving the quality of working life. They appeal to managers now, however, because they hold out the promise of creating a more interested, motivated and innovatory workforce, taking more responsibility for the results of their own work. It is perhaps not surprising that approaches which held out the promise of meeting such a wide range of objectives from such a range of disparate groups generate some cynicism. Seen as we will view them here – as attempts to increase the benefits side of the manpower costs equation – they have a clear rationality, and can be expected to spread. Unlike the 1960s, however, the emphasis in these schemes is now more on improvements to efficiency than on improving communication or 'process skills'. Control at the local level, in work organization, is still shared only in a minority of organizations. In most it is exercised by managers, under the constraints of workforce and trade union reaction. This is perhaps most clearly manifest in matters of discipline.

During most of the 1970s managers were on the defensive in matters of discipline. This was to some extent a response to greater union confidence at the workplace; but in the main, of course, it was a reaction to the spate of employment legislation. In the 1980s, this position has changed, and the successive Employment Acts of the 1980s have reflected and reinforced that fact. There is still a huge diversity in the way managers treat discipline, but it seems clear that one result of the legislation has been a formalization of procedures.[11] Many managers, however, are beginning to operate such procedures according to harder criteria.[12] The offences of not obeying orders within the contract, or not carrying out contracted duties are becoming more common.

An instructive sidelight on this issue is shed by the 1982 statutory sick pay provisions. They were a spur to management to get to grips with the problem of absence control and to continue developing viable procedures to reduce levels of absenteeism. The predictable presence of employees is obviously a necessary prerequisite to efficient use of them.

It is no accident that the early 1980s saw a number of major disputes related to efficiency – working practices and manning levels became key issues in organizations as diverse as British Airways, Birds Eye, the Ministry of Social Security and London Weekend Television. We have indicated some elements of the debate about the output side of the equation here. We examine these issues in detail, with examples, in chapter 3.

Efficiency and working time
A second aspect of the efficiency criterion concerns patterns of work.

Within the workplace the argument about efficiency can be linked with the continuing introduction of new technology, new production methods and new service industries. The introduction of computers into many organizations led to the introduction of a new pattern of work for white-collar employees – shift working. The reason, that the organization could not afford to have equipment of that value standing idle, is one which is increasingly likely to be generalized. Managements are starting to compare factors such as the cost of new technology with the on-going costs of their plant and premises. In the public sector, for example, our hospitals are utilized on a 24 hour, 365 days a year basis, but our Town Halls are only used between say 8am and 10pm, only on weekdays and not during Bank Holidays, over the Christmas period and so on. And in the education sector our schools and colleges are used for less: only 24 or 30 weeks a year in some cases. Can we afford this? The developing countries use their schools and colleges much more intensively.

As well as increased utilization of workplaces and equipment, however, there are social movements pulling in the opposite direction. We might instance the demand for a shorter working week, the concept of job-sharing and the use of part-time workers. Managements have to understand, reconcile and adapt to these differing requirements.

Longer-term social changes are also affecting employing organizations. People are not expecting to be in employment for so long; they are hoping for (or in some cases fearful of) earlier retirement. They may have to accept a number of different careers during the course of a lifetime: they will need extensive retraining periods, they may be asking for sabbaticals – months or years off work just to do something else. We discuss the responsibilities of management, and some of the possible responses, to all these changes in the pattern of work in chapter 4.

The other side of this efficiency equation is more traditional, but has not been untouched. The narrow focus on the pay package has been widened and is still extending. Again, the more sophisticated managements are moving away from a crude objective of minimizing wage costs towards a series of objectives concerning a wider view of efficiency. The switch towards white-collar employment which we noted in chapter 1 has amongst other things led to a re-evaluation of all wage structures in terms of manpower planning. The question now being asked is 'what manpower do we need, and what sort of reward structures should we be aiming for in order to achieve that?' Thus the content of the package, including cash and all the range of associated benefits, is being reassessed.

Wage packages are being renegotiated in form as well as in size. In the past, and still today for many organizations, bargaining parameters would be set in terms of overall targets. How the wage costs were packaged, what percentage is basic, shift, various allowances or benefits, was seen as less important. The more explicit focus on efficiency is changing all that. Managements are beginning to see the benefits in careful calculation of the content of the wage packet. This needs more complex planning in unionized organizations than in non-union ones.

Many managements have responded to the new economic circumstances and to trade union concerns by restricting their negotiations to simple basic elements of pay. Others, however, have seized the opportunity to link pay more directly to productivity. These managements are themselves putting novel and hitherto unconsidered elements into the bargaining package. They are, for example, inviting the unions to join them in assessing and distributing added value, previously an issue held as confidential by management in its preparation for negotiations. They are bargaining with unions on payments for improved quality – the work side of the wage–work equation. Previously discussions had concentrated on the wage side (in its widest sense) with the form, type and output of work being left to a combination of custom and practice, and management fiat. These issues are being increasingly linked, at management initiative, to rewards and incentives.

There is an interesting discrepancy between these moves towards a more comprehensive payment on the basis of results for all types of employee and the much admired 'Japanese' approach to management. (Though it should be said that the mixture of myth, folklore and misinformation which makes up most British managers' views of the Japanese approach is unlikely to be recognized in Japan.) The Civil Service is, in the 1980s, being pushed towards a system of payment on the basis of results. This will foster specialization and short-term employment; it will militate against commitment to service, life-time contracts, interchangeability and the 'company union'. One of the British institutions that shares many of the structural features of the 'Japanese' is moving away from them.

The form and duration of the agreement is also important. Britain is unusual in having agreements that abjure detail, that leave items not included in them to subsequent negotiation and that last, typically, one year or, occasionally, less than that. This basic pattern has been complicated by an extension of the number of agreements; many organizations now have several dozen, covering a range of topics from pay to the introduction of new machinery and pensions to job evaluation. These agreements have tended to grow incrementally with even personnel departments often seeing little relationship between them. They could all, however, form parts of a planned approach to relationships with employees and unions.

Along with a new look at the make-up and format of agreements is a new emphasis on elements within the package that will aid rather than hinder efficiency: flexibility between tasks, buying out of restrictive practices, a concentration on performance-linked rewards. There is also, to activate a later argument, a move towards longer-term agreements lasting two or three years.[13] These will increase stability and predictability. Overall managements are beginning to take a more pro-active look at the reward side of the work-reward package. We examine this in detail in chapter 5.

The criterion of control: alternative forms of contract

Efficiency is not the only criterion managements will be guided by in their industrial relations policies. Another important one will be their ability to control the employees' output (in whatever form their work takes). This thread will run throughout most of the industrial relations policy, but is in one respect leading away from industrial relations altogether. Definitions of industrial relations assume that people are working under a contract of employment. This may not be a safe assumption. Historically it is only very recently that the idea of 'working' has been linked to 'being employed'; geographically, the vast majority of people in the world still work only for themselves. It seems unlikely that we shall be able to repeat the strange circumstances of the first thirty years after the Second World War, when there was more employment available than people to fill the jobs. The UK will have to adapt to continuing high levels of unemployment, or to redefine the relationships between work and employment (or both).

The relationship between work and employment is always being redefined. We can characterize this by talking about contracts of employment and contracts for service. The former consists of the terms and conditions under which the majority of the British working population goes to work. Contracts for service are specific limited arrangements for particular pieces of work to be carried out: control by contract. In some areas this is an accepted mode of operation; lawyers operate this way, so do management consultants and window cleaners and garages. Contracts for service are becoming more widespread. A substantial 'black economy' has been identified in the UK,[14] and there are growing numbers of people working outside the usual employment contract.

Some industries, such as construction and the exhibition industry, have always used sub-contractors. 'Temps' in offices are now commonplace. And more recently local authorities have been sub-contracting many of their services: most offices and factories sub-contract cleaning, security and other services. There is a growth of employment agencies. Manufacture in the UK started with a 'ganger' system, where whole aspects of the process were contracted out. Two hundred years later some of our more sophisticated companies are looking at such a system again. A wide range of services are increasingly being offered by specialists in all fields. Many of these 'freelance consultants' have been made redundant by large employers and are now selling their skills, in an increasingly competitive market, to other organizations. For managers the assumption that work has to be done by currently employed staff or by new recruits is no longer valid.

Chapter 6 considers these aspects of the casualization of work and the effect they have on organizations.

Stability: channels of representation

A third criterion that we identified in industrial relations policies is stability. Like efficiency and control this applies to all aspects of the policy and various manifestations of it have already been discussed. In particular, however, it will apply in employee representation and to the collective bargaining arrangements.

By stability we mean that the industrial relations procedures are well-established and used consistently to resolve problem issues. All groups of employees will have their terms and conditions of employment regulated through a small number of accepted channels. The channels can be kept to a minimum because the industrial relations policies will aim to reduce the number of issues and range of differential conditions as far as possible. This will be seen as being cheaper to administer, to have motivational benefits and, most importantly, to reduce the range of topics that can lead to dissatisfaction and, potentially, to unpredictability.

It is not necessary to be unduly cynical to see most of the steps that are being taken to increase worker participation as being related directly or indirectly to the efficiency criterion. Directly because communication, consultation and negotiation on aspects of the business can lead to innovative ideas being jointly developed and implemented with the cooperation of the workforce. Indirectly in that through the participative medium, a climate can be created which is conducive to adaptation and change. At present most of these steps will lead to increased participation by the workforce (or elements of it) in working methods, in responsibility for the activities of fellow workmates and, sometimes, in financial success. They very rarely include participation in the overall control of the organization.

The pressure for stability also requires managers to have some warning of the expectations and fears of the rest of the workforce – and how these may be manifested. There will therefore be a more substantial element of managerial information-gathering than exists at present in many organizations. And there will be a more extensive, and more controlled, circulation of specific information.

For many items collective bargaining will continue to be appropriate. The relationship between the bargaining levels and the organization's structure are crucial. There is a continuing debate about the value of centralizing negotiations compared to the value of disseminating them to the various locations at which employees work. Chapter 7 discusses the management of consultation channels and collective bargaining.

The changing trade unions

This debate takes us on to consider the role and influence of the trade unions. In a highly unionized country such as the UK, the unions will continue to be an important factor for most managements. The decline in union membership and power will not develop to a point at which the unions can be ignored. They will continue to influence labour utilization at all points; from manpower planning through to control at the workplace. Despite the newspaper stereotype, the unions are changing – and rapidly.

Some managements are aware of these changes and their potential impact, understand how they might affect the power balance at the workplace, and appreciate how they can themselves influence the changes. These managements will be able to exercise more control over their industrial relations than managements which are less forward-looking.

One way of increasing stability and predictability is to keep the trade unions out of the organization. This is a policy which requires constant vigilance and work by the personnel specialists and knowledge and effort on the part of line managers if it is not to lead to greater unpredictability. It is fraught with peril but gives managements potential benefits. An alternative approach is to accept the unions and to ensure, as far as possible, that they cover all staff, are truly representative, and are involved in relevant decisions. Policies that fall between these alternatives seem to lead to less stability.

Where there are unions, management will be trying to achieve stability and simplicity. This implies that the management accept a responsibility for preventing splits within the unions or allowing new unions in. They may, in certain circumstances, take steps to reduce their number, or at least the number of channels through which they consult and negotiate. The trade unions, and management's options in dealing with them, are the focus of chapter 8.

Predictability: managerial roles and the need to plan
Our discussion so far has indicated that industrial relations can be managed. We have already pointed out however that management is not a homogeneous whole with all managers thinking and acting alike. For the organization there are important issues about the role of line management and of personnel and industrial relations specialists. In order for the first three managerial objectives of efficiency, control and stability to be realized senior managers have understood the need to plan industrial relations and develop appropriate policies that will guide all members of management.

This planning has the same constraints as planning in other aspects of the organization's operation: that much of the value lies in the planning process itself rather than in the plans that result. It is the discipline of establishing the present situation, developing targets, projecting possible alternatives and assessing what needs to be done that is beneficial. Eventual outcomes will be more controlled and closer to optimum than they might have been otherwise, though the plans will never be fully achieved.

Managements will be attempting this planning through the mechanism of industrial relations policies integrated into the objectives and overall strategy of the organization. The issues we have discussed so far, and will discuss in the rest of this book, need to be integrated with each other, so that the industrial relations policy is coherent and consistent; and with the overall organizational objectives.

This has two implications for industrial relations. First, it becomes in one sense less identifiable. It will be absorbed into the general management strategy – a factor in all cases, but rarely a separate item in its own right. It is in this sense that the classic finding by Winkler[15] that Boards of Directors do not address industrial relations issues should be understood. Second, and also relevant to that analysis, industrial relations in the broad terms that we will be using it in this book becomes less of a specialist area and more one for all managers – but in particular for the senior management team. It is only at this level that industrial relations can be integrated into the organizational objectives: only at the lower management level that it can be integrated into operational management. We discuss managerial roles in industrial relations in our final summary chapter.

References

1 C. J. Brewster, G. G. Gill and S. Richbell, 'Industrial relations policy: a framework for analysis', K. E. Thurley and S. Wood (eds), *Industrial Relations and Management Strategy* (Cambridge University Press, 1983), p. 62.

2 Ibid., p. 63.
   C. J. Brewster and S. Richbell, 'Industrial relations policy and managerial custom and practice', *Industrial Relations Journal*, vol. 14, 1 (1983), pp. 22–31.

3 W. E. J. McCarthy and N. D. Ellis, *Management by Agreement* (Hutchinson, 1973).

4 *Royal Commission on Trade Unions and Employers' Associations, 1963–68* (HMSO, 1968).

5 S. Wood, 'The study of management in British industrial relations', *Industrial Relations Journal*, vol. 13, 2 (1982), pp. 51–61.
   D. Winchester, 'Industrial relations research in Britain', *British Journal of Industrial Relations*, vol. xxi, 1 (1983), pp. 100–14.

6 C. Brookes, *Boards of Directors in British Industries*, Research Paper 7, Department of Employment (1979), p. 53.
   W. Brown, *The Changing Contours of British Industrial Relations* (Basil Blackwell, 1981), p. 27.

7 J. Purcell, 'The management of industrial relations in the modern corporation: agenda for research', *British Journal of Industrial Relations*, vol. xxi, 1 (1983), pp. 1–16.

8 C. R. Littler and G. Salaman, *Class at Work: The Design, Allocation and Control of Jobs* (Batsford, 1984), p. 8.

9 J. Hasek, *The Good Soldier Svejk* (Penguin, 1973).

10 A. Fox, *Beyond Contract* (Faber and Faber, 1974).
   A. L. Friedman, *Industry and Labour* (Macmillan, 1977).

11 W. W. Daniel and N. Millward, *Workplace Industrial Relations in Britain* (Heinemann, 1983), p. 163.

12 The industrial tribunals are adopting economic and business criteria in their judgement of unfair dismissal cases too. See, for example, *Industrial Relations Law Reports*.

13 See Income Data Services Report, 429 (July 1984).

14 G. Mars, *Cheats at Work* (George Allen and Unwin, 1983).

15 J. Winkler, 'The Ghost at the Bargaining Table: Directors and Industrial Relations', *British Journal of Industrial Relations* vol. xxii, 2 (July 1974), pp. 191–212.

3
Flexibility of task

Future industrial relations historians may characterize the 1980s as the decade of 'dissolving demarcations'. This view will be derived in particular from the significant steps taken in one industry – shipbuilding – which has most often been connected with historic job demarcations. Vertical and horizontal interchangeability between jobs certainly has progressed in all sectors in the 1980s although many organizations had made substantial moves in this direction in previous years. The productivity agreements of the 1960s had anticipated this trend toward flexibility of task.

Economic circumstances and rapid developments in technology lie behind these changes. As one study put it

> 'The twin pressures of the drive for efficiency and the impact of technology have pushed flexibility and the associated concepts of interchangeability and mobility onto the bargaining table, if not for the first time, then with renewed force.'[1]

In this chapter we will focus initially on these economic circumstances and these developments in technology. We will then describe how moves toward enhanced flexibility of task have affected particular groups in employment – semi-skilled, skilled and white collar 'staff'. Finally, we will examine how managements can improve flexibility of task within their organizations.

Economic pressures

As we have noted in chapter 2, the current pressures on organizations to reduce costs are intense. In the public sector, 'rate-capping', penalties for over-spending and cash limits have generated such pressures. For manufacturing industry the economic pressures derive, as we have seen, from competitive forces operating in an international trading context. Improving flexibility of task can make a significant improvement towards cost effectiveness. It does this firstly through its implications on manning levels. Over-manning has been closely associated with demarcation, and the continuation of demarcation lines has thereby contributed toward lack of competitiveness. Employing two people on work which occupies each for

DOI: 10.4324/9781003193043-3

50 per cent or less of their time when one (with training) could cover both jobs increases the costs of a particular product or service. In his writings on inter-craft flexibility and the transfer of minor maintenance work from craftsmen to semi-skilled employees in the productivity agreements of the 1960s, Flanders says that their main objective was savings on manpower,[2] although he also stresses the role of such Agreements in regaining 'control' over pay and work systems which had been 'lost' as a result of the 'enhanced power of work groups'.[3] The harsher economic circumstances of the 1980s and the implications of unemployment on work group power has placed the objectives of task flexibility firmly on improving cost effectiveness rather than diminishing 'informality, autonomy and fragmentation of local bargaining'.

Flexibility of task by reducing unnecessary boundaries between jobs can also improve productivity through reduced waiting time and reduced lost output through absenteeism. For example if the wages clerk is absent, it is less critical if the administration clerk is trained in wages duties and can cover for this absence. Improving overall performance in this way is seen in the 1980s as fundamental to the future stability and growth of the organization. There may be some gains in job satisfaction from this trend, but, again to draw a comparison with the 1960s, the emphasis is on cost effectiveness rather than job enrichment as the prime goal.

This trend can be seen operating in the non-manufacturing sector. The insurance salesman will deal in loans, stocks and shares; the milkman will deliver eggs and orange juice; the plasterer will paint the walls. Organizations operate more efficiently, customers receive better and quicker service and the employee will, hopefully, have a more interesting job.

There are other economic pressures acting as a catalyst for task flexibility, including in particular the increasing pace of product development. In many different fields, consumers demand and get a wide variety of product choice: in colour television sets, in telephones, in personal computers, in food and drink, in banking services and so on – the range of choice is enormous and widening. The consequence for the organization of this variety is that the workforce has to be capable of responding flexibly to changed requirements.

As market requirements change within the range of services on offer, so the workforce will need to adjust to meet these changed requirements. This creates considerable demands for flexibility of task within broad groupings of similar jobs. Thus the semi-skilled operator will increasingly be required to assemble different products requiring different fixtures and fittings; the clerical worker will be required to move between a wider range of activities; the service engineer will need to adapt to servicing a wider range of products.

These developments have major implications on reward systems and we will return to this aspect in chapter 5.

Technological changes

We described in chapter 1 the rapidity of technological change and referred to the widespread application of microelectronics. Of particular importance in the context of flexibility of task is the way technological changes have blurred the distinctions between many jobs; it is this factor which underlies many of the movements toward flexibility of task. This blurring of the boundaries between jobs can be seen operating at many levels. In an Order Processing Department, for example, traditional divisions between 'telephone ordering' and 'written orders' can be removed once VDUs are installed as part of a computerized order processing system. Inputing data to a computerized payroll system will require similar skills to inputing data to a computerized bought ledger system. CNC machine operators can be trained in programming skills. Craftsmen may be required to diagnose faults in complicated equipment, blurring the distinction between them and 'technicians'[4] and leading to the development of the mechanical technician or electronic technician from the ranks of the craftsmen. In other instances the division between semi-skilled and skilled will be blurred; for example it was envisaged that NC machines would be operated by semi-skilled employees.[5] There are, of course, limits to this blurring of job boundaries:

> We are all for some form of demarcation, but in management language we call it specialization. We don't want the electricians to fix our plumbing and we don't want the welders to build our wooden decks.[6]

The continuing spread of microelectronics is increasing the range of operations that can be automated. The visions of the 'electronic office' and the 'factory of the future' with its emphasis on robotics, flexible manufacturing systems and computer aided design are fast becoming reality.

Trade union responses to new technology

Although expressing a number of reservations about the spread of new technology, unions have generally given a favourable reaction to these developments.[7] The Association of Professional, Executive, Clerical and Computer Staffs (APEX) for example, have produced a number of well researched booklets on the implications of new technology particularly in the office environment, and have said that they accept

> the argument that a negative approach to new technology would not be in the long term interest of the living standards or employment prospects of trade union members.[8]

The unions generally emphasized the importance of consultation in the introduction of new technology, and have formalized their position through the introduction of new technology agreements. Although the emphasis in these differs between unions, they essentially contain clauses on consultation prior to the introduction of change and on handling the manning implications of such changes. 'No compulsory redundancy' clauses figured more prominently in earlier drafts: economic circumstances generally in the 1980s meant few organizations could afford to accept such blanket concepts. Instead many have accepted that consultation is fundamental to the successful introduction of technical changes, and have agreed to explore voluntary redundancy, retraining and redeployment, natural wastage and so on as methods to handle any job displacement, with compulsory redundancy as a last resort.[9]

The implications of new technology on job content, and on moves toward flexibility of task, have been considered by the unions. The TUC in its report *Employment and Technology* stated, for example, that

> Technological change by blurring or even obliterating the boundaries between jobs has implications for trade union organization and structure. Structures and practices are needed which promote unity and closer working between unions and their members.[10]

Individual unions at national level have responded differently, depending on whether the trend in new technology was generally favourable to their membership or not. Thus the Electrical, Electronic, Telecommunications and Plumbing Union (EETPU) whose members stand to gain much from the introduction and spread of electronically controlled equipment, has generally supported the introduction of new technology.[11] The Amalgamated Union of Engineering Workers (AUEW) given the direction of change, has been understandably more cautious, but has, for example, recognized the need for workers to learn several skills during their working life, and the need to train workers with the skills to apply and operate microelectronics equipment.[12]

Flexibility of task: practical implications

So far we have described how economic pressures and technological developments are combining to generate further pressures towards flexibility of task. These pressures can lead to inter-job flexibility, between such groups as craftsmen and semi-skilled; or to intra-job flexibility, for example, within craft jobs or within clerical jobs. Such flexibility of task can therefore be horizontal or vertical within the organization. We now turn to examining flexibility of task in practice, starting with semi-skilled employees. From this we will review craft flexibility and flexibility amongst white collar grades.

Semi-skilled flexibility

Flexibility of task amongst semi-skilled workers, which mainly affects manufacturing industry, can fall into the following categories:

1 Horizontal flexibility, bringing together what were traditionally separate jobs at a similar job demand level into one generic semi-skilled job.

2 Vertical flexibility: semi-skilled job holders undertaking other semi-skilled work which has traditionally been graded as less or more demanding. In this category, too, can be grouped semi-skilled workers taking on work previously undertaken by supervisors, or minor craft tasks, or taking on unskilled work.

3 A combination of horizontal and vertical flexibility.

Before examining each of these three categories in turn it must be emphasized that not all semi-skilled jobs will move in these directions. There will remain a need for specialist one-off, semi-skilled jobs where for reasons of experience and training, flexibility of task would not be practical. For those jobs where the operation can become more cost effective as a result of greater interchangeability, however, the first issue is to define the area of overlap:

> A particular job may be defined either narrowly or widely; however from the point of view of skill utilization the most significant question is what portion of a job can be performed by a worker from another job. The extent of overlap – the area of potential flexibility – may not be large but even a small amount of interchangeability can contribute significantly to increased efficiency. Thus skill utilization can be explored in terms of the manner in which work components are clustered into jobs and the extent of overlap in these clusters.[13]

Horizontal flexibility demands the employee taking on different jobs, or tasks, at broadly the same job demand level. This is particularly relevant where the pace of product change is significant, since production operators in this context are required to move quickly from one model to another. Similarly, replacement operators are often required to be entirely flexible across the range of semi-skilled jobs in order to cover for absence of employees at any work station.

Vertical flexibility involves the employee taking on jobs or tasks which require lower or higher demands than that on which he is currently engaged. This may involve taking on inspection work or quality control or even certain supervisory tasks. This type of flexibility is increasingly sought as a way of removing barriers between types of work, to improve efficiency and cost effectiveness. It often has manning implications, and it can add to the satisfaction of the employee concerned if the additional tasks are at a more responsible level, for which training is provided.

A combination of vertical and horizontal flexibility can be found in the many examples of group working introduced in recent years. These used to be referred to as semi-autonomous work groups, but may now be called production clusters, minimum work teams or self regulating groups. These aim to relate small groups (generally fewer than 20) of employees to groups of activities in a particular production process. While it may be relatively easy to relate a work-group to key activities, the question of where the boundaries between workgroups are drawn may be more problematic.

Typically, technically interdependent jobs are grouped together, including production and maintenance. Part of the vertical interchangeability required in group working is that minor first line maintenance can be resourced from amongst the production operators, although craftsmen may also be directly associated with the workgroup. The opportunity within a small team for the production operators, craftsmen, technical support (not specialist support which will probably remain part of back-up services) and clerical staff to work together can lead to improved communications, improved productivity particularly through absence cover and enhanced flexibility of task both vertically and horizontally. This concept of group working is particularly associated with Volvo where groups can include 15 workers sharing 150 jobs, with workers rotating within and between groups.[14]

A number of industrial relations issues arises in connection with semi-skilled flexibility including

1 payment implications;
2 union representation;
3 common conditions; and
4 retraining.

We will explore each in turn.

The payment implications arise in at least two ways. Firstly, if individuals are required to undertake more demanding work, should this be rewarded? Secondly, if individuals take on less demanding work, does this reduce the overall evaluation of the job? On the first point, it is rare for payment to be directly related to flexibility – more commonly, general flexibility agreements are tied into annual review increases.[15] However, flexibility may figure more prominently in multi-factor payment schemes, and this is described in more detail in chapter 5. On the second point, it would hardly secure greater flexibility if job grading and hence pay were reduced as a result of developing a generic job description covering flexibility of task. In practice jobs are unlikely to be evaluated at lower levels, since the 'core skill' will not change, and it is the core skill which is influential in job evaluation terms. Nevertheless, the concept of flexibility does pose a challenge to the principles of job evaluation and we will consider this separately later in this chapter.

Issues associated with union representation revolve particularly around the manual union/white collar union interface, although barriers to task flexibility can be created by the existence of different unions at any level in the organization. The issue can be seen at its sharpest if a new post embodying flexibility of task is created which is 50 per cent 'manual' and 50 per cent 'staff' – the question then is into which bargaining unit does it fall, manual or staff? Generally this can be resolved at local level by reference to the traditional spheres of influence of particular unions as defined for example in recognition agreements and union membership agreements. Barriers created by union recognition are eased where management has encouraged joint union working on the site. Otherwise management have requested discussions between officials of the various unions involved where demarcation issues cannot be resolved locally. One of the main advantages of single union agreements is that such inter-union difficulties are removed. There is in particular great union sensitivity to semi-skilled employees undertaking craft work; although this can be alleviated by restricting semi-skilled activity to the routine maintenance work necessary to keep production going.

Common conditions in this context refers to problems that might arise in breaking down work barriers between employees if conditions of employment are significantly different between work groups. Thus if an organiz-

---

Example 3.1   *Some cases of the development of flexibility of task*

Principle of flexibility at BL

It is agreed that there will be full cooperation in the movement of labour to ensure the efficient continuity of production. In consequence, any employee may be called upon to work in any part of his employing plant and/or to carry out any grade or category within the limits of his abilities and experience with training if necessary.[17]

Esso-Fawley: full utilization of capabilities

. . . when . . . workload and efficiency considerations, advances in technology or changes in organization require new skills, new working practices or the assignment of individuals to different work areas in the Refinery, the only limitations would be

- the skill which people have or can acquire (with new training if necessary);
- the time available to perform any new or additional tasks; and
- the requirement of safety.[18]

British Shipbuilders

2.0 Composite group working

2.1   It is agreed that composite groups shall be formed within which there will be complete interchangeability and flexibility in order to eliminate waiting time and enable the group to undertake the entire range of tasks required to complete the job. The main features of 'composite groups' are:

   (a)   Composite groups shall be formed to operate in shops, assembly areas and on board ship.
   (b)   The composition of the group shall be determined by reference to the target manhour content of the complete job or task to be undertaken by the group. The manning of the group shall reflect the craft and ancillary breakdown of the manhours content of the job.

ation requires a semi-skilled operator to be flexible by undertaking a certain amount of clerical work associated with the production process, yet clerical workers receive more holiday entitlement, then the semi-skilled employees may insist upon equal conditions as a precondition for such flexibility. Many organizations have pursued a policy of harmonizing conditions of employment to avoid such problems arising; others will need to evaluate whether flexibility of task can be impeded by different conditions applying to different groups, and whether this is in the organization's long-term interest. Of course, questions of short-term costs and 'knock on' effects may still arise.

Retraining is critical for flexibility of task. This is a subject which is

---

(c)　The make up of a composite group will vary according to the target manhour content and will alter to reflect changes in planning and developments in production processes and work organization.

　　　The following are examples, by no means exhaustive, of areas where composite groups can function:

(i)　Integrated pipe working squads;
(ii)　Cabin module manufacture; and
(iii)　Outfit module construction.

3.0　*Interchangeability and integration*

3.1　(a)　Subject to the experience and skills of the individual there will be full interchangeability and integration within trades and trade groups.

(b)　Ancillary workers will be fully interchangeable within the ancillary workers groups as required, this will include where necessary integrated groups.

(c)　Staff employees will be used in those areas where their knowledge and experience is most effective, and therefore shall be interchangeable as required, according to their individual skills and experience. Integrated teams of supervisory, technical and commercial staff in planning, production, engineering and drawing office departments will be supplemented, where appropriate, by the inclusion of hourly paid workers with appropriate skills.

(d)　Area supervision shall be operated with full acceptance by staff and hourly paid.

4.0 *Balanced labour force*

4.1　To balance shortages and surpluses of manpower with workload requirements, tradesmen subject to their skills and experience shall supplement other trades subject to consultation.[19]

being highlighted more and more in discussions with trade unions, since flexibility has to be within the limits of the employees' abilities and experience, unless further training is provided. The general emphasis as far as semi-skilled employees are concerned will increasingly be on problem-solving techniques, associated with the development of new technologies. Depending upon the type of equipment used, however, more specific training may be required. If production operators are involved in NC programming, for instance, training in the necessary computer skills will be required. This might involve a minimum of one week's classroom training and three weeks on-the-job training if operators are to become responsible for programming, setting, operating and quality inspection.[16]

See Example 3.1 for some illustrations of organizations which have developed flexibility of task amongst semi-skilled workers. They are included to illustrate the scope and content of agreements on flexibility of task.

Craft flexibility
Most attention in the area of flexibility of task continues to be given to the craftsmen. In many organizations, craft demarcation lines are well defined, especially between electricians and those with mechanical skills. As one study commented, 'an electrician would not remove a motor, and a millwright would not disconnect one',[20] although the situation will differ between workgroups, and informal practices allowing for a degree of flexibility will undoubtedly exist in many organizations.

However with the introduction of new production equipment, such as the CNC machines and maintenance by automatic insertion equipment mentioned earlier, there will be an increasing demand for skills in electronics, hydraulics and pneumatics. With relatively less emphasis also being placed on the traditional toolroom and machine setting skills, the trend toward the multi-skilled craftsman is clear. One commentator pointed out that

> predominantly line-based companies favoured a wide ranging mechanic diagnostician who is simultaneously process worker, craftsman and technician. Others preferred a more straight forward mix of existing skills, especially electrical and mechanical.[21]

Although most references are to 'multi-skilled' craftsmen, there are in fact a number of different directions of enhanced flexibility for craftsmen. These include:

1 A single core skill remains, but greater flexibility is achieved through the craftsman gaining an appreciation of other aspects of the job. Machine setters for example may be required to be capable of undertaking a limited range of mechanical maintenance work on their machines. The requirement for greater flexibility between plant and maintenance electrician would come into this category as would

the requirement for mechanical maintenance craftsmen to be able to undertake minor electrical work, requiring a modest appreciation of electrical engineering.

2 'Dual skill': again a core skill remains, but the craftsman is also equipped with skills in a different discipline. This would be at a level above the appreciation level identified above. It could be achieved by a mechanical craftsman, for example, agreeing to undertake an electrical training module, although demarcation lines do remain stronger between mechanical and electrical skills than between the various mechanical trades – toolmakers, fitters, machinists:

> There were signs that demarcation within mechanical trades was being broken down increasingly, but by no means yet invariably; and there seemed to be little resistance from mechanical trades to acquiring hydraulic and/or pneumatic skills. [22]

3 At the next level is the genuine multi-skill craftsman. This term is often very loosely defined but is taken here to include those craftsmen with generalized skills of a wide-ranging variety. For the mechanical craftsman (including hydraulic and pneumatic skills anyway) and the electrical craftsman (including electronic and diagnostic skills) to become a multi-skilled craftsman requires formal training in electronics, electrics and mechanical skills. Other skills, such as programming, may also be added to this. This group would include the multi-skilled service engineer or the workshop engineer in many small organizations whose job demands skill in a wide variety of disciplines. This genuine multi-skilled employee may also have the responsibility for operating costly production equipment with specialist backing within the engineering department if this is required.

Both the two main unions involved in this area – the EETPU and the AUEW – have supported, at national level, flexibility and multi-skilling. As one EETPU statement (1983) put it,

> in the future the multi-skilled craftsman will be a very real force in the engineering industry. While recognizing that the phasing in of this new craft status will not be without problems, the sub-committee feels that in order for British industry to survive and remain competitive these problems must be confronted and overcome at the earliest opportunity. [23]

Union anxieties about craft flexibility remain, and four main issues can be identified:

- the attitudes of the craftsmen themselves;
- the problem of trade union membership;
- the relationship between craftsman and technician; and
- the training implications.

The attitude of the craftsmen themselves affects flexibility of task in a number of ways. First, some craftsmen may view this development as personally threatening, and may fear failing to achieve the required standards in a new discipline. Returning to a technical college after many years, or possibly attending for the first time, will not be to everyone's liking. Secondly, demarcation lines generally arose on the union side from a desire to restrict access to jobs and skills. This craft exclusiveness, of which adherence to the apprenticeship tradition is a part, is based on strengthening job security. There will be fears that flexibility of task will lead to job losses. Thirdly, because not all craftsmen can develop into dual or multi-skilled jobs, distinctions inevitably will arise between the level of craft job and this runs counter to the collective orientation which has characterized craftsmen's thinking in the past.

Against this, many craftsmen will welcome the challenge implicit in the updating and broadening of their skills. There is potentially greater job satisfaction available to the dual or multi-skilled craftsmen.

The 'problem' of trade union membership reflects the fear of some unions – particularly the AUEW – that long-term trends may result in a further decline in membership. However this is not proving a significant barrier to change as:

> Companies are largely stopping short of complete multi-skilling in favour of a core-skill to be supplemented. The AUEW or the EETPU therefore do not face losing members who pick up additional skills. [24]

The relationship between craftsmen and technicians may prove more intractable. As the EETPU put it:

> In order for our membership to benefit . . . [we] . . . regard it as essential that as a Union we should take action to keep multi-skilling within the craft ambit. Already technicians are moving into this area of work. This is largely due to the fact that traditionally the technicians' sector is less well organized and there is therefore less resistance to traditional trade union practices. [25]

As the concept of a generic technician/craftsman role emerges, covering both diagnostic skills as well as traditional manual skills, so the relationship between craft unions and staff unions will become more complex. The insistence of the manual unions on only their craft members 'using the tools' will continue to be a factor determining union membership at this craft/technician level.

The training implications for dual and multi-skilled craftsmen are related to the wider questions about apprenticeship and skill training. This includes discussion about entering craft apprentice training at any age, about training to standards and about module training. Consideration has been given to moving away from the predetermined time served system to one of standards and modules. Multi-skilling is most easily achieved by a basic two-year training period followed after the apprenticeship by further training at periodic intervals; with an emphasis on defined technical standards reached through a variety of modules which could be chosen to relate to the particular needs of the organization concerned. What is clear is that the process of retraining will be continuous and long term.

Organizations faced by pressures to develop any of the four levels of craft flexibility identified above need to formulate a strategy for introducing and maintaining such flexibility of task. This would include identifying the direction of technical change, the requirements of new equipment and the training which will be necessary. This can only be handled in sufficient detail at local level. Consultation at this level will be critical to the successful introduction of change:

> you discuss fully with the workpeople involved at management level, as high as you can go, as fully as you can, as early as you can, the problems that are important. . . .[26]

Example 3.2 illustrates many of the aspects of craft flexibility.

Flexibility amongst white-collar staff
Flexibility of task is not an issue confined to manual employees. Such flexibility amongst white-collar employees can be crucial to an organization's effectiveness. Job descriptions for 'staff' employees have tended to be more broadly defined than those for manual workers and this has – amongst other factors – facilitated flexibility. In recent years white collar employees have however been more inclined to adhere to the detailed terms of job descriptions. To reverse this trend jobs are being increasingly described in broad, general terms with an emphasis on principal accountabilities rather on the detailed requirements of each job. Job evaluated grading structures consisting of a small number of broad bands also promote flexibility of task within each grade. Amongst clerical employees there has been a movement towards more generic jobs, covering say the activities of sales ledger, clerk/typist and progress chaser in one job. Each employee may retain a core skill in one of these areas too. Thus, if one employee is absent, work does not simply build up, but can be covered to a degree by another employee.

Examples can also be found at more senior levels:

> Rigidities are also identifiable within staff grades. Here lack of interchangeability as between planning, production engineering and drawing room functions, for example, with each operating as a separate rather than integrated unit, and resultant duplication of effort and resources, can serve to limit communication and efficiency.[28]

Flexibility of task amongst white collar employees may also mean supervisors taking on elements of the task that they are supervising. Economic pressures and developments in technology will affect all job boundaries, particularly between production, product engineering and maintenance. The job supervisor will change markedly as the supervisor is required to manage multi-disciplinary groupings, including planning and technical aspects of the job. Supervisory jobs will be merged where comparable technologies have been introduced in what were previously separate sections. Supervisors will be required to respond to such requirements for

---

Example 3.2 *Craft flexibility at ICL*

In the Mainframe Systems Development Division of ICL agreement was reached with AUEW (representing mechanical trades) and EETPU (representing wiremen) to develop two levels of 'Engineering Workshop Technician'. It was the job of the first level to:

> provide an integrated skilled technician service across the following activities: assembly/wiring; bench fitting; machining; welding; sheet metalwork; support work in a project environment; printed circuit board assembly and modification; and finally computer and system installation.[27]

The senior level also included quality control, estimating and basic planning.

The training
At the heart of the training programme lies the strategy of increasing the basic skills of the existing workshop craftsmen through a series of training modules providing progression to the technician grade.

The programme is built on a number of clear principles. Defined as being 'positive' in nature – individuals are not only expected to acquire the skills to the required standard but to use them on a day to day basis in the workshop – the training is monitored, assessed and underwritten by the EITB. Based on a modular approach, it is also specific to the extent that it is tailored to ICL workshop requirements.

It comprises two concurrent courses – day release over a 39-week period at a local (Openshaw) technical college; and 'in-house' and external tuition (carried out by a combination of MSC instructors, and Openshaw technical college staff) for an intensive 3-week period. Both are followed by 12 weeks of consolidation training in the workshop itself.

For those wanting to progress to senior technician, this programme can be supplemented by the quality control and basic planning courses. The former involves an in-house course of 4 days' intensive tuition – by the Production Engineering Research Association (PERA) – plus 12 weeks of consolidation training. The basic planning programme consists of a week's intensive course with ICL tuition, plus 12 weeks of consolidation.

Throughout the training programme skill requirements, training standards and goals are specified. Each individual is required to maintain a log book and, throughout, progress is monitored, controlled and assessed by a combination of tutors, local management and supervisors.[27]

flexibility, and this will involve considerable retraining. In each managerial function, opportunities will be taken to merge jobs. In personnel, too, the generalist personnel manager who can cover recruitment, management development, manpower resourcing, employee relations and remuneration is becoming more sought after than the specialist.

In the services sector, requirements for white-collar flexibility are equally pronounced. This ranges from the need of the airline pilot now to navigate the plane with the aid of new technology (in some airlines they are also required to load baggage!) to that of the insurance salesman to handle every type of policy.

Improving flexibility – a strategy for change

Organizations need to begin by analysing where further developments in flexibility of task will be required. This means studying particular technological developments and the manning requirements of these, as well as the effect on jobs of market developments, rationalization and reorganizations. Tasks should be grouped into broad job categories, with all aspects itemized in general terms. Then the payment implications, training implications and any recognition issues can be examined. In most organizations there are barriers to achieving improved flexibility of task, including job evaluation schemes, different conditions of employment applying to different grades and separate pay structures. Trying to encourage flexibility of task between blue and white-collar employees, for example, will be more difficult if there are significant differences in conditions of employment between these groups. The attitude and abilities of employees themselves will also be critical. Many will see attempts to achieve flexibility of task as undermining their job security and will resist it accordingly. In this situation, the principal duty of management is to communicate and consult with employees and their representatives about the necessity for such changes. Many aspects will be subject to negotiation including any payment for such flexibility and how any employee surplus is to be handled. Overall, flexibility of task is closely related to the achievement of organizational objectives generally. In facilitating improved flexibility many other organizational dimensions are relevant, including payment systems, the annual reviews, job evaluation, union recognition, discipline and management style.

Payment systems are important in that many manual workers' schemes remain tied to quantity, and this is often at the expense of rewarding flexibility more directly. Single factor (quantity) schemes are being increasingly replaced by multi-factor schemes which stress flexibility as a component to be assessed as part of an overall performance review process. This emphasis on flexibility in a payment system highlights the importance of this dimension, especially if it receives a substantial weighting in relation to the other factors.

The 'annual' review itself provides an opportunity for directly linking basic wage increases to improved flexibility of task, and this has been adopted by many organizations in recent years. One of the most notable amongst these was British Shipbuilders, whose 1984 review award of £7 was conditional upon the improvements in flexibility described above. This is analogous to the productivity bargaining of the 1960s. It can be disadvantageous in that payments are made for improvements which should be secured anyway and often such agreements are only notional with little changing at local level. A further 'buy out' of the same practices may be required in future years and employees build up barriers to 'sell' at the next round. In addition, linking such trade-offs to the annual review has the danger of jeopardizing the successful negotiation of the review increase, whilst in future years it may be necessary permanently to link the review to improvements to flexibility to avoid a relaxation or even reversal of previous gains. Against this, it could be argued that the review increase has to be paid for by improvements to operating efficiency, and tangible improvements to flexibility may for some organizations be critical to this. A measure of control can be retained by insisting that local managements have to be satisfied that the commitments in principle will become commitments in practice before the review, or other buy out, is payable.

Job evaluation schemes can be influential in facilitating improvements in flexibility. Detailed job descriptions categorizing every aspect of a job may actually have the effect of 'freezing' or limiting the job to the one described. Additional tasks not so described have to be recorded on new job descriptions and be evaluated anew – sometimes this process has to be worked through and a salary increase result before a job holder will take on the additional duties required by the job. Pressure to re-evaluate jobs where such flexibility is demanded may result in enormous delays as the job evaluation system tries to cope with the backlog. Where there are a larger number of grades, such that a small change in job demand might lead to a regrading, pressure for re-evaluation may be greatest.

Where job evaluation schemes are operating in this way, the solution might lie in deliberately briefer job descriptions, coupled with statements to the effect that the list is not exhaustive and employees will be required to undertake whatever duties are reasonably required by management, subject to these being within the employee's capabilities and experience. Once again we are back to the concept of 'core skills' being evaluated, rather than the job in totality. Where these additional requirements are substantial the job may be re-evaluated in the normal way.

Job evaluation itself, of course, is based on the scientific management principles of specialization – breaking down tasks into discrete units. The value of job evaluation in establishing a felt fair relationship between jobs is well recognized; it is also valuable in providing a basis for measuring job change. However it may actually militate against flexibility of task since it has emphasized describing tasks in detail – if the scheme cannot recognize and reward a job holder taking on significant extra tasks, this may prevent moves toward greater flexibility. In future managements may be more prepared to adopt the Japanese practice, avoiding job descriptions and job evaluation to encourage maximum flexibility of task.

In the UK many organizations have sought to structure their relationships with employees and trade unions by specifying in, for example, recognition agreements, that maximum flexibility is required. This approach tends to be more relevant in a 'greenfield site' where the workforce from the inception of the organization understand the policy that has to be followed. Union recognition itself may be conditional upon such terms being accepted.

Questions of discipline also arise in connection with flexibility of task. Management must determine, generally at supervisory or departmental manager level, what flexibility is required. Whether this is described in general terms, or in detail, management need to be prepared to discipline and ultimately to dismiss employees who are not flexible in the way the organization requires. This is subject to the requirements being within the employee's capability, and after counselling and training as appropriate. Such disciplinary action may be crucial in demonstrating the seriousness of managerial intentions. Where such action is taken in the context of joint agreement to flexibility of task it will be more effective.

Finally, issues of management style arise. The organization needs to structure employee and trade union attitudes towards flexibility. Approaches which include full communication of the business needs for such flexibility, harmonized conditions of employment, a consultative approach to new requirements for flexibility, appear to be more successful in generating a commitment to improving flexibility of task.

Conclusions

Developments in flexibility of task have proceeded apace, driven by economic circumstances and technological changes. It is not surprising that organizations such as the British Steel Corporation and British Shipbuilders have been at the forefront of such initiatives in the early 1980s, since their economic circumstances have made such flexibility essential:

> At Llanwern production workers change shear blades without calling in craftsmen, tradesmen drive cranes and do their own heavy lifting, crane drivers do cleaning. . . .[29]

Many organizations in the UK, particularly in the white-collar service and central and local government sectors, have long had such flexibility, and this has often been established from the beginning as part of an organization's policy. Interchangeability is, of course, well established in the civil service and at a time when many aspects of this organization's approach are being questioned, they provide a lead for other managements in their approach to flexibility of tasks. In Japan and other countries overseas, interchangeability of task is more common – a factor which has contributed generally to the UK's relative lack of competitiveness. In Japan, for example,

corporate paternalism emerged, incorporating team working and shop floor control over many aspects of production. A generalized semi-skilled worker emerged, able to play a key role in developing product quality and willing to agree to a wide degree of flexibility.[30]

In many organizations, trade union objections to flexibility of task will remain; these objections often stem from manning implications of such flexibility as well as fears that management may abuse these provisions or that individuals could not cope with the demands. In tackling this, an open, consultative approach, backed up by a determination at all levels to achieve such improved flexibility, appears to be most successful.

In summary, increasing flexibility of task is a critical element in the organization's strategy for improving cost effectiveness. Managements in the vanguard organizations are attempting to develop pay structures which encourage task flexibility – or at least do not hinder it. They are at the same time encouraging patterns of trade union representation which minimize the barriers between jobs.

Given the traditions of industrial relations and the patterns of collective bargaining in the UK managements do not achieve such changes easily. But, as the examples in this chapter have illustrated, progress in increasing task flexibility in the 1980s has been real enough.

References

1 'Flexibility agreements – the end of who does what', *Industrial Relations Review and Report* 316 (March 1984), p. 2.
2 A. Flanders, 'The Fawley experiment', in *Management and Unions – The Theory and Reform of Industrial Relations* (Faber and Faber, 1975), pp. 51–65.
3 A. Flanders, 'Productivity bargaining prospects', in *Management and Unions*, p. 70.
4 B. C. Roberts, R. Loveridge and J. Gennard, *Reluctant Militants* (Heinemann, 1972), p. 17.
5 B. Wilkinson, 'Technical change and work organisation', *Industrial Relations Journal*, 14, 2 (Summer 1983), pp. 18–27.
6 S. Paulden and B. Hawkins, 'Whatever happened at Fairfields?' (Gower Press, 1969), p. 121; quoted in R. McKenzie and L. Hunter *Pay, Productivity and Collective Bargaining* (Macmillan, 1973), p. 119.
7 K. Robins and F. Webster, 'New technology: a survey of trade union response in Britain', *Industrial Relations Journal*, 13, 1 (Spring, 1982), pp. 7–26.
   A. Manwaring, 'The trade union response to new technology', *Industrial Relations Journal*, vol. 12, 4 (July/August 1981), pp. 7–26.
8 *APEX Office Technology: The Trade Union Response* (1979); quoted in Robins and Webster, 'New Technology'.

9 TUC, *Employment and Technology* (1979).
   'The union and new technology', *Report of a Trade Union Conference in the use and impact of micro-electronics* (Aston University, 1981).
10 TUC, *Employment and Technology*, Report to the 1979 Congress.
11 EETPU, 'New electronic technology: a programme for the 1980s' (1981).
   'An ideal technology agreement for EETPU stewards' (undated).
12 T. Duffy, 'Co-operation between Management and Trade Unions', *AUEW* (1979); quoted in Robins and Webster, 'New technology'.
13 McKenzie and Hunter, *Pay, Productivity and Collective Bargaining*, p. 118.
14 M. Linton, 'The caring sharing business approach', The *Guardian*, 27 May 1983.
15 'Flexibility agreements – the end of who does what', pp. 7–8.
16 C. Wyles, 'People – the forgotten factor in automation', *Works Management* (March 1984), pp. 17–19.
17 A. Manwaring, 'The motor manufacturing industry in Britain – prospects for the 1980s', *Industrial Relations Journal*, vol. 14, 3 (Autumn 1983), p. 18.
18 'Oil industry – Fawley leads again', *Industrial Relations Review and Report*, vol. 282 (October 1982), p. 11.
19 'British shipbuilders pay and flexibility package', *IRS Pay and Benefits Bulletin*, vol. 107, 6 (March 1984), pp. 2–4.
20 EITB *Maintenance Skills in the Engineering Industry: the influence of technological change*, Occasional Paper No. 2 (1981), p. 28.
21 D. Goodhart, 'The dissolving demarcation', *Financial Times*, 27 February 1983.
22 EITB, *Maintenance Skills in the Engineering Industry*, p. 30.
23 EETPU National Industry Committee for Engineering, 'Multi-skilled craftsmen', 1983.
24 *Financial Times*, 27 February 1983.
25 EETPU, 'Multi-skilled craftsmen', p. 4.
26 TUC Minutes of Evidence 61 and 65 to Royal Commission on Trade Unions and Employers Associations (The Donovan Commission) (HMSO, 1967).
27 'Flexibility at ICL', *Industrial Relations Review and Report*, vol. 311 (January 1984), p. 9.
28 'Flexibility agreements – the end of who does what', p. 3.
29 B. Groom and D. Goodhart, 'Enter the jack of all trades', *Financial Times*, 17 August 1983.
30 A. Manwaring, 'The motor manufacturing industry in Britain', p. 19.

4
Initiatives in working time

In the UK initiatives in working time have concentrated largely on 'flexitime' and part-time working. In the period of labour shortages in the 1960s and 1970s flexitime appeared to offer an attractive option for employees, one which provided for a measure of personal control over working time. There were fewer advantages for managers, indeed the management of flexitime systems can be time-consuming and create operational difficulties. Part-time working too was often introduced in a context of labour scarcity, to attract on to the labour market people – especially married women – who would not otherwise wish to work. This had more appeal to managements, since part-time working provided an opportunity to relate working hours more flexibly to operational requirements.

Generally, however, employees continue to be employed in blocks of eight hours (or thereabouts), irrespective of the operational requirements of the business. These operational requirements rarely, of course, operate in blocks of eight hours. As a result there are two well-known consequences – 'waiting time' and overtime. Employees may be 'waiting' for work for long periods, then working long hours of overtime as the supply of work or, in service industries, the requirement for labour fluctuates. Both phenomena may be apparent in the same day or week – periods of inactivity in the normal working day followed by periods of overtime subsequently.

Of course, some jobs require continuous attendance in a way that means blocks of time are suitable; for example, machine operators in a continuous production process. Many others, though, can be operated more cost effectively by introducing greater flexibility in working time. This chapter will focus on those initiatives in working time which can improve cost effectiveness by better relating employee hours of work to the organization's requirements. We will concentrate here on:

- the development of an annual hours contract;
- the introduction and/or extension of shiftworking including 12-hour shifts, and five-set working;
- part-time working; and
- Saturday/Sunday contracts.

We focus on these initiatives because they contain significant oppor-

DOI: 10.4324/9781003193043-4

tunities to improve operational effectiveness for organizations in both the public and private sector. We will outline what these opportunities are and how they contribute to improvements in efficiency. We will then describe these approaches in some detail and call upon relevant examples of current practices in a number of organizations at the vanguard of initiatives in working time. In one of the areas we discuss – the annual hours contract – there are, at the time of writing, few examples of its use in the UK. We include it, nevertheless, because it does seem to us to open up further possibilities for tailoring working time to the needs of the business.

We begin with an examination of working time in the UK, including a brief examination of how the main development in working time in the early 1980s – the reduction of the length of the working week – was handled. We also touch on developments in Europe. Our central emphasis, however, is on initiatives in working time for operational reasons, rather than on handling a reduction in working time. This reflects our concentration on cost-effective strategies in industrial relations.

Working time in the UK

Many managers viewed the breaking of the 40-hour 'barrier' during 1980/81 as highly significant, leading, it was felt, to an irresistible momentum towards the 35-hour week.[1] By the mid-1980s, however, events had tempered this earlier view. It is true that the TUC officially retains the goal of a 35-hour week. Further reductions in working time have been claimed in many organizations, as manual unions have sought in particular to remove the hours differential between manual and non-manual employees – which remains largely a UK phenomenon in working time. For the unions, certainly their claim at national level for a reduction in working time is linked to their view that jobs will be created as a result;[2] others have disagreed with this view.[3] Clearly, pressures to reduce working time will continue, even if the timescale for such reductions may be slower than many trade unionists hoped or managers believed. In the UK further reductions in working time have been agreed in certain sectors – many chemical firms, for example, have reduced their working week to 38 hours; a few introduced a 37½-hour week. By 1984, a 37-hour week had been introduced in electricity supply, a 37½-hour working week in electrical contracting and newspaper printing. There were other reductions to 37, 35 and even fewer hours.

It is interesting to note that a minority of organizations have retained a 40-hour week. This is also true of some countries. Japan has retained a working week of 40 hours, and basic hours of work are indeed higher in other Far Eastern countries. It is this factor, amongst others, which has concerned managements faced with continuing competitive pressures on costs. A reduction in working time in the UK which is not matched by international competitors will produce an adverse shift in competitiveness. The unions for their part have shown a willingness, at least at national level, to discuss ways of reducing working time which minimize this danger. The possibility of trade-offs between smaller pay increases, shorter hours and job creation has been publicly aired by some leading trade unionists.[4]

It is worth placing the debate about the shorter working week – or life – into the context of patterns of work in the UK. The following points are relevant:

1   There is relatively little regulation of working time in the UK compared with, for example, other European countries. Only women and young persons and some occupations such as driving have legal hours limitations. There is in the UK no legislation restricting overtime, whereas in other countries in Western Europe weekly or daily limits are often set. These daily limits can be at very low levels, say 1 or 2 hours maximum.[5]

2   Overtime working remains high in the UK, even in the context of the recession of the early 1980s. In 1984 52.5 per cent of all male manual employees worked overtime. As an average of the entire male manual workforce 5.1 hours overtime per week were being worked. For those male manual workers actually working overtime, the average number of hours worked was 9.6. The average overtime level for all employees working overtime was 4.4 hours a week.[6]

3   In the NBPI report of 1970, 22 per cent of the manual labour force in all industries and services were working shifts; the figure for manufacturing was 25 per cent. In 1979, one study estimated that the manufacturing position had increased only slightly to 26 per cent.[7] Most surveys indicate that the common shiftworking patterns are of 8 hours duration (including a meal break), generally consisting of 'double day' shiftworking (06.00–14.00 hours, 14.00–22.00 hours), three shift systems over five days, or three shift systems over seven days. The number involved in shiftworking may be slightly lower in the UK than in Europe; it is lower than Japan where, it has been reported, 37 per cent of manufacturing employees work shifts.[8]

4   There is a high level of part-time working in the UK. Four-and-a-half million workers, 3.7 m of whom were women, were part-time in 1981 out of a workforce of 21 m. In Western Europe, only Denmark exceeded this proportion and the UK accounted for 41 per cent of all part-time employees in the European Community.[9]

5   A distinction generally remains in the UK between manual employees on 39 hours and staff employees on 37/37½ hours. There are, of course, exceptions and the harmonization of hours of work has been achieved in some organizations. The reduction of working time in the early 1980s did narrow the differential a little, and the opportunity was taken in many cases to equalize starting and

finishing times. Nevertheless, hours of work generally differs still between manual and staff employees.

So the picture emerges of a legally unregulated pattern of working time, with a significant number of employees (primarily manual) working shifts of 8 hours' duration with a high level of overtime and with a high proportion of part-time working in certain sectors.

Handling the reduction of the working week in the early 1980s

Since 1980, reductions in the length of the working week in the UK have affected over 8 million employees. In handling this reduction, few organizations took the opportunity to introduce alternative patterns of work. Without doubt, most implemented the reduction from say 40 to 39 hours by an earlier finish on a Friday afternoon.[10] This was certainly the proposal most favoured by the workforce, and few employers fancied the 'failures to agree' which would have resulted from their insistence on alternative methods of reducing working hours, especially if productivity improvement had been secured anyway. There were isolated examples of more unusual approaches, including the introduction of a '168 hour' fortnight, aggregating the reduction as half days off every four weeks, or the introduction of 'five shift' working. These examples were generally linked to a reduction of working time greater than one hour.[11]

Though little attention was being given in the early 1980s to more imaginative initiatives in working time, it was a condition of most agreements reducing working time that it had to be self-financing – funded by improvements to productivity. In some cases, the reduction at local level was not implemented until management were satisfied that the necessary productivity improvements had occurred.

Discussions in the early 1980s therefore concentrated on this question of productivity improvements, and on when in the working week the reduction would be taken. The impact on unit costs of a one hour reduction of the working week varied between organizations depending upon the proportion of labour costs to the total costs. For many organizations, about a 1 per cent increase in unit costs could be predicted if no increase in productivity occurred. In the context of public sector cash limits or private sector improvement plans, 1 per cent seemed to many hardly worth a separate study. For others, the reduction had been 'given away' at national level with consequent difficulties for management locally in negotiating effective productivity trade-offs.

The majority, however, sought – given the competitive pressures on unit costs – to improve productivity such that output or service could be maintained at the previous level even though working time had been reduced. For direct employees on measured work this was relatively straightforward. Taking for example a reduction from 40 to 39 hours a week, the employees' output target was maintained even though working time was reduced by 1 hour, thus involving an increase in work values. In certain other cases, there was a reduction in relaxation allowances or 'contingency' allowances to compensate for the overall reduction in working time. Tea breaks were sometimes shortened or – particularly on Friday afternoons – abolished. If the productivity improvement could more easily be identified for workers on measured schemes, this remained a source of some industrial relations difficulties because the manual employees often felt they were 'paying for' the decrease in working time whereas 'staff' were not.

For white-collar employees it was presumed they would produce the same results in the reduced working week as they had done previously with no increase in staffing levels or in overtime working. This assumption was theoretically sound although difficult to establish. Many words were committed to paper about flexibility between jobs, minimizing non-productive time, reduced lateness and absenteeism and so on in order to secure productivity improvements.

Overall, the reduction in working time in the early years of 1980s was handled smoothly, if unimaginatively, and with agreement locally on measures to ensure the reduction did not increase unit costs. The patterns of working time were largely unaffected – the characteristics of working time in the UK as described above were unchanged.

Developments outside the UK

Developments in working time have occurred outside the UK, particularly in many other countries of Western Europe. Social and legislative pressures have led to many initiatives, including the extension of part-time shiftworking in Belgium and greater labour flexibility in Holland. Some of these initiatives have been stimulated by the EEC. In 1979, for example, the European Council of Ministers called for a directive to create a European framework for a reduction of annual working time. This was aimed at alleviating high rates of unemployment. Since that date, unemployment in the European Community has increased from over 8 million to over 12 million people. Although a European approach in terms of a directive was not pursued, in late 1983 a draft recommendation was published on the reduction and re-organization of working time.

This draft recommendation emphasizes that the reduction and re-organization of working time can help improve employment, provided in particular that

- a more flexible and intensive use of the means of production is achieved;
- unit production costs are not increased; and
- bottlenecks in the supply of labour are avoided[12]

and Member States are invited to consider combining reductions in individual working time with the re-organization of patterns of work and this it was felt should:

> result in the more efficient and flexible utilization of capital equipment, in particular, where applicable by lengthening production time. Working time changes should be fully exploited where they can increase viable opportunities for investment in new technologies and help to maximize the returns on that investment. . . .
>
> Reductions in individual working time may involve reductions in hours worked daily, weekly or annually, or in the amount of time spent working over an entire lifetime. . . .[13]

Another key element of this draft recommendation is the stricter limitation of systematic overtime. Time worked beyond normal hours should increasingly be compensated by time off in lieu.

What has been happening in the Member States? In the early 1980s most developments have occurred in Belgium, France, Holland, Italy and West Germany. In Belgium, with 17 per cent unemployment, the government proposed a reduction in annual working time of 5 per cent. Employers were required to increase the size of their workforce by 1½ per cent per year. Employment could however still be cut back, as long as 1½ per cent extra persons were recruited. As we have said this requirement has led directly to many initiatives in the area of part-time work including four, five- and six-hour shifts. In Belgium the graduated tax system means that significant cuts in hours worked leads only to marginal decreases in basic pay. In the UK of course, such cuts, because of the wide tax bands, generally involve a pro rata cut in pay. In France the 39-hour week was introduced in 1982, with a further obligation to reduce gradually by another hour. Cost pressures in France have led to initiatives on the re-organization of working time. At Renault, for example, a Friday–Saturday–Sunday contract has been introduced. In the Netherlands, government pressures have led to many company agreements to reduce working time involving greater labour flexibility and many different forms of part-time work have also been generated. In Italy an annual reduction of 40 hours was agreed for 1984/85 and in West Germany a reduction from 40 to an average of 38½ hours was agreed with effect from spring 1985. This was in a context of unemployment at around 9 per cent.[14]

Operational issues in working time

Notwithstanding such developments in the rest of Europe, organizations in the UK have been more concerned with a number of operational issues which influence working time rather than with a further reduction in hours of work. These operational issues include

1   increasing output/service provided;

2 utilization of capital equipment;
3 responsiveness;
4 maintenance;
5 fluctuations in workload; and
6 unpredictability.

We will examine each of these issues in turn.

Output/services
Although manufacturing output overall has significantly fallen in recent years, in certain sectors and for certain products there are pressures to increase volume. This can be seen particularly in the semi-conductor industry, or in personal computers. In the leisure and other service industries, demand remains buoyant in many areas. A good example of pressure to extend a particular service can be seen in the moves towards weekend working introduced by some of the clearing banks and retail stores. Changes in demand for goods or services were often being satisfied by overtime working.

Capital utilization
As the scale of investment in expensive equipment increases, and as the pace of technological change accelerates, so pressures to ensure such equipment is fully utilized are increasing. Computerized equipment is being installed in organizations throughout the country, whether this is for booking holidays or modelling and testing new designs. Individual items of equipment can often cost hundreds of thousands of pounds and system costs can run into millions because of the pace of technical developments – and such equipment may be obsolete within a few years of its installation. Faced by such investment, organizations must ensure they are fully utilized.

Responsiveness
To win orders or contracts, organizations have to be responsive to the needs of the customers. If the customer sets a tight deadline for a particular order or retains the right to vary the level of the order, then development and production lead times may have to be cut in order to accommodate this. Such demands may also mean changing working patterns in order to speed up development and production time. Service organizations too are under pressure to speed up their responsiveness to customer requirements.

Maintenance
Many organizations are experiencing high levels of overtime working amongst maintenance crews. The high cost of machine downtime means that there are pressures for maintenance work to be undertaken outside of normal hours – especially during weekends for organizations with five day working. With the increasing pace of technical change in processes, more

installation work will also be required and this often means, again, Saturday or Sunday working. Similarly, contractors will find increasing demands for their services at weekends.

Fluctuations in workload
Fluctuations in output relate to many factors, of which four in particular are most common:

1 *Seasonal* commercial patterns, which can be most clearly seen in the hotel and catering sector, in food and drink and other consumer fields.
2 *Environmental* changes: thus demand for different types of clothing is related to certain times of the year; energy demands are similarly related to environmental changes. In one industry, sugar beet, 24-hour working occurs for four months after the harvest, then only maintenance is required for eight months.
3 *Budgetary* patterns: many organizations are faced by 'end of year' buying, i.e. purchasing by customers finding themselves underspent on budgets at the end of their financial year.
4 *Key events:* these may produce enormous variations in workload for an organization. A typical example involves the production of end of year financial reports in the finance departments.

Unpredictability
In some industries there is considerable uncertainty about the supply of work. The leisure or retail industry cannot predict very far ahead how fashions may change. An advertising campaign, for example, may produce a demand for work considerably in excess of what was predicted; a terrorist bombing campaign in central London may have the reverse effect on tourist business. Such pressures are not new, although technological change, competitive and financial constraints may make them more relevant now, nor is the solution to be found solely in the working time area.

These current operational issues in working time are, as we have indicated, often handled by overtime working; although the use of temporary labour to meet fluctuations in the supply of work is also increasing (we cover this aspect in chapter 6).

In the 1960s the regular use of overtime had much to do with labour shortages with overtime being used partly to boost pay levels in order to attract and retain workers.[15] Maintenance and installation work, as we have already noted, generally is achieved by overtime working.

Is overtime working efficient? In a NBPI study, about two-thirds of managements surveyed said there was no difference in productivity between normal hours and overtime hours.[16] If overtime working appears not to be necessarily associated with lower productivity, poorer quality or high levels of absenteeism, it may still be an expensive way of handling flexibility in working time.

It is also clear that once introduced to handle variability in the supply of work, overtime may not subsequently revert to previous levels. Instead it can become institutionalized, and the flexibility to use overtime again to meet peak demands is reduced.

An analysis of the costs of overtime working and the extent to which overtime levels do genuinely relate to changing operational circumstances may well show that there continue to be instances in which overtime working is cost effective, especially to meet short-term difficulties. However, such an analysis may well reveal that overtime costs are unacceptably high. The options then include (i) introducing alternative patterns of work that relate standard working hours more appropriately to operational requirements; (ii) increasing manning levels; or (iii) attempting through investments in new equipment or additional capacity to meet changing patterns in the supply of work.

There are many approaches to tackling the operational issues in working time that we identify above, and in the process reduce high levels of overtime. We will, however, concentrate here on introducing alternative patterns of work, beginning with the annual hours contract.

Annual hours contract

The annual hours contract provides a mechanism for relating standard working time more directly to operational requirements. We define it as:

> a contract which enables the employer to vary the number of hours worked in a defined period (daily, weekly, quarterly, yearly,) within a context of the agreed standard working hours for the year.

This definition clearly distinguishes annual hours from flexitime, since in flexitime schemes it is the employees who decide on their pattern of work to suit their requirements. In the annual hours contract the managers determine the working pattern to suit the organization's requirements; essentially involving working longer hours in the busy period and shorter hours in the slack period. This can accommodate fluctuations in workload in a more cost-effective way than has often been the case by, for example, cutting the costs of overtime, reducing time spent waiting around, reducing costs (for manufacturing industry) of producing only for stocks – including savings on storage and transportation – and providing better guarantees that higher levels of output/service can be met in the peak periods.

The use of an annual hours contract can be shown diagrammatically (see Figure 4). These charts represent a deliberately simplified model of production against sales. In the upper a seasonal pattern of sales – high in winter and autumn and low in the spring months – is illustrated. Production is spread evenly across the year (we have smoothed a number of other fluctuations which typically affect production levels). Periods of excess sales over production require overtime working, the use of temporary employment and drawing from stock to meet demands (assuming the product can be stored). Periods of excess production over sales result in, for example, stock build-up or waiting time.

In the lower chart of Figure 4 the annual hours contract has provided a mechanism to better tailor working time – and therefore production time – to the pattern of sales. Such an exact relationship as we show in this simplified example will be difficult to achieve in practice since there are – as we will come to describe – limits to the flexibility of labour under an annual hours contract. But if overtime levels can be reduced, stock build-

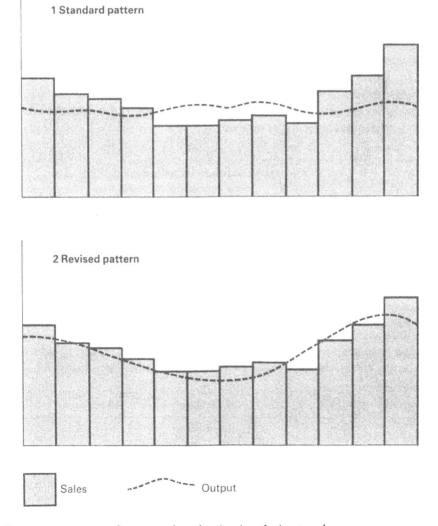

Figure 4 *An annual pattern of production in relation to sales*

up reduced and periods of 'waiting' minimized, variability in working time introduced under such a contract can be cost-effective.

Approaches to an annual hours contract

There are two basic approaches to achieving variability in working time within the concept of an annual hours contract: varying the length of the working day/week or varying the number of days worked across the year. The extent of variations in the length of the working day, and possibly the length of the working week, will depend upon both operational requirements and industrial relations realities. In this approach to the annual hours contract management determine the length of the working day/ week within pre-defined limits negotiated with trade unions. In one recent example a limit to such variability had been agreed allowing for working up to nine hours a day, or forty-five hours a week. In this case Saturday-Sunday working was not included in the annual hours contract.

One company where such variability is reported as being introduced is ICI Ltd. (See Example 4.1)

Another example of its use can be seen in a department involved in order processing where there is a high demand for orders in the first half of the week in comparison with the second:

	Approximate number of orders to be processed
Monday	1150
Tuesday	1150
Wednesday	1000
Thursday	850
Friday	850

Such a 15 per cent variation may traditionally be covered by recruiting extra staff part-time in the first part of the week, by overtime, or by allowing bottlenecks to develop which can be handled later in the week. The annual hours contract enables daily hours to be varied to meet such fluctuations:

	Hours worked (under annual hours contract)	
Monday	9	
Tuesday	9	
Wednesday	7	
Thursday	6	
Friday	6	(37-hour week)

This may avoid some of the inefficiencies and costs associated with the traditional pattern of work.

The second approach involves varying the number of days worked across the year, but maintaining the length of the working day. In its simplest form this could involve a marginal lengthening of the working day, which is then worked for five days during the busy period and for four days during the slack period. Alternatively, and more radically, long periods of continuous working could be followed by long breaks, for example, over a two-week period:

Traditional pattern: 5 days on; 2 days off; 5 days on; 2 days off.
New pattern: 10 days on; 4 days off.

More sophisticated approaches which allow variability of working time within the annual hours for the year can be considered, including varying the daily hours worked *and* varying the number of days worked across the year. Periods when the length of the working day is extended to meet peak demands are compensated by days off (or half days off) in lieu of this extra time. These days off (or 'shift free' days) are ideally fixed at a time that is both operationally advantageous and attractive to employees. Fixing such days either side of a summer break may be such a time.

The annual hours contract therefore provides the opportunity to adapt working time to varying operational requirements. There are, however, certain operational and industrial relations implications of the use of an annual hours contract to consider.

Implications of introducing an annual hours contract
Beginning with the operational implications, there may be difficulties in gearing suppliers/customers to the more flexible patterns of work associated with an annual hours contract. In addition, there will be different work cycles for different functions/sections within an organization – or even in manufacturing establishments for different products within product families. One annual hours pattern may not suit all the diverse operating requirements within an organization. Yet to adopt different annual hours patterns within the same locations may become overcomplicated, creating problems for supervisors, site services and so on. Each organization will need to analyse the pattern and predictability of its workload by function, including marketing and sales, development, pro-

---

Example 4.1 *Varying the length of the working week in part of ICI Ltd*

In the plant protection division . . . the work is very seasonal and an average of 37.5 hour week has been achieved by working 35 hours a week during the quietest six months and 40 hours during the busy season.[17]

duction and administration in order to determine the most appropriate form of annual hours contract.

Difficulties may also arise in the use of an annual hours contract in shiftworking organizations. Those working double day patterns of work can vary the length of the shifts to some degree, but for organizations using three shifts working over five days, the options with traditional eight-hour shifts involve considering Saturday or Sunday working – and this has proved difficult to negotiate. Shiftworking organizations using 12-hour shifts (of which more below) have more scope to use the annual hours contract since the number of shifts, or half shifts, can be varied. The annual hours approach is, however, of proven value in a shiftworking context where the calculation of annual production hours is the critical starting point for determining shift rotas and crewing. It has been most associated with the British Paper and Board Industry Federation.

In a discussion paper on reduced working time the TUC referred to more flexible patterns of daily working and working 'larger blocks of time'. The TUC acknowledge this 'may better serve leisure purposes and save on travelling expenses to work'. On the issue of competitiveness the TUC said shorter hours can 'focus attention on the need for a better use of resources within basic hours by introducing better patterns of work organization and working time. . . .'[18] However, the extent to which employees will be attracted to the annual hours concept as a new form of work organization will depend partly upon the form of the contract. Longer basic working hours in the summer may be operationally necessary if one is in the ice-cream industry, but may not be welcomed by employees. They would most likely prefer to maintain high overtime earnings in this period.

Indeed the subject of overtime in relation to the annual hours contract clearly presents certain industrial relations difficulties. For some employees there will be significant losses in overtime earnings. This arises under the annual hours contract because on most schemes an overtime premium is not paid until after the pre-defined daily or weekly upper limit has been worked. Yet if an overtime premium is payable after the current standard working hours in any week the potential savings arising from the annual hours contract will be markedly reduced. There are negotiating possibilities between these positions, of course, and at organizational level much will depend on the attractiveness of any overall package being negotiated.

A number of more detailed administrative questions need also to be covered. Since it is preferable that pay levels are unchanged across the year this gives a potential problem with starters/leavers. Rules may be necessary if the 'swings and roundabouts' effect does not work as it should. In addition, consideration needs to be given to how much notice of the required pattern of work is to be given to employees. The options range from three months to as short as one month – this is a matter for joint determination at domestic level.

We have concentrated so far on the annual hours contract because of our view that it may prove a cost-effective option to meet many of the issues in working time we identify above. A number of operational and industrial relations implications need to be examined by each organization but the advantages to both employer and employee may make the effort worthwhile.

Introduction or extension of shiftworking

Turning to alternative *weekly* patterns of work, we begin by focusing on extending or introducing shiftworking. Shiftworking has long been recognized as a way of increasing volume, and improving the utilization of expensive capital equipment. By extending production time, it can also, for example, reduce lead times. There are extra costs involved in shiftworking – headcount, shift allowances, provision of services and the possibility of increased maintenance as equipment is used for longer periods.

The details of shiftworking have been well covered elsewhere.[19] We discuss here a number of more imaginative approaches to shiftworking which may be cost-effective. This includes the use of 12-hour shifts and 5-set working.

Twelve-hour shifts

There is nothing new about 12-hour shift working. In the NBPI survey of the late 1960s, 18 per cent of alternating day-night shift systems had shift lengths of at least 12 hours.[20]

There are of course Factory Act regulations related to women and young persons which restrict the potential coverage of 12-hour shift working. We include this shift working pattern here because organizations are re-appraising the length of shifts and 12-hour shift working may be more attractive to both managements and employees than has hitherto been the case. Certainly for the manager with 5-day shift working faced by increased demands for the product and pressures to obtain improved capital utilization, 7-day working significantly increases production time. Improved utilization can ensure costs of extra employment are absorbed. If 7-day working is desirable, then operating on a 12-hour shift basis is one possibility and one which may be more popular with employees than 8-hour patterns, because of the longer breaks involved. Absenteeism, too, may be lower as a result of this. In addition, there are only two shift changes every 24 hours rather than the three in 8-hour shifts. This is operationally advantageous and facilitates improved communication since both shifts come together at say 6am and 6pm.

Twelve-hour shift working has been seen as most appropriate for tasks which require low level motor skills and are repetitive. However, as technological changes are increasingly reducing the physical dimension to jobs, 12-hour shift working may become more common.

One example of the recent introduction of 12-hour shifts has occurred at Esso-Fawley. Introduced in the context of a move to 5-crew working (of which more below) employees were given the choice of 12-hour or 8-hour rotas. All groups opted by ballot for the same 12-hour shift pattern confirming our belief that this will then prove a more popular shift arrangement. The details are shown in Example 4.2.

5-set working

To resolve many of the issues in working time listed in our earlier analysis, some companies took on extra crews. The idea received much coverage in the early 1980s and a number of options were canvassed including moving from 3 to 3½ crews or 4 to 4½ crews. A half set is operationally useful in that it has built-in opportunities for absence cover; it therefore assumes a degree of flexibility in tasks between the crews. However we concentrate here first on the introduction of an extra full shift, and secondly the use of a fifth crew in a double day pattern of either morning or afternoon shifts.

Many organizations involved in 7-day continuous working adopt the 4-set, 8-hour pattern of working. This provides for the normal 3-shift pattern over 7 days, for example:

> 0600–1400
> 1400–2200
> 2200–0600

but operated by 4 crews on a rapidly rotating basis. Thus the 21 shifts of the week, worked by 4 crews, provide for an average number of shifts of 5¼ per week, as follows:

> Week 1 – 5 shifts
> Week 2 – 5 shifts
> Week 3 – 5 shifts
> Week 4 – 6 shifts

spread over a 12-week rota. Average working hours take into account the extra shift every 4 weeks.

Problems with 4-crew working revolve around the difficulties associated with absence, since in continuous operation all absence has to be covered.

Example 4.2   *12-hour shiftworking at Esso-Fawley*

Each shift crew works an eight day rota comprising two 12-hour day shifts, two 12-hour night shifts and four shifts off. The pattern is repeated over a 10-week period at the end of which there is an 18-day break before the cycle starts again. . . . Employees receive a constant weekly wage across the year, inclusive of shift supplement . . . which is not related to the particular shift worked in any one week.[21]

Example 4.3 *Elements of 5-shift working at American Can*

For most of the year each shift group works blocks of five eight-hour shifts, followed by a three or four day break. However, the actual number of shifts worked in a block varies between four and seven. Late night, daytime and early evening shifts are worked in rotation. Every 15 days the daytime shift is operated by two teams. This allows routine maintenance and cleaning without disrupting production which continues 24 hours a day for all but four days a year (in the Christmas period). [23]

This generally involves high levels of overtime working. In non-process controlled environments, such overtime working can lead to fatigue and higher accident rates. [22]

As a result a number of organizations have introduced 5-shift working. These include American Can (UK) and Esso at Fawley. Details of the American Can system are illustrated in Example 4.3.

A rather different approach to 5-crew working has been reported from Westlands. Faced with a £5 million investment in computer-aided design equipment, the company required full utilization through new shift patterns. Wanting maximum cover within the 18-hour period, 6am–midnight over five days a week, one chosen cycle involves five crews working four weeks on, one week off over a five-week cycle (see Example 4.4). In summary, moving to a 5-crew shift system can give the following advantages:

1 Overtime costs for covering personal holidays, sickness absence and start-up shifts can be significantly reduced.

2 Holidays can be built into the five-shift rota, thus increasing production time and therefore output and (assuming the extra volume is demanded) unit costs can be reduced accordingly.

3 The increase in staffing levels may 'save' otherwise redundant jobs or at least be viewed as socially important in a context of high unemployment.

Against this are the following disadvantages:

1 The labour costs involved in recruiting an extra shift, which may

---

Example 4.4 *5-crew working at Westlands*

Employees work a double day pattern of either morning or afternoon shifts, over the course of the shift cycle, working hours average out at 32.5 a week. . . . . Providing four weeks of consecutive time shift working followed by a week off, it makes the most intensive use of technicians' skills when they are working while, at the same time, providing employees with periodic lengthy breaks. [24]

involve up to 25 per cent extra people unless spare operators can be absorbed, will be high.

2 Because working hours reduce on average, basic pay levels will drop pro rata unless in negotiation it is agreed to hold current weekly rates. If this is so, hourly rates will increase.

3 Overtime earnings will clearly fall and this may prove difficult to negotiate.

4 It involves changing shift patterns and this can be unsettling.

Overall, 5-crew working is a means by which high levels of overtime associated with absence cover can be reduced and an increase in job opportunities provided.

Part-time working

In the search for better methods of relating employees' working time to the operational requirements of the organization, part-time working has considerable relevance. It enables hours to be varied to meet specific peak demands, especially if these periods are of short duration. Thus in the UK part-time working is already common in certain service occupations, especially in hotels and catering, and cleaning. In retail work too, part-time working is frequently employed to cover variations in business needs and peak periods.

Part-time working can also provide a means of extending production hours by for example a 'twilight' shift at the end of the day shift. This may be a more cost-effective alternative than recruiting a full shift. Many part-time workers are also prepared to extend their hours to meet peak requirements – a further advantage.

It has been found that the performance levels of part-timers are likely to be higher than their full-time equivalents, that absenteeism is likely to be lower and that part-time employees generally are adaptable and more responsive to change.[25]

For these reasons the focus on part-time working has not been restricted to the UK but can be seen occurring in, for example, the US, Japan and the rest of Europe:

Between 1970 and 1983 the share of part-timers in Japan's workforce rose to 10.5% from 6.7%. . . . From 1970 to 1982 in the United States, says another study, the number of employed rose by 26.5% while the number of part-timers rose by 58%.[26]

Developments in part-time working include the more widespread use of shifts of the following kinds:

- one week on/one week off or two weeks on/two weeks off;
- 6 hour shifts, operating up to 4 crews;

- a mixture of shifts of different lengths, for example:

  Monday   9 hours ⎫
  Tuesday   6 hours ⎬ 21 hour week
  Wednesday 6 hours ⎭

- use of 2 × 10 hour shifts

Many examples of such patterns can be quoted from Europe. In West Germany, for example, the electronics firm Siemens has been discussing with employees' representatives a flexible working arrangement involving full-time employees volunteering to sign part-time contracts for 32, 30 or 24 hours a week.

> This would allow management to add a second shift and raise utilization of the production line to 60–70 hours a week. Staggered shifts totalling 12–14 hours a day could then be created in ways that could suit individual worker's preferences. An employee's 32-hour week could be divided into four eight-hour days, giving him a three-day weekend. . . . In one electronic components assembly line about 100 workers – mainly women – have 20 hour per week contracts that let them alternate one five-day, eight-hours-a-day shift with a free week or work three eight-hour days one week and two the next.[27]

At the National Westminster Bank in the UK:

> Part-time staff are employed on a wide variety of working arrangements. For example, clerical staff may be engaged on alternate weeks or fortnights, mornings (generally 9.00am to 1.00pm) or afternoons, and many other combinations of hours per day and days per week. Most commonly, they work 20–25 hours per week. Arrangements are flexible to cater for both the operational requirements of the branch and circumstances of the individual.[28]

It is this combination of management advantages, particularly through increased flexibility, with the opportunity to meet individual preferences in working time which makes part-time working so attractive. These advantages for the organization outweigh the marginal extra costs of recruiting part-time labour.

For full-time employees, however, while the transition to part-time work may provide more leisure it does involve a proportionate reduction in pay. For this reason, few are likely to be attracted to this option. In other countries, as we have indicated, a more graduated tax system means that a reduction of hours worked is not so disadvantageous on take-home pay.

Trade unions have sought to negotiate pay and conditions for part-timers pro rata to full-time employees, together with their inclusion in training schemes and removal of barriers to the promotion of part-timers. The degree of union membership amongst part-timers remains low.[29] EEC proposals on part-time working also aim to guarantee part-time workers equal benefits on a pro rata basis.[30]

Part-time working therefore can be attractive to both employers and employees. It also has significant social implications in that more jobs can be created through restructuring full-time into part-time work. For these reasons interest in part-time working will continue.

Saturday/Sunday contracts

Turning to a rather more unusual form of 'part-time shift working' brings us to the concept of a Saturday/Sunday contract. This envisages employees being recruited solely to work on a Saturday and/or a Sunday. It could involve a 12-hour Saturday and a 12-hour Sunday. It is perhaps an alternative to the 4-crew or 5-crew options for 7-day working.

The main reason why a Saturday/Sunday contract might be considered rather than say 4-crew working is that it can be cheaper. Whether this is so depends on what payment is made for Saturday/Sunday. Most collective agreements on overtime provide for payments of time-and-a-half for Saturday working and double time for Sunday working. On this basis, a Saturday/Sunday contract would mean 24 hours worked for 42 hours' pay. An expensive option indeed! Since, however, it could be argued that the Saturday and Sunday working in this case is not 'overtime' but part of a rota which happens to cover Saturday and Sunday, then this pay level might not be deemed appropriate. Payment at flat rate would certainly mean such a contract is more cost-effective than using 4-crews since the use of a 4-crew uplift would be avoided. If flat time for weekend working is difficult to negotiate, then even with a 'weekend supplement', such patterns may still be cost-effective. Even if such a contract is cost-effective, other operational difficulties might arise. Sickness absence and holidays could be more difficult, and costly, to cover. It might prove difficult to integrate such weekend workers into the organization. Questions of maintenance and supervisory cover for weekend workers also arise.

Other initiatives

We have concentrated on those initiatives which tackle the operational issues in working time we identified above. Greater responsiveness to customer requirements, for example, can be gained through the annual hours contract; improved utilization through shiftworking. There are other initiatives in working time which are being considered including sabbaticals and early retirement. The latter is potentially of considerable importance in the context of the social pressures we referred to. Not everyone wishes to retire early of course, but one survey in recent years found that 60 per cent of people would like to take earlier retirement.[31]

Many organizations have introduced voluntary early retirement schemes, generally from age 50 or 55. Most stipulate a certain level of 'actuarial' reduction in the individual's pension to reflect the early retirement – this is often around 5 per cent a year. A minority of organizations, including some of the financial institutions, have provided for early retirement without any reduction, with pension being based on salary and years of service at the actual date of retirement. This is a costly option both in terms of loss of employee contributions, loss of investment income and because the pension would be payable for a longer period. It can only be financed either by an increase in employer contributions, an increase in employee contributions, or both. With continuing cost pressures on organizations, employers will be reluctant to increase their pensions costs; employees similarly will not be keen to increase their level of contributions notwithstanding the social aspects of the change.

Changes to the state pension ages of 60 for women and 65 for men which were set in 1940 are being considered and one report has recommended a pension age of 63 for both men and women.[32] This is a longer term option.

Summary

Operational pressures in working time are leading organizations in the private and public sector to review their patterns of work. The key question is what pattern of work does the organization require to meet its customers' requirements in the most cost-effective way. The answer to this may involve better relating working time to the pattern of demand/service of the organization; there may be pressures to introduce shift working. Increasingly, management staff and technical staff will be required to work on shifts, especially when engaged in using expensive capital equipment.

Flexitime as an approach to working time has increasingly fallen out of favour. It provides for employee controlled flexibility – organizations in the 1980s will require such flexibility to operate more in the interests of the business. Such flexibility is particularly apparent in the concept of an annual hours contract and in part-time working. The annual hours contract is a novel one, and more experience is needed of working under this arrangement before firm conclusions can be drawn. At this stage, it appears to offer an attractive option to organizations whose work requirements vary daily, weekly or monthly.

This chapter has presented a number of options in working time – there are others which could have been included. The 1980s will see further initiatives in working time aimed at improving organizational effectiveness. These will form a major part of the organization's cost-effective strategy in industrial relations.

References

1 In one survey 35 per cent of managers felt this way. See M. White, 'Shorter working time through national industry agreements', *PSI Research Paper No. 38* (1982), p. 37.
2 At a TUC Conference on working time in 1984 it was reported that 100,000 jobs in France and 30,000 jobs in Belgium had been created or saved. See *Financial Times*, 4 February 1984.

3 See, for example, Richard Allen, 'The economic effects of a shorter working week', *Government Economic Service Working Paper No. 33* (HM Treasury, 1980).

4 Mr Len Murray, for example, has been reported as saying:

> There is a trade-off here. It is a trade-off between incomes and jobs. Not cuts in pay in return for shorter hours. We reject that. But workers choosing between pay increases alone or smaller pay increases with shorter hours. We have got to get the balance right.

Quoted in *Financial Times*, 4 February 1984.

5 See *Long suffering British workers: working time in Europe* (Labour Research Department, 1981).

6 Department of Employment, *New Earnings Survey*, 1981.

7 NBPI Report No. 161, 'Hours of work, overtime and shiftworking' (December 1970). NEDO, *The Introduction and Extension of Shiftworking* (1980), p. 6.

8 NEDO, *The Introduction and Extension of Shiftworking*, p. 6; quoting M. Maurice, *Shiftwork* (ILO, 1975).

9 R. Duney and E. M. Szyszczak, 'Protective legislation and part-time employment in Britain', *British Journal of Industrial Relations* (March 1984), p. 79. O. Robinson and J. Wallace, 'Growth and utilization of part-time labour in Great Britain', *DE Gazette* (September 1984), p. 392.

10 This was confirmed statistically in a study by the Policy Studies Institute; see M. White, 'Shorter working time through national industry agreements', *Research Paper No. 38* (1982).

11 See for example, *IDS Study No. 224* for details of the different options. (IDS, June 1981).

12 Draft recommendation submitted to the EEC Council of Ministers by the European Commission on 16 September 1983; reproduced in *European Industrial Relations Review*, No. 118 (November 1983), p. 23.

13 Draft recommendation submitted to the EEC Council of Ministers on 16 September 1983, p. 24.

14 Draft recommendation submitted to the EEC Council of Ministers on 16 September 1983, p. 16.

15 'Hours of work, overtime and shiftworking', p. 20.

16 'Hours of work, overtime and shiftworking', p. 33.

17 C. Wyles, 'Shorter hours need not cost any more', *Works Management* (November 1983), p. 45.

18 Extract from TUC Discussion Paper on Reduced Working Time. See 'Shorter Working Week – an IR-RR Review', *Industrial Relations Review and Report*, vol. 312 (January 1984), p. 2.

19 See, for example, *The Introduction and Extension of Shiftworking* (NEDO, 1980). M. Maurice, *Shiftwork* (ILO, 1975).

20 'Hours of work, overtime and shiftworking', p. 60.

21 'Shiftwork 2: reducing working hours', *Industrial Relations Review and Report No. 308*, 22 November 1983, p. 3.

22 See 'New technology and five-shift working at American Can (UK)', *Industrial Relations Review and Report no. 228*, January 1983, p. 8

23 'New technology and five-shift working at American Can (UK)', pp. 7–9.

24 See '32.5 hour shiftworking at Westland', *Industrial Relations Review and Report No. 321*, 5 June 1984, p. 8.

25 For further information on those aspects of part-time working see 'Part-time workers', *IDS Study No. 267* (June 1982); 'Part-time work survey', *Industrial Relations Review and Report No. 320*, 22 May 1984.

26 'What the boom in part-time work means for management', *International Management* (May 1984), p. 38.

27 'What the boom in part-time work means for management', p. 39.

28 See *IDS*, 'Part-time workers', p. 26.
29 See 'Part-time work survey', p. 7.
30 For details on EEC proposals see 'Part-time work survey', pp. 7–8.
31 M. Stafford and R. Hould, 'Retirement and the older Worker'; quoted in *Industrial Relations Review and Report*, vol. 291, p. 2.
32 *Age of Retirement Vols. 1 and 2*; Third report from the Social Services Committee, 1981–82 (HMSO, 1982).

5
Changing patterns of reward

Central to any organization's approach to industrial relations is the 'reward package'. It is pay and other rewards which are particularly influential in determining whether the right people are recruited and retained by the organization. Pay, even in highly capital intensive businesses, remains a significant part of total costs, and a part which is more directly under management's control than most other costs. But pay is far more than just a cost item. Through pay structures, management influences employee reactions. This relationship, between pay and the contribution the organization seeks to stimulate, links pay firmly to business objectives. It is a central theme of this chapter that the criteria for this contribution are changing – from output to quality and flexibility; from time/attendance to improved performance.

This very centrality of pay and other rewards, however, with all its cost and 'knock-on' implications throughout the organization, means that changing established pay structures is a task which managers approach with considerable caution. Such moves, especially if linked to the 'annual' review, place the organization in an unusually vulnerable position. It requires deep understanding within the organization of what the objectives of the payment system are to be, how any changes are to be negotiated and what the short- and long-term costs are.

In this chapter we explore those factors that organizations are seeking to encourage and reward. This will be examined in relation to individual and group payment structures and will cover both manual and white collar 'staff'. We will refer to a number of developments associated with the wage review itself, such as the renewed interest in long-term agreements and the continuing momentum towards harmonization of conditions. In all this there will be a stress on the objectives of the organization, and our earlier analyses of flexibility of task and initiatives in working time will be particularly relevant. We will concentrate on how enhanced competitive pressures in the 1980s – economic and technological – has changed the emphasis within reward systems in general and pay systems in particular. As Angela Bowey has put it:

> The reward system is a major mediating mechanism between the requirements of those planning the organization and the desires and interests of the employees.[1]

DOI: 10.4324/9781003193043-5

The requirements of those planning the organization are changing because of the pressures on them that we have identified in earlier chapters. The reward system will need to change to reflect this.

Traditional emphases within pay structures

Most organizations have traditionally encouraged and sought to reward the following factors:

- output;
- time at work;
- length of service;
- improvements in individual performance; and
- improved productivity on an individual or group basis.

We explore each of these factors in turn.

Output

Those pay systems which maintain a direct relationship between pay and output or effort

> have one underlying assumption: namely that where the worker can vary his output according to the effort he puts into his work, and this can be related to his earnings in a way he can understand, the payment of increased earnings will induce him to work harder.[2]

The implications of piecework arrangements on costs (through wage drift), on quality and on industrial relations are well known.[3] The attempt to provide greater stability of pay and industrial relations generally, especially in the context of changes in technology, has led to the extension of Measured Day Work (MDW) schemes, a move described as 'a central feature of change in payment systems' in the late 1960s and early 1970s.[4] Such schemes remain popular because the key ingredients, of pay stability linked to work measurement, are still relevant.

Time

Schemes which pay for hours worked with no direct pay/performance link are also common. In this approach employees generally receive a rate for the job (payable after a learning period, which may be as little as one week). There is no scope for individual progression – all individuals doing this job are paid this rate. This approach is seen most frequently amongst skilled men, but can also apply either to semi-skilled employees, where it may be referred to as a 'high day rate', or to white-collar staff where it is more often referred to as a 'spot rate' or just a 'salary'. Employees whose performance is below the required standard are subject to disciplinary action rather than penalties within the pay system.

Length of service

Encouraging staff continuity through rewarding length of service is an approach to payment structures most often associated with the public sector. Underlying such schemes is the view that where measurement of performance is difficult, rewarding service is an appropriate substitute since it recognizes that the individual's contribution can increase with experience. This increased contribution is limited in such pay systems through the use of ceilings on upward incremental progression.

Performance

Pay structures which reward performance or merit usually operate in the context of a variable incremental system; they relate incremental progression to performance, as judged by management. Typically, progression through a scale can be advanced or retarded, depending on assessments of performance, though other options such as salary range with no fixed incremental points, also exist. These options are often associated with cash limits on the sums available for performance increments.[5]

Productivity

Finally organizations may seek to encourage improvements in individual or group productivity. Increasing use has been made of 'added value' – a direct financial measure of productivity linked to pay increases.[6] Other approaches to paying for group productivity include rewarding factors such as an increase in sales revenue or the achievement of cost reduction targets (for example on manpower), or meeting delivery targets. We return to techniques for rewarding a group contribution below.

Such a list is not exhaustive, and examples exist of schemes including more than one of these elements – such as an individual time-related scheme together with an 'added value' bonus scheme.

Changing emphasis in pay structures

It will always remain a fundamental objective of pay structures that a level of income must be provided that will attract and retain employees capable of carrying out the work that the organization requires. This objective may be difficult to achieve. Considerable market pressures exist in certain sectors – particularly for electronics engineers and software specialists at present, for example. On the other hand, pressures on costs within organizations mean that the necessity to pay high wages to the few cannot be allowed to lead to higher salaries for all employees irrespective of their market scarcity or performance. These diverse pressures imply maximum flexibility in pay structures.

Having said this, the factors that organizations seek to encourage and reward are changing fast. Through the reward system managements are defining and measuring the required *contribution* and linking pay and other rewards directly to it. For manual workers, for example, this contribution has in the past been essentially output based. While this still remains relevant in many organizations, the employee's contribution is increasingly being defined, and rewarded, against a wider range of factors. For 'staff' this contribution was often as we have said an assumed one; if years of service are increasing then, probably, so is the employee's contribution. Now for staff the focus is more on incentives, merit and performance. These changing emphases within pay structures are summarized in Table 2.

Table 2   *Changing emphases on factors to reward*

	Factors being rewarded	
	Away from	*Toward*
Manual employees	Output	Machine utilization Quality Flexibility Group working Job knowledge/skill
'Staff' employees	Time Service Age	Direct incentive schemes Merit/performance assessment

Some further exploration of the contents of this table is required. For manual employees in the manufacturing sector in particular, the trend away from encouraging and rewarding high levels of output reflects the influence of technological developments. Computerized control of the manufacturing process has proceeded with great rapidity and is changing the nature of semi-skilled work in many organizations from hand-work to machine-minding. Of course, the range between being solely engaged in manual assembly tasks and being solely engaged in machine-minding is wide – until totally automated plants are widespread, people will continue loading and unloading automated equipment, for example.

Nevertheless, as one study put it, the spread of process controlled operations has challenged the basis of payment by results schemes.

> Their relevance – dependent as they are on the individual's ability to control his output personally – will be brought into question by the more widespread introduction of robotics, computer-controlled machine tools and flexible manufacturing systems where the immediate control of rates of input and the work done on the product piece are determined by the computer system.[7]

So the emphasis is changing from a focus on volume to a focus on the importance of keeping equipment running, reducing downtime, improving yields and improving quality standards. On quality, specifically, many organizations are now emphasizing 'first time right', given for example the costs of re-working faulty products, and the cost of scrap. While quality has often been referred to in quantity based payment schemes, it has not received the attention it is now getting.

Also in the manual workforce area, we noted in chapter 3 the importance of the reward system in promoting flexibility of task and the encouragement of group working. With technological changes blurring the boundaries between many jobs greater vertical and horizontal interchangeability is possible, and necessary, if manpower is to be utilized effectively. Of course, far from encouraging group working, pay structures can have the effect of preventing it; different pay systems operating within a potential group can create different levels of payment and reward different features. Establishing links between pay systems can make it easier to develop a workgroup concept. Although this could have considerable cost and 'knock-on' implications, some organizations have pursued this strategy and one – Cummins Engines – is described below (see Example 5.1).

Payment systems will also have to adapt so as to facilitate the changes in working time we described in chapter 4. Organizations currently generally pay for alternative patterns of working by way of 'adds-on' to the basic/incentive structure, using monetary or percentage shift allowances. Where specific amounts of money are related to specific work patterns organizations resort to complicated shift protection arrangements or 'red-circling' when alternative patterns of work are introduced. A system which rewards the individual for shift-working in a very general way, and which is not related to specific times or patterns, would better facilitate flexibility in working time.

Finally, in the manual area, organizations are increasingly seeking a better qualified workforce, and are in many cases paying for this directly by rewarding particular qualifications or the completion of skill modules, or indirectly through references to job knowledge in performance assessment schemes.

For staff Table 2 indicates an emphasis on performance assessment, reflecting the desire of many organizations to reward the individual's contribution in as precise a way as possible. The ideal measure, presumably, is profit; but profit-sharing schemes remain relatively unusual. Instead, where the contribution can be directly measured – as in the case of many salesmen – direct incentive schemes have been introduced. Recently, incentives in kind such as gift vouchers and holidays at home or abroad have been used.[8] Where direct measurement remains difficult because of the nature of the job, performance assessment schemes that categorize employees into levels of contribution have been further developed. Pay increases are then linked to such an assessment.[9]

Changing structural parameters

The emphasis on the factors to encourage and reward is changing, and so

are the structural parameters of pay systems. Examples of such changes
are itemized in Table 3.

Table 3 *Changing structural parameters of pay systems*

	Structural parameters	
	Away from	*Toward*
Manual employees	Single factor schemes	Multi-factor schemes
	Work measurement	Performance assessment
	Job rate	Scope for individual progression
'Staff' employees	Automatic progression	Variable progression
	Fixed salary ranges	Open-ended salary ranges
	Fixed increment size	Variable increment size

Within PBR or MDW schemes, the single factor most often emphasized
has been, as we have seen, output. The increasing spread of machine
controlled technology and pressures to improve cost effectiveness, have
made other factors relevant and led to the introduction of multi-factor
schemes. These schemes relate payment to performance against a number
of predefined categories, including:

Quality of work   Established from inspection or quality information

Job knowledge   Depth of knowledge of process and machinery in use

Flexibility   Number of different tasks/jobs performed

The targets can be set through work measurement, or alternatively employees can be assessed at set time intervals against these factors and
awarded points accordingly. Points are then translated to pay. The factors
can be weighted to reflect the particular contribution which the organization wishes most to reward. Given the pace of technical change, the concept
of work measurement itself is increasingly being questioned. The value of
such an approach in terms of control and monitoring of performance levels
remains valid but work measurement in its traditional forms is highly
labour-intensive and costly. Hence interest is increasing in schemes which
instead employ a concept of performance assessment.[10] Although relatively uncommon amongst semi-skilled staff, the example provided by
Inmos may be indicative of future developments:

> Manual workers . . . are appraised annually, during April and May. The
> appraisal is carried out by the immediate supervisor using a standard form.
> This lists such criteria as: quantity of work, quality, initiative, conduct and
> attendance. The supervisor writes in a comment under each of these headings
> and then makes an overall assessment at the end. Employees are rated on a five
> point scale, ranging from 'unsatisfactory' to 'outstanding'.
>   The appraisal form is completed in advance and then discussed with the

employee, the discussion usually lasting between 20 minutes and half an hour. . . .[11]

The third development we identify in Table 3 is the movement away from a job rate structure to one allowing scope for individual progression. This provides management with greater scope to reward enhanced individual contribution. While simple to operate and having a certain 'equity' in the treatment of employees, job rate structures may prove a strait-jacket in practice. Retraining job-holders or changing the nature of the job often means negotiating a new job rate, and this enhanced rate can quickly become the norm for employees elsewhere in the organization – even if these do not require the retraining or job changes applicable to the original group. It is often difficult to promote particular individuals to enhanced salary levels because the rest of the work group on the particular job rate will expect comparable treatment. For this reason, employees of ability may be held back in career and payment terms by the operation of job rates, while the organization may be reluctant to re-negotiate the job rate because of the knock-on effects. In addition, if a job rate becomes out of line with the market, it is again difficult to increase this rate above others in the organization since internal differentials might be jeopardized.

It has to be added that a job rate structure may maximize flexibility, since all job-holders are paid the same irrespective of what they do.

'The rate for the job' is, of course, a strongly held trade union principle amongst skilled unionists. It is now, however, a principle honoured more in the breach than in the observance. Where the principle has been observed, care and the provision of safeguards for the lower performers, have proven to be necessary in negotiating a change away from this criterion.

By the mid 1980s, competitive pressures and technological developments had led many organizations to introduce new or revised pay structures. Example 5.1 is included because it seems to us to illustrate in more detail many of the themes we have been examining.

Changing white-collar pay systems

For white-collar 'staff', the emphasis of salary structures is also changing. In the 1970s salary structures were introduced or developed in a context of high rates of inflation, rapid growth of white collar unionization and incomes policies. The consequence was a leaning toward incremental structures emphasizing service rather than merit. These were obviously preferred by the trade unions, who disliked schemes providing discretion to management. They were also felt to be more 'incomes policy proof'. Because of high rates of inflation, incremental progression was perceived as less important than the size of the general increase. This reinforced the separation of the general increase from incremental awards and further

Example 5.1 *New pay structures at Cummins Engines (1984)*

With an objective of reducing costs by 30 per cent in 30 months, Cummins Engines introduced a new pay structure in 1984. The key elements were

harmonization, a 37½-hour week; abolition of the bonus scheme; extension of group working; a new system of pay progression through individual acquisition of skill modules; and the restructuring of job classification into pay 'bands' with an integrated staff/manual pay structure

There is a key requirement for flexible working:

In support of the philosophy of the new pay and productivity scheme which is designed to increase skill and thus achieve greater levels of productivity, it is agreed that all AUEW employees will continue to apply without reservation, the skills they currently practise, and newly acquired skills from the modular training as and when required within the organization

The application of skill modules is of particular interest, once employees receive their revised 'particulars of employment', including job title:

The departmental manager/supervisor will discuss with job holder(s) the proposed new skill requirements for that particular job title . . . and develop those into skill modules. . . .

the supporting training programme will be produced and a schedule of training published. . . .

Individuals will be required to undertake one skill module per annum up to a maximum of six or until Grade ceiling is reached. . . .

the appropriate method of assessment will be developed. The assessment process will be used to determine the ability of the job incumbent to practise specified skills. . . .

Incremental payments are effective on successful completion of the skill modules.[12]

---

diminished the importance of merit payments where this was the basis of incremental progression.

The new emphasis on rewarding higher levels of contribution directly has led to a move away from automatic service or age-related progression to variable progression based on performance.[13] There are pressures, even in bastions of the incremental approach such as the Civil Service, to develop systems in which progression is linked directly to performance assessment.

The transition from fixed salary ranges and fixed increment sizes to open-ended salary ranges and variable incremental movements also reflects a desire for greater flexibility, particularly to enable the organization better to reward, and hopefully therefore retain, key staff. There may be high performers who would be demotivated by reaching their ceiling, or employees with skills in short supply for whom extra payments are needed to prevent their being 'poached' by competitors. While fixed salary ranges provide a basis for ensuring comparability and limiting wage drift, organizations are increasingly seeking the greater flexibility inherent in open-ended structures.

One study saw a variable approach as providing

> an effective basis for motivation by relating pay to performance, that . . . is in line with the concept of management accountability, that . . . is both fairer and more cost effective in relating pay increases to contribution and that . . .
> provides more flexibility to match pay to the individual in the face of greater job mobility and changing conditions. . . .[14]

Movements in the public and private sector toward a greater link between pay and performance reflects these factors.[15] This trend amongst white collar 'staff' is illustrated in Examples 5.2 and 5.3.

Rewarding a group contribution

In our earlier analysis of the traditional emphases within pay structures, we listed improved productivity on an individual or group basis as a factor being encouraged and rewarded in many organizations. As the emphasis on rewarding contribution to the organization's objectives is sharpened in the 1980s, so interest in the link between pay and group productivity has also grown. Although clearly not as powerful a motivator as individual incentive arrangements, schemes covering groups of employees can encourage and reward certain factors while taking account of the interdependence of operations.

Example 5.2   *Changing salary structures at BL Cars Ltd (1982)*

As part of a two-year agreement reached in 1982, BL Cars Ltd replaced its system of incremental salary progression with individual salary awards. The important points of this emphasis on variability in salary payments are:

- a 'rolling review' basis, with not less than 12 months normally elapsing between awards; and

- provision for increases ranging from the minima to 15 per cent depending upon an individual's 'performance and skills, salary position in the range, size and timing of last award, the level of salaries in the department, etc.'.[16]

Example 5.3 *Rewarding clerical and administrative staff at Legal & General Assurance (1981)*

Appraisal of staff
The assessment form for those in grades 01 and 02 involves rating on a five-point scale for (i) understanding of job; (ii) quality of work; (iii) quantity of work; (iv) use of initiative; and (v) attitude to job. An overall performance rating on an eight-point scale is also made.

The appraisal of staff in grades 03 and above is more comprehensive, including performance in key tasks, rating on nine personal qualities, setting of objectives, and identification of training needs and longer-term career development possibilities. An overall performance rating is given. Managers are expected to assess all those of their staff who have been in post for more than a few weeks.

Budget allocated
Heads of department are each allocated a budget representing a certain proportion of the salary bill for their staff (in recent years this has been 4 per cent of salary band midpoints). The overall performance rating is used to assist managers to determine the level of merit award and they also take into account the relative position in the salary band. (The overall 4 per cent has resulted in individual increases of between 0 and 6 per cent – and, exceptionally, 8 per cent).[17]

One instructive example is provided by the still growing interest in 'added value' schemes. Added value (AV) has been defined as:

> the money value which is added by the production process to raw materials and production purchases. It is a measure of the income generated by the application of employees' skills and company investment to bought in materials.[18]

Hence it is applicable only to production industry companies. Payments are generally related to a ratio determined by expressing payroll costs as a percentage of the added value. A base ratio is needed, established by monitoring company performance in terms of added value, against which future bonus payments can be related. Alternative added value ratios have been used, including relating AV to each £ of payroll costs, or to the number of employees.[19]

Added value is as valuable as a vehicle for communication about the nature of the business and its finances as it is for rewarding employees. It is less appropriate for manufacturing organizations with uncertain, flat or declining output. Introducing an AV scheme which subsequently pays

---

Example 5.4   *Lump sum bonus schemes at British Steel Corporation*

In the January 1981 review the emphasis was placed on lump sum bonus schemes as the only way of increasing pay levels. In one case the bonus scheme

> related to improvement in the ratio of added value to employment costs, and this is linked to an examination of existing demarcation lines.

Certain principles were laid down, including:

- production operatives to be involved in first line inspection and checks, and simple maintenance;
- senior process and maintenance grades are to accept greater responsibility, particularly in taking over certain supervisory duties. . . . ;
- manual grades are to record information;
- all operatives are to use computer terminals as appropriate;
- senior operatives control work groups without immediate staff supervision;
- agreement to use of contract services where necessary;
- reduction in overtime; and
- payment by credit transfer.[21]

---

little or no bonus can be more demotivating than not introducing the scheme at all.

Other group or company wide productivity schemes can be based on, for example, net sales invoiced, a productivity index reflecting volume of deliveries, or an index based on quality improvements.[20] Rewards for such contributions have in some cases replaced a general cost of living pay award. The most well known example of this trend is the British Steel Corporation (see Example 5.4).

Example 5.5   *Productivity scheme at Massey Ferguson (1984)*

The Agreement incorporates the terms of the company wide 'tractor division bonus plan' based on net sales invoiced. . . .

Assuming sales targets are achieved the scheme is designed to yield £1.50 a week at base level with another £1 a week being paid for every additional 5 per cent increase in sales. The bonus is additional to the general pay increase and is calculated quarterly. This amount is paid as a lump sum which is not consolidated into basic rates. . . .[22]

Such a movement away from general pay increases has so far only been possible in a context of severe economic difficulties such as those besetting BSC in the late 1970s and early 1980s. However, for many organizations there may be significant and as yet unrealized opportunities to develop the link between pay increases and productivity improvements.

Another such link in the private sector, with a different criterion, is shown in Example 5.5.

The most direct means of rewarding a group contribution is through profit-sharing schemes. These and savings-related share option schemes are increasingly in use, though as yet hardly a typical approach. They provide the opportunity for companies to reward staff for improved business performance. These may be introduced as part of a benefits package or as part of a strategy for employee involvement. Such schemes may involve distribution of a proportion of 'profit' to employees as a cash bonus; putting money aside to buy shares or allocating profits to a trust fund which acquires shares on behalf of employees. [23]

A profit-sharing arrangement was agreed recently at British Airways (see Example 5.6).

Non-contributory elements of pay determination

So far we have concentrated on the relationship between pay and the contribution from the employee that the organization is seeking to encourage and reward. We have shown how the factors that define this contribution are changing, from output to machine utilization, quality and flexibility, and from service to performance and merit. However, in the determination of pay and other rewards, there are many elements which do not relate to the contribution of a particular employee or group of employees. These we call the non-contributory elements of pay, and recent developments in this area include

- a renewal of interest in long-term agreements;
- a concentration of settlement dates;
- continuing interest in flat-rate increases;
- renewed interest in cost of living arrangements; and
- the use of comparability, particularly within the public sector.

We explore each of these issues in turn.

Example 5.6 *Profit-sharing at British Airways*

for every £50 million operating surplus over £150 million employees receive one week's pay, e.g. £300 million surplus equals three weeks' basic pay. For every million pounds over the trigger figure, a fiftieth of a week's pay is paid. [24]

Long-term agreements
'Annual' reviews of pay are a relatively recent development, promoted particularly by higher rates of inflation in the 1970s. With inflation at considerably lower levels in the mid 1980s, the possibilities for long-term agreements are again being explored. These offer a number of advantages – of which the attainment of pay stability for a two- or three-year period is foremost. Organizations can plan their future costs with greater certainty. The 'annual' review is always a time-consuming affair for both management and trade unions, and this time can be avoided altogether for at least one cycle. This provides the opportunity for discussion on other priorities, such as erosion of demarcation lines, away from the tactical considerations and pressures of the 'annual' review.

This was the thinking behind, for example, the three-year agreement secured by Scottish and Newcastle Breweries in 1983. They wished to achieve the following objectives:

1   To rationalize the pay/grade structure for all groups of employees;
2   To create logical, justifiable and defensible relationships across and within work groups; and
3   To move towards a more 'common' pay and conditions package as the vehicle for embracing and achieving these changes; to change the aspirations of the various bargaining groups in relation to these same differentials, to persuade each group to recognize the legitimacy of each other group's right to a logical and defensible place in an agreed heirarchy of pay and profits.

Their three-year agreement with the unions ensured that

> acceptance of the first phases of changes in conditions could be monitored alongside work practice changes before moving to the next phase.[25]

In general, there is evidence that the pay increases necessary to achieve long-term agreement may be higher than those in a one-year format, especially for the second year of a two-year deal. For organizations who already have a fair degree of industrial relations stability, paying this extra price may not be cost-effective. If rates of inflation fall below the predicted levels, and these predictions formed the basis of the level of settlement in the long-term agreement, such arrangements may prove costlier.

Concentration of settlement dates
By the mid 1980s the concept of the fixed national 'pay round' had lessened. This was a product of the periods of incomes policies in the late 1970s. It has not disappeared, as the desire of many organizations to change their review date from the August–October period in any year to the following January–April clearly demonstrates.[26] Now there is a concentration of review dates in the January–April period, and this trend can be expected

to continue. No organization likes to be a front-runner, with the publicity and bargaining pressure that accompany that position. Moving review dates requires negotiating a review agreement of more or less than 12 months; for example, a 1 October review date being moved to 1 March requires an 18-month or a 6-month agreement. The former may be difficult to negotiate, and requires substantial managerial determination in negotiation – effectively making such a change a precondition for the annual review offer. A shorter period of agreement will be more acceptable to the trade unions, but may prove costlier overall.

Flat-rate increases

Many settlements in recent years have incorporated flat-rate increases. These take one of two forms; a combination of percentage increase or monetary increase with each employee receiving whichever pays most in their case, or a single monetary increase. An example of the former includes the 1984 first-stage agreement at British Airways which provided for 4 per cent or £6, whichever was the greatest. An example of the latter was agreed by Honeywell in 1984 providing for a flat-rate increase of £6. This approach is attractive to the trade unions in that it improves the relative position of the lower paid in the bargaining group. Of the two options, negotiators will generally prefer the mixture of a percentage and monetary increase since single monetary increases disturb percentage differentials for higher paid workers.

Cost of living arrangements

Lower and more stable rates of inflation in the mid 1980s have raised again the concept of cost of living arrangements, a familiar component of pay deals in the 1970s. Management negotiators have generally been pleased to see the back of them, remembering the loss of control over their labour costs which was a consequence of such arrangements. Yet in the context of lower inflation they may prove attractive. There are essentially two forms of cost of living arrangements.[27]

1 A detailed predefinition of the circumstances in which additional increases are payable. This may take the form of an improvement payable after a defined increase in the retail prices index – say above 6 or 7 per cent over the period of the review agreement. Flat rate or percentage payments can also be stipulated.

2 The use of re-opener clauses. That agreed by General Motors in 1984 (in the context of a two-year agreement) is a good example:

> in the event that the figure for annual inflation as measured by the RPI exceeds 6.5 per cent between May 1985 and the expiry date of the Agreement (April 1986) the company agrees that the trade unions may re-open negotiations on base pay.[28]

Comparability

Management negotiators well understand that relative pay levels are as important to employees as absolute pay levels. While in the private sector internal comparability is more important than external comparability, in the determination of public sector pay, external comparability continues to have relevance. One survey has shown that 78 per cent of public service workers think that they are lagging behind over pay.[29] Police pay is related to an earnings index covering a number of organizations; and review bodies such as those for nurses and teachers in Scotland have incorporated comparisons with external groups.

Comparability, therefore, remains a factor in pay determination, but one which we believe will lessen even in the public sector. Here, pressures to focus on merit and on linking pay and productivity will become sharper as the 1980s progress.

So the scope and context of the pay review is itself changing, reflecting the changing economic and bargaining pressures of the 1980s. Gone are the days when

> The company, with minimal regard to trading performance, would pay the going rate or even more commonly, the maximum allowance under whatever pay policy was in force.[30]

Managements in all sectors are increasingly testing pay, and the non-contributory elements of pay outlined here, against a rigid criterion of cost-effectiveness. This has inevitably led to union opposition. But not to as much as might have been predicted at the beginning of the 1980s. It has proven to be possible better to control wage and salary costs and increase productivity.

The same criterion has been applied to conditions of employment beyond those directly related to salary. In the case of *harmonization* of conditions and *career* progression these moves have in general been welcomed by the trade unions: the relationship with *manpower planning* may, however, have more long-term significance and more potential for dispute. We consider these three topics next.

Conditions of employment

Harmonization

The subject of harmonizing conditions of employment has been with us a long time, although Britain is still far behind most of its developed country competitors in this respect. In the 1980s, it has received considerable attention in the context of rapid technological and organizational changes, which it is felt could be impeded by artificial distinctions on conditions of employment between work groups. Yet just at the time when movements towards harmonization are most desirable, cost pressures have inevitably led organizations to question, and possibly slow down, developments towards such harmonized conditions.

What is harmonization? In 1972 it was said that

Differences in the conditions of employment and status of different categories of employees and in the facilities available to them should be based on the requirements of the job. The aim should be progressively to reduce and ultimately to remove differences which are not so based.[31]

In 1982, definitions of harmonization were even broader, moving away from the link between differences in conditions and requirements of the job. For example, harmonization was defined as 'the process of reducing or eliminating differences in the basis of particular conditions of employment.'[32] The ultimate outcome of such developments is the concept of 'single status' where differences in all basic conditions of employment have been eliminated.

For most organizations, harmonization moves take place within the overall objective of a more integrated workforce. Differences in conditions of employment between groups can obstruct utilization of employees across job boundaries.

One study has suggested four main aims in moving towards single status:

- Changing employee attitudes – status distinctions reinforce a 'them and us' philosophy amongst manual employees. This can inhibit cooperation and change.

- Improved workforce utilization.

  The elimination of systematic overtime, reductions in manning, easing of demarcation lines and other restrictive practices, and generally improved flexibility are all goals which have prompted harmonization in companies.[33]

- Improved recruitment and retention – as a result of improved morale.

Example 5.7 *Harmonization moves at Berger Paints*

By 1977 this company had already harmonized pensions and sick pay, and . . . it agreed on a 'package' which provided a mechanism for the manual workforce to achieve harmonized conditions by 1 December 1983. The introduction of the new conditions – a 37½-hour week and 25 days' annual holiday – is controlled and monitored by joint working parties in each bargaining group.

The speed of the introduction of the new conditions will depend upon when the groups identify and quantify savings which will offset their cost. . . . The company has agreed with the manual unions a list of working practices which will be eliminated including such items as: new overtime rates abolishing the 'one in, all in' system; changing manning levels, more flexibility of individuals and groups to avoid bottlenecks in production . . . and more extensive use of contract labour.[35]

- Achieving an extrinsic return through collective bargaining.[34]

Of this list improving workforce utilization is critical to management in the 1980s, and 'trade-offs' between harmonized conditions and productivity improvements have frequently occurred. The details of one such 'trade-off' are described in Example 5.7.

There are two main negative issues for management to consider on the subject of harmonization – cost and the effect on the staff unions of narrowing or eliminating differentials.

Costs will differ depending on the conditions being harmonized, the gap to be reduced or eliminated, the time scale over which the harmonization is to be completed and what cost saving conditions can be directly attached to each improvement. For example:

On holidays
Increasing annual entitlement has clear cost implications. This can be alleviated by phasing the increase over a period of years, and by insisting that extra days of leave are fixed by the company at times which suit business requirements. Fixing days to bridge the period between Christmas and New Year statutory holidays, to provide for a long break has many cost saving advantages for the organization which otherwise would open for only a skeleton staff.

On sick pay
Costs generally arise from paying normal earnings from the first day of sickness; from an entitlement to sick pay (of say up to four weeks) in the first year of service; and from increases in the maximum length of time over which the employee is entitled to sick pay. Here attempts can be made to tighten up on absence control procedures as a trade-off for improvements in sick pay provision. Such tightening up would include notification procedures, self-certification, and joint monitoring of length of sickness absence.

On overtime
Harmonization has, of course, often been in 'reverse' with 'staff' gaining an overtime premium previously enjoyed by manual workers. Costs can be reduced by linking harmonized moves to cuts in overtime working – possibly through the use of a maximum monthly entitlement. As we showed in chapter 4 there is much scope for savings in overtime costs.

Pensions
These costs can be the most significant expense arising from harmonization. If employee contribution rates increase, and employer contributions are a percentage of this, then pension costs will increase. Similarly, bring-

ing previous years of pensionable service in the manual workers' fund up to the level of the staff scheme would also be very costly. The alternative is to create a new combined pension scheme, harmonized for the future but without retrospective adjustments.

It is unlikely that harmonization of hours of work will be achieved easily, largely on grounds of cost. There are some who would argue that harmonization of staff hours upwards to equate with the hours of work of manual workers is the most desirable course of action!

Further cost savings can also be secured by extending the principle of harmonization to the method and cycle of wage payment. Payment by credit transfer on a 4 weekly/monthly basis is an aspect of harmonization with many advantages to management. Savings arise from

- interest on money left in the bank for longer periods (this may be expressed as reduced interest charges on overdrafts);
- savings on security costs;
- savings on staff time in the make up of wage packets and in coin analysis; and
- savings in bank charges for withdrawals of cash.

There are, of course, the important security advantages to employees of payment by credit transfer as well as the advantages of the facilities provided by the banks. So a cost-effective strategy for harmonization of conditions would include the harmonization of the method and cycle of wage payment.

There are process, as well as content, issues to be considered here. The effects of moves towards harmonization on staff unions, as differentials narrow, can be a difficulty. It is less of a problem in practice than is often feared. It is hard for one union to sustain long-term an objection to other unions securing an improvement in their conditions. There are negotiating tactics to minimize this impact of differentials – for example by marginal improvements to staff conditions which immediately become 'red-circled'. This, however, has further cost implications.

Careers

Career development is an aspect of manual/staff integration which is often omitted from consideration, yet in terms of effective utilization of manpower it can be important. There is a broad general assumption that manual workers will undertake one occupation all their lives, with real earnings reaching a peak in their thirties and forties and then declining as they 'slow down', or in some cases move to more secure but less well-paid jobs. Non-manual workers on the other hand are expected, through increments and promotion, to move up the organizational ladder and reach peak earnings in later life. The same pattern, though more marked, is expected for managerial staff. Managers, and to a lesser extent clerical workers, are encouraged to think in terms of their own development and career progression, encouraged to undertake training and look for enlarged jobs. Manual employees, in general, are not. Training for them is usually strictly job-related.

On a vertical dimension there too are distinctions. Because non-manual and managerial jobs are generally rewarded on the basis of seniority, service and grade, an employee switching to another area – from sales to stock control for example – will generally suffer no financial or pay-related loss and may well increase his or her promotion prospects. This is true despite the fact that the UK uses 'job swap' or job rotation far less than most competitor countries. For a manual worker, however, a job change may mean less opportunity to earn bonuses and incentive payments; a loss of pay during training and reduced chances of promotion. This disparity may apply however good the retraining that individual has received.

The development of career structures for manual employees which cross manual/staff boundaries will be facilitated by integrated pay structures and common conditions of employment.

Reward 'packages' and manpower planning

Manpower planning, theoretically about planning human resource requirements, in many organizations amounts to little more than trying to establish a rate for the job that will attract appropriate recruits. Yet it is also argued that manpower is a crucial resource, and one which therefore needs to be husbanded carefully. The speed of change is increasing and, in certain industries at least, the opportunities for employees are expanding – this at a time when unemployment is generally high. These factors combine to make it easier to recruit certain staff; and often easy to lose them too. In these circumstances a vanguard of organizations are moving towards a more long-term and planned approach to manpower. These organizations identify the kinds of staff they need, where and when they need them, and the form in which they need them. They identify relevant reward packages for those kinds of staff.

The focus is on overall reward packages rather than just cost or pay. Thus in addition to the usual 'pay and conditions' package they consider cars, holidays, office furniture and support services, pensions and medical benefits, bonus and shares schemes, assistance with house purchase or rental, school support, nurseries – anything, in fact, which achieves their organizational objectives.

With this wider view of reward the organization can tailor a reward package to the types of staff that it plans to have. There will be a number of jobs where long-term employees, committed to the organization, are vital. For them packages may include a comprehensive, service-linked pensions and insurance scheme, assistance with house purchase and other loans, and perhaps a share option scheme. Salaries may be competitive, but this competitiveness may wane as other non-cash benefits become important.

Other employees will be required who can perform to a high level almost immediately, are young, aggressive and effective, but whom it is recognized may be 'burnt out' or headhunted fairly swiftly. They will be attracted by a high basic salary with short, steep scales, and the trappings of success – travel, holidays, school fees paid; expensive perhaps, but all short-term commitments by the organization.

For some employees, particularly those in the financial sector with the information necessary to make such choices, a 'cafeteria' approach may be attractive. This defines overall cost but allows employees to choose amongst different packages.

Associated with these approaches will be other, non-reward elements, including training and development. For the company-committed, long-service employee, development and career progression are crucial. They will be achieved often through a process of exposure to new situations, job enlargement and job rotation rather than through a series of courses. As in the reward package there will be a consistent focus on internally relevant training and a rejection of anything transferable.

Many other groups, a majority in large numbers of cases, will receive no training. They will be identified as 'short stay' or as merely labouring jobs. Whether at the top or bottom of the employment hierarchy, the assumption will be that the reward package attracts appropriate candidates from the marketplace.

With the decreasing size of company workforces, increasing proportions of service industries and of small, more professionally orientated, white-collar employment such integrated approaches to manpower planning and reward packages are spreading.

Changing patterns of reward

We have examined the changed emphasis in pay structures in the 1980s, developments in conditions of employment and the concept of reward packages with its link to career development and other non-reward factors. We now pull together the following related developments in pay and other rewards by way of concluding remarks:

- the move away from automatic increases;
- the desire for stability;
- rewarding key objectives;
- moves in harmonization; and
- the necessity for control over costs.

The move away from automatic increases stems from the desire of organizations better to link pay and the employee's contribution. Automatic increases based on service or age do not relate pay to performance except in the sense that increments can be withheld if performance is poor.

This only applies to a handful of employees. Such schemes, as we have seen, are under pressure and have been replaced in many instances by arrangements providing for discretionary payments based on performance. Similarly, the general increase itself has to be justified in relation to performance – of the individual, work group, division or organization as a whole. In this context there has been a continuing focus on 'added value' and other productivity schemes, and on profit-sharing.

The desire for stability has been reflected in a resurgence of interest in long-term agreements and in the concentration within organizations of settlement dates. Within payment systems this desire has been restated in a continuing interest in measured daywork schemes.

Rewarding key objectives reflects renewed interest in factors such as quality and flexibility which are critical to the business objectives of the organization. Other objectives relate to the desire to retain staff with highly marketable skills or to reward team working, and these factors are being reflected in reward systems. In many cases, however, factors such as output/effort will remain key objectives.

Moves toward harmonization of conditions will progress in a more cost conscious manner than that which characterizes the 1970s. The abolition of hourly paid conditions will be slowly followed by the abolition of weekly paid conditions exception of hours of work.

In the area of pay and other rewards, control over costs remains fundamental to organizational success. To improve cost effectiveness, we have stressed the emphasis on the employee's contribution to organizational objectives. Cost control can also be exercised through cash limits, the use of the kitty principle, or through self-financing productivity arrangements. For all except those few organizations whose pay is a very small percentage of total costs, this is a key challenge.

References

1   A. M. Bowey, 'Installing salary and wage systems', in A. Bowey (ed.), *Handbook of Salary and Wage Systems* (Gower, 1975), p. 57.
2   D. Grayson, *Progressive Payment Systems*, Work Research Unit Occasional Paper No. 28 (February 1984), p. 5.
3   NBPI, *Payment by Results Systems*, Report No. 65 (1968), p. 3.
4   NBPI, *Payment by Results Systems*, p. 8.
    See also NBPI Report No. 28, pp. 10–17;
    IDS *Guide to Incentive Payment Schemes* (1980), p. 6.
    Royal Commission on Trade Unions and Employers' Associations 1965–68, Cmnd 3623 (The Donovan Report).
    Office of Manpower Economics, *Measured Daywork* (HMSO, 1973), p. 8.
5   For a full description see Office of Manpower Economics, *Incremental Payment System*, (HMSO, 1973), pp. 14–24.
6   E. G. Wood, *Added Value, the Key to Prosperity* (Business Books, 1978).
7   D. Grayson, *Progressive Payment Systems*, p. 17.
8   I. G. Smith, *The Management of Remuneration: paying for effectiveness* (IPM, 1983).

9 Office of Manpower Economics, *Incremental Payment Systems*.

10 'Merit pay for manual workers' *Industrial Relations Review and Report* No. 319 (May 1984), pp. 2–6.

11 'Merit pay for manual workers', p. 5.

12 *Incomes Data Report* 432 (September 1984), pp. 10–12.

13 'Salary progression systems', *IDS Study* No. 246 (July 1981).

14 Office of Manpower Economics, *Incremental Payment Systems*, p. 34.

15 'Low inflation and low turnover put pressure on incremental systems', *IDS Report* No. 403 (June 1983).

16 *IDS Report* No. 394 (February 1983), p. 15.

17 'Salary progression systems', *IDS Study* No. 246 (July 1981), p. 12.

18 'Added value schemes', *IDS Study* No. 189 (March 1979), p. 2.

19 Engineering Employers Federation, *Practical Applications of Added Value* (1977).

20 For further information see 'Productivity bargaining', *IDS Study* No. 162 (January 1978) and F. Wilson, S. Haslam and A. Bowey, 'Bonuses based on company performance', in A. Bowey, *Handbook of Salary and Wage Systems*, pp. 321–48.

21 'Productivity improvements', *IDS Study* No. 245 (July 1981), p. 12.

22 *IDS Report* No. 432, September 1984, p. 13.

23 'Profit sharing and share options', *IDS Study* No. 306 (January 1984).

24 J. Higgins, 'Sharing out profits', *Personnel Management* (May 1984), p. 29.

25 J. Benson, 'The long-term agreement: offering stability in return for change', *Personnel Management* (October 1983).

26 For example the dispute at Vauxhall in September 1984 over the company's desire for an 18-month agreement in order to defer their review date; see *Financial Times*, 3 September 1984.

27 'Cost of living arrangements', *IDS Study* No. 200 (August 1979).

28 *IDS Report* No. 425 (May 1984), p. 8.

29 Unpublished study by Policy Studies Institute; referred to in P. Bassett, 'The long shadow of the miners' strike', *Financial Times*, 21 August 1984.

30 Esmond Lindop, 'Taking stock at the start of the pay round', *Personnel Management* (August 1984), p. 21.

31 *Industrial Relations Code of Practice* (HMSO, 1972), para 42.

32 'Harmonization of Conditions', *IDS Study* No. 273 (September 1982), p. 1.

33 Institute of Manpower Studies, 'Staff status for manual workers', Company Manpower Commentary No. 9 (University of Sussex, 1981), p. 9.

34 'Staff status for manual workers'.

35 IDS, 'Salary progression schemes', p. 2.

6
Alternative forms of contract

We have concentrated on cost-effective strategies affecting the workforce, including flexibility in working time and flexibility of task. Yet the size and shape of this workforce is itself changing fast. The number of permanent staff working under a full-time contract of employment is diminishing. Referring to the number of full-time jobs in existence, Handy, for example, has said

> of the approximately 30 m adults of working age in Britain today, only about 16 m (or 53 per cent) have them. The rest are self-employed (2½ m and growing), part-time workers (5 m and growing), registered unemployed (3 m and likely to grow) and what the OECD quaintly calls 'unpaid domestic workers' (3.5 m, most, but not all, women). [1]

For the organization, flexibility extends to the use of alternative forms of contract with a number of contractual options available to suit different needs. Within a context of alternative *permanent* contracts of employment, there are contracts covering job-sharing and/or part-time working. There are alternative *temporary* contracts of employment, including the use of fixed-term contracts. There is scope for organizations to sub-contract work to self-employed individuals or to companies providing a particular service. There are contracts that provide for work to be undertaken *at* home, there are others providing for work to be undertaken *from* home. These homeworking contracts could, in turn, be linked to self-employment. There are more traditional forms of outworking.

This chapter will examine these alternative forms of contract. We will try to develop some of the more practical implications of these developments whilst not losing sight of the general trends that they suggest.

These general trends include a concentration within organizations on the 'core' workforce − a 'committed, versatile, skilled and knowledgeable group, who know the organization's problems and products'. [2] To employees, however, these developments represent a trend towards the casualization of work, a trend which has both advantages and disadvantages, depending in essence on the market for a person's knowledge and skills.

In examining the alternative forms of contract, we will be stressing their operational significance for management − the opportunities to reduce

DOI: 10.4324/9781003193043-6

costs and enhance flexibility of working. However there are also major social implications of these concepts. An increase in part-time working and job-sharing, for example, can have a major effect on unemployment. The stigma of unemployment too may be lessened if we could loosen the current association between 'work' and 'employment' – this link, after all, is of relatively recent origin. The breaking down of the link between being in 'work' and being in 'employment' (usually taken to mean working under a contract of employment) may be accompanied by a weakening of the barrier between work and leisure. It is the hallmark of many professional jobs that this distinction is a fine one – leisure and work cannot be easily separated, either by tasks or by time. In this context there is a higher degree of personal freedom – the freedom to work when one feels like it – be it Sunday or Wednesday, rather than working Monday to Friday 9am to 5pm. Of course there is another side to such 'freedom' – the self-employed will tell you that there may be freedom to choose when you work, but in practice, one is always at work. The distinction between work and leisure is indeed removed – there is no leisure!

Structural changes in employment

Within an organization, the employees with a continuing contract of employment are being defined as having 'primary employment'. These employees are distinguished from 'secondary employment' groups of 'peripheral' workers, which include staff on short-term contracts. A third group is sometimes added, consisting of people employed by a third party who are engaged on a particular task on a sub-contract basis, with no short- or long-term allegiance to the organization itself. This structural change in the nature of employment has been characterized as:

> the fragmentation of the internal labour market into increasingly peripheral and hence numerically variable groups of workers clustered around a numerically stable core group of employees, responsible for the key . . . activities of the organization.[3]

Such developments are motivated by a desire to concentrate the organization's skills on those things that are vital to it – what the Americans call 'sticking to the knitting'. Staff who are central to these activities are being drawn into the organizational fold, developed and cherished. Staff who are less central – who do not get a positive response to the question 'do we really need to do this ourselves?' – are being seen as 'peripheral'. We will return to this subject later when we examine the reasons for growth in self-employment contracts. Suffice it to say here that for managements the use of such employees has a number of advantages, particularly where work cannot be sustained long-term. Temporary staff, for example, can be more easily 'let go', sub-contract work can be terminated and so on. This position is often tacitly supported by the unions covering the permanent staff although they are nevertheless seeking comparable terms and conditions of employment for the 'peripheral' groups. This may provide complications for the unions in that these groups of workers are difficult to organize and the transitory nature of their employment provides them with little bargaining power.

The 'core' employees are working to a relatively traditional contract of employment of a continuing kind, subject to termination by notice from either party. The quest for enhanced flexibility is leading to explicit references in these contracts of employment to management's right to vary the employees' tasks, and place of work, according to the needs of the business. This also includes references to changing patterns of work, including shiftwork. This contractual authority to vary the terms of the contract is still not of course providing managers with complete freedom of action. Tribunals will continue to apply the test of reasonableness to such contractual terms, and 'key' employees will continue to be in a stronger position to limit the full application of such flexibility.

What characterizes such employment contracts, however, is their relative stability. While these employees are still affected by changes in patterns of demand for the organization's services, and to technological changes, they do have greater security in comparison with the 'peripheral' employees. Thus primary employment has been described as being about

> permanent commitment on both sides. It offers security, fringe benefits and the
> chance for training and career development.[4]

The employee who opts for the contract of employment in this way is seeking to maximize job security. Others will prefer to maximize what can be called 'market freedom' – the freedom to pick and choose work in the labour market to maximize income or opportunity for more work activity. These employees may, too, be motivated by what we call personal freedom, i.e. the freedom to choose to work on tasks at a certain time and place to suit the individual's personal preferences. Such people become freelance workers – self-employed – maximizing market and personal freedom but at the expense of job or income security.

Few, of course, are in a position to flourish in this freelance mode. Orchestral players, designers, writers and others can survive, but often at the cost of overwork. This is because the absence of job or income security tends to lead people to take on every work opportunity as it arrives lest it is their last. Others – not possibly at the top end of their profession – earn from this freelance mode a spasmodic income. Market freedom does not automatically lead to income being maximized. Personal freedom remains, but at the price of lower incomes and no job or income security.

So, at one end of our spectrum is the employee on a contract of employment of a permanent, ongoing kind. At the other extreme is the freelance 'consultant' operating under a contract for services – self-employed and casualized. The former offers job and income security. The latter offers considerable market and personal freedom. In between – at the employed end – are contracts of employment of a temporary nature, or contracts that are limited in time, either by reducing the hours worked (part-time working) or by specifying the duration of the contract (fixed-term contracts). Towards the self-employed end we find 'regular casuals' or individuals working on a 'first call' contract. We will explore in this chapter these different contractual modes, beginning with self-employment.

Self-employment

Inevitably there are problems of definition in examining self-employment. Legally, the key concept is that of the contract of employment, the absence of which distinguishes the self-employed from the employed.

The self-employed operate under a contract for services, which provides discretion to the contractor as to how and when to meet the work requirements of the contract. The exact determination of contractual status – employed or self-employed – has exercised tribunals and the minds of legal specialists for decades. A multiple test is now favoured, emphasizing for example the degree of control exercised by the employer, the extent to which the worker is 'integrated' into the business and the intention of the parties.[5] This is no academic question since the self-employed are liable for Schedule D income tax assessment rather than Schedule E. Tax is levied retrospectively on profits in the previous accounting year. Since payment is retrospective, because of inflation tax payments can be lower in real terms. A much wider range of tax deductible allowances can also be claimed, including the cost of travelling and hotel expenses, if incurred exclusively for business purposes.[6]

For the employer, there may be cost savings, since no national insurance payments are made in respect of the self-employed, no occupational pension scheme contributions are payable and many indirect costs of employment such as recruitment and training costs, holidays and sick pay, are reduced or avoided altogether. Whether self-employment is in fact cost-effective for the organization will depend on the level of fees demanded by the contractor and the quality of work provided. In many cases the fee demanded is 'grossed up' by the contractor to compensate for the absence of holiday, sick pay and other benefits and may result in self-employment being more expensive than contracts of employment. However the other benefits for the organization that we have noted mean that self-employment may still be cost-effective overall.

Growth of self-employment
Self-employment covers sole traders (i.e. one-person businesses), partnerships and individuals operating as limited liability companies. Also included under this heading are those operating a business under a franchise, which means the contractor has bought the right to market a

branded commodity or service. Some occupational groups have a long tradition of self-employment – lawyers and window cleaners, management consultants and taxi-drivers. Some kinds of unskilled workers, who hire out their labour or work on a commission-only basis in selling, operate on a self-employed basis. The 'lump' system in construction and civil engineering, whereby a nominally self-employed person sells his labour as a sub-contractor rather than as an employee, is perhaps the most notorious example in this field.[7]

How many people are self-employed? Putting to one side the size of the 'black economy' . . .

> The new estimates indicate that there were 2,057,000 self-employed people in Great Britain in 1981. . . . It represents an increase of . . . 12 per cent over mid 1979. . . . By mid 1981 self-employment represented almost 9 per cent of the employed labour force.[8]

The UK still has – at 9 per cent – a lower proportion of its labour force in self-employment than other European countries, whose average is 12.5 per cent. In Japan 19 per cent of the workforce is self-employed. In the UK under 10 per cent of self-employed work in manufacturing, 60 per cent work in services.[9] However, given that self-employment grew only slowly between 1961 and 1975 and then fell back slightly between 1975 and 1979, this increase of 12 per cent between 1979 and 1981 is striking and deserves further comment. At least four factors are relevant here:

- the desire of organizations to focus on activities which are central to their objectives;
- the cost-effectiveness of self-employment, particularly at senior levels in an organization;
- the link between redundancy, unemployment and self-employment; and
- the opportunities for the self-employed to maximize market freedom and personal freedom.

We examine each in turn.

Concentration on central activities
Many organizations in the 1980s have looked critically at their operations with a view to concentrating only on central activities. This concentration could then involve selling off activities that are not mainstream to that organization's purpose. These organizations also review the reasons for employing many one-off specialist occupations in their midst. Examples here include the organization which keeps its own printing facilities and buys in expensive equipment and expertise to produce printed articles, thus deflecting funds from its main activities: or the provision of catering facilities or of a security service. Increasingly, organizations are seeking to sub-contract such activities to individuals or companies who are special-

ists in these fields, and who can take over the administration of such services. This frees the parent organization from the financial and administrative commitment of providing services in which it has no particular expertise. Such changes within organizations have led to the widespread growth of freelance self-employed labour described above, particularly in printing and publishing (copyediting, proofreading, illustrating, etc.), medical services, legal services, cleaning and in maintenance.[10]

Cost-effectiveness

As we have already suggested, sub-contracting these activities may also be cost-effective:

> Add . . . the social costs and the attendant bureaucracy which governments load onto the wage contract and it is hardly surprising that most organizations calculate the true cost of employment at double the wage actually paid. It is simpler by far – and cheaper – to pay a fee not a wage.[11]

Rank Xerox, in relation to their 'networking' concept (of which more below) calculated that the true cost of an employee with a basic salary of £10,000 would be nearly £27,000 when facilities and employment costs were taken into account.[12] In this example, self-employment allied to homeworking has been less costly. Using freelance labour can also be a more efficient mode of operation, since the organization retains maximum flexibility to employ the contractor only at times when the workload demands it.

The link between redundancy, unemployment and self-employment

With over 3 million unemployed and continuing cut-backs, particularly in manufacturing industry, are redundant workers setting up businesses on their own account? From the available evidence it appears that this is happening only on a small scale – perhaps only rarely have more than 5 per cent of redundant workers made this transition.[13] The evidence tends to relate to manufacturing industry whereas self-employment is considerably greater in the services sector, and therefore the numbers of redundant workers becoming self-employed may be greater. Given that sub-contracting can be cost effective to the organization, consideration needs to be given by management to assisting employees to set up on their own account.

Opportunities for greater freedom

Finally, the growth of self-employment has been linked to the greater degree of personal freedom it provides, allowing the individual to control pace, type and duration of work for example. There may also be opportunities to maximize income, which would not be available to the employee operating under a contract of employment. The notion of self-employment as personally satisfying has however been critically examined in recent years. The self-employed are required to keep basic accounts, to negotiate agreements, handle advertising and so on. They can easily run up large bills for professional services; they are always subject to cash flow problems. We have already noted that casualization of employment has the major implication of generating insecurity – insecurity of work and insecurity of income. For these reasons, possibly, those who are self-employed tend to be a distinct social type – independent minded, egocentric and opposed to government, trade unions and large bureaucracies generally.[14] For the organization considering assisting current employees to transfer to a contract for services, these personal elements need to be taken into account.

Outworking and 'networking'
In one recent study just over 100,000 outworkers were identified, over half of them being employed in the service sector:

> outworkers were used predominantly for three types of work, clothing and leather work . . . packaging and repetitive assembly work, secretarial and clerical work. Only one-quarter of plants used outworkers for other types of work, including 'professional' work (such as research, teaching, legal and design work) driving and deliveries and sales agent work.[15]

The majority of organizations using outworking employed it in response to seasonal or other fluctuations in demand. Thus outworking is another form of flexibility of labour. The use of outworking also enables the organization to save the cost of providing a place of work – and in many large cities this could be a very big saving indeed.

This factor has certainly figured prominently in the Rank Xerox 'networking' concept, which combines homeworking with self-employment. Costing their London operation, for example, Rank found that one-third of total costs were related to facilities – rent, rates, etc. In addition many of these cost factors were outside of the organization's control.

Rank Xerox had also noticed a trend in their organization of individuals leaving secure jobs to go into business on their own. The management believed they could harness this motivation by offering self-employment contracts, while cutting their indirect costs by homeworking. They therefore set up their 'networking' scheme. Networkers were obliged to form limited liability companies and the networking contract formed by Rank Xerox is with those companies, not the individual. This clarifies the legal/tax position.

Rank themselves comment that to maintain the entrepreneurial independence of the networking company is the key to success of the concept and, in consequence of this:

1   The individual forming the company receives substantial training in selling his or her skills to other companies, in marketing and sales and in microcomputer skills.

2 All networking contracts are defined in terms of the output required, quantity, quality and timescale. How the job is done is a matter for the limited company involved.

3 No networking contract is given where completion of the task may require more than 100 man days, this being considered the maximum consistent with retaining the independence of the smallest size of limited company involved.

4 Completion of the task involved to a satisfactory standard results in payment of an agreed fee for the job. [16]

Great care is therefore taken that the individual should not work more than half his time on Rank Xerox business, so that independence is maintained. Many jobs formerly considered full-time have since proven to be capable of being performed in far less time once the individual is working for his or herself and from home.

This has been a major productivity gain, while the reduction of travelling time is important to the individual concerned. In order to specify requirements in detail Rank also found that a rigorous work analysis was required, and this too has proved beneficial to the organization.

On a more personal level, a number of factors have also been identified. The initial adjustment to networking, lasting around six months, seemed to be the hardest period, whilst isolation from work colleagues proved initially a difficulty. Weekly meetings in the company, the inclusion of networkers on mailing lists and regular social events minimized this problem, however. The networkers were described as 'determined', 'outward going' and 'resilient'. These people were clearly orientated towards self-employment, although career guidance consultants and counsellors are nevertheless required to identify potential 'networkers'. [17]

While each organization will have job holders in positions where their place of work is unimportant, we believe that this approach allied to self-employment has most potential for certain senior specialist jobs where the individual motivation is most pronounced. This is especially relevant to discrete tasks where standards can be easily set and monitored. Because self-employment appeals to a certain 'type', and because most organizations are concerned about control over standards and maintaining continuity over self-employed workers, organizations will be understandably cautious in extending the networking concept beyond the one-off specialists engaged in one-off activities. What may well grow at a faster pace is homeworking itself – under a more conventional contract of employment.

Homeworking
The availability at increasingly low cost of 'new technology' linking the office to the home through microcomputers connected to ordinary telephone lines and television sets is facilitating homeworking. Modern microcomputers can hold and relay messages as well as entering and re-

trieving data. The influence of such developments on systems analysts, systems installers, software engineers, sales representatives, service engineers, insurance agents and so on is enormous. Some of the problems encountered when working under a contract of employment but on a homeworking basis involve the homeworking employee, others are for the purchasing organizations. They include for the employee the allocation of sufficient space at home; the need for considerable preparation for the possible upheaval, domestic or otherwise, of such a change in work style; and the need for social contact. For the manager, there are questions to be dealt with about the implications of working at home on insurance, taxation and similar matters; the monitoring and control of staff and their time (planning and time accounting) and the need to be very specific on target setting.

Table 4 summarizes the advantages and disadvantages of homeworking from the management point of view:

Table 4 *Advantages and disadvantages for management of homeworking*

Advantages
- Allows more flexible working environment, particularly for tasks requiring concentration;
- Savings can be made on office rent, heat, light, etc.; and
- As work suitable for homeworking would likely be a discrete task, performance measurement may be made easier.

Disadvantages
- Only a single job could be undertaken at any point, thus allowing little or no opportunity for task switching;
- Because of this limited sphere of working, it would make assessment of promotional potential more difficult;
- Training new staff could be difficult – and would probably require a period of office-based work at the outset; and
- Selection of individuals suitable for homeworking needs careful attention, to ensure that factors such as possible domestic upheaval, ability of individual to be self-disciplined, and psychological effect on individual, are dealt with.

Trade union responses to self-employment and homeworking

While the trade unions have not specifically responded to the recent interest in self-employment, their views on sub-contracting generally are well known. In relation to 'the lump', for example, one writer has said that the main union argument against it was that it led to wage cutting and to the complete undermining of national trade union conditions. The trade unions stood against the lump because

> it undermined their ability to regulate uniform time, wages and secondly because . . . [the lump] . . . was traditionally the employers' method of breaking trade union control of the labour process. The lump was understood to be an

attempt to lower the standards of training in the industry. In this sense it was a practice that aimed at lowering wages.[18]

For other writers, self-employment is seen to divide workers, to lead to a higher level of accidents, to lead to fewer apprentices, to lead to reduced standards and to overwork.[19]

In many sectors outworkers and freelancers are non-unionized.[20] as the relevant unions have been opposed to such contractual forms for the reasons described above, little effort has been put into recruiting them. The unions may be forced into adopting a less defensive posture. Handy has argued that something like a return to the old guild system is required as employment returns to the format of sub-contracting and outworking that characterized the pre and early Industrial Revolution. The unions could develop in this direction – the (TUC-affiliated) Writers' Guild of Great Britain may be an indicator.

In other sectors, such as the music industry, a post-entry closed shop exists which provides for union membership for self-employed workers. Although this gives the Musicians' Union a certain national standing, membership participation in its affairs remains low.

Within companies and public organizations the trade unions concentrate on defining the grounds on which sub-contract labour can be used. This generally falls into two categories. First, where because of peak demands on the organization, internal resources, even with maximum overtime, cannot cope. Second, where a job requires particular skills and knowledge, and these are not available within the organization. The unions generally require to be consulted prior to the introduction of sub-contractors, to satisfy themselves that one of these two criteria is being met. The absence of consultation, or the use of sub-contract staff contrary to these or other agreed criteria has often been the cause of industrial action, including national stoppages.[21]

Union opposition to the extension of contracts for services, unless for reasons referred to above, is another reason why organizations will proceed cautiously in this area. However, while tax advantages for the individual remain, and while market freedom can continue to be, exploited by the self-employed, the unions' ability to control developments in self-employment will remain limited.

The TUC have defined homeworking as 'work done in the home for another person or for sale to another person'.[22] They drew the distinction between homeworking and outworking – the latter being work done on premises away from the home, but not in a factory as such. They are concerned about the social isolation of homeworkers and seek to develop greater legal regulations of homeworking, particularly through legal minimum terms and conditions of employment. In general, the TUC note, homeworkers are 'self-employed'. In their policy proposals, they argue that unions should insist that homeworkers become employees of the company concerned and PAYE and national insurance contributions are deducted from wages.

Temporary employment

In the search for greater flexibility of labour there has been a considerable increase in the use of temporary employment in recent years. This has been particularly noticeable in the use of agency staff for typing and other office work.

In its typical form, this can be distinguished from self-employment in that temporary workers are engaged on a contract of employment for a short, usually unspecified, time period. Other temporary workers may be genuinely 'casual' – employed for very short periods, less than four weeks. Some people may be regularly employed by one employer but for discontinuous periods of less than four weeks at a time: 'regular casuals'. These are particularly found in the hotel and catering industry and in the performing arts. Still other contracts may be temporary in the sense that a specified period of time is described in the contract. These are generally referred to as fixed-term contracts.

Temporary employees are taken on for a variety of reasons, of which the most common is to meet seasonal peaks in demand, which are of short-term duration – warehouse staff just before Christmas, airline staff in the summer, and so on. Managements are increasingly using temporary staff to meet requirements for increased output which is not necessarily seasonal – it may be simply a number of new orders where, however, the increased production cannot be guaranteed in the long term. Management in such circumstances prefer to take on temporary staff who can be made permanent if the higher volume of work is sustained. This avoids redundancy announcements, consultation periods and the like which would be necessary if permanent staff were taken on, only to be subsequently declared redundant.

Temporary workers are also used, more traditionally, for holiday, sickness and maternity cover, although their use in holiday and sickness cover is becoming less common as organizations insist upon the flexible use of their workforce to cover such circumstances.

Most organizations accept that pay rates for temporary workers should be pro rata to permanent employees. However, surveys have shown that while holidays are sometimes provided to temporary employees at the same level as permanent employees, sick pay is less common – and those that do provide it generally require a qualifying period of three or six months before employees become eligible.[23] Statutory sick pay is of course payable after three months' service.[24] Occupational pension schemes are rarely open to temporary employees.

Although the use of temporary workers may provide an additional element of flexibility, the organization using them needs to assess carefully whether temporary employees are cost-effective. Doubts arise because of the cost of recruiting and training temporary staff, measured especially in terms of lost production during training. At the point when temporary staff become effective, they may be laid off. This training cost may diminish if some temporary workers are recruited into similar work on successive occasions and indeed it would seem sensible to develop a pool of 'permanent temporary' staff in order to minimize the indirect costs of using temporary labour. This is a common practice in the air transport industry, for example, where such 'temps' are also used as a source of recruitment to permanent posts.

Trade unions have generally accepted the use of temporary staff to meet seasonal patterns of demand or to cover absence. They generally seek to ensure such staff receive the same pay and conditions as permanent staff. Unions also seek information about the employment of temporary staff. Some union agreements limit the number of temporary staff and the level of job which they carry out; others try to ensure that temporary workers are included in closed shop agreements.[25] Trade unions have in recent times developed policies which accept the need for temporary labour only as stand-ins for permanent staff.[26]

Proposed EEC directive on temporary work
The European Commission adopted a proposal for a directive on temporary work in 1982. An amended proposal was published in 1984. Extracts from this revised directive are summarized in Table 5. Most importantly, this draft directive sets a maximum duration for temporary contracts of three months, renewable once, although an extension beyond six months may be authorized. This directive has produced widespread opposition from employer organizations, largely on the grounds that the directive restricts flexibility in deployment of labour. It has been welcomed by the TUC.

Job-sharing

Interest in job-sharing as an alternative form of contract has grown in the 1980s. Management are attracted to a scheme which has significant operational advantages as well as wider social benefits. Union interest in job-sharing is less marked, but support has been given by a number of unions.

Job-sharing can be defined as an arrangement whereby

two people share the responsibilities of one full-time job, and, share the pay and benefits between them in proportion to the hours each works.

This distinguishes this form of contract from part-time work in that it is two people sharing one job rather than one person working reduced hours. It is important to maintain the distinctiveness of job-sharing since contractual requirements are included in the job-sharers' contract which would not normally be part of the contract of a part-timer.

Table 5 *Extracts from EEC Draft Directive on Temporary Work*

Art. 3

Labour supply contracts may be concluded only

(a) to cope with a temporary reduction of the workforce present in the undertaking; or

(b) to perform occasional tasks of a transient nature; or

(c) for other legitimate reasons which justify the limited duration of the contract.

Except in the case of (a) the maximum duration of each assignment shall be three months, renewable once. An extension beyond six months may be authorized by the competent authorities if shown to be justified by exceptional circumstances.

No post may be occupied by successive temporary workers after expiry of the above periods.

Art. 6

Unless collective agreements applicable in the temporary employment business or covering the temporary employment sector otherwise provide, the remuneration of a temporary worker must be comparable to that of workers with equivalent occupational skills, experience and duties in the user undertaking.

Art. 8

When intending to have recourse to temporary workers the user undertaking must inform worker representatives in good time – telling them the reasons, the duration, the numbers, the nature and location of the assignments – and must answer relevant questions raised by the worker representatives. This information must also be given periodically to worker representatives in the form of a general report.

Art. 9

Unless collective agreements reached by temporary employment businesses otherwise provide, temporary workers must be subject to the same working conditions (whether laid down by law, collective agreement or customary practice) – as regards shift work, night work, weekly rest periods, work schedules, public holidays, safety, health and industrial medicine – as employees of the user undertaking. They must also have access on the same terms to any communal transport services or other communal services (such as canteen facilities).

Job-sharing is likely to be of most relevance as an alternative approach to filling vacancies. This focus on vacancies rather than existing employees reflects our view that few employees are likely to accept an arrangement involving a 50 per cent reduction in pay. There may be some limited scope for job-sharing, particularly in a redundancy context, but organizations who choose to introduce job-sharing for existing employees may be disappointed. We believe it is more realistic to focus on vacancies. The advantages and disadvantages of job-sharing are identified in Table 6.

The most important advantage is the opportunity to cover all holiday absence and possibly sickness absence by requiring one partner to stand in for the other during these periods. Clearly covering for all sickness absence may prove impractical, because of the short notice one partner would be given. Cover for all holidays, and sickness absence of more than three days, is a typical contractual requirement however. Wording similar to the following is often used in the offer letter or written statement.

It is a feature of this job-sharing contract that if your partner is absent on holiday, you must be prepared to work additional hours so that the job is fully covered for the normal contractual hours.

In addition, you are required to cover for sickness absence of your job sharing partner whenever reasonably required by management. You will be given not less than two days' notice of this requirement.

The extra costs identified in the disadvantages are not significant. There are certain practical problems to be overcome, particularly in connection with the compatibility of sharers and achieving a balance in such things as overtime working both between partners and between job-sharers and full-time staff.

Table 6   *Operational advantages and disadvantages for management of job-sharing*

Advantages
- Opportunity to cover all holiday absence in a contractual way;
- Opportunity to cover long-term sickness, and possibly short-term sickness, in a contractual way;
- Absence levels may be lower with commitments covered by periods off work (absence levels of part-timers less than that of full-timers anyway);
- Performance levels likely to be higher because of shorter periods at work;
- Can use job-sharing partners to expand output quickly if required;
- Job-sharers form an experienced pool of labour available for switching to full-time work if required; and
- Job-sharers likely to be more cooperative and responsive to change.

Disadvantages
- Marginal extra recruitment costs;
- Some extra training costs – both at point of recruitment and subsequently as products/technology changes;
- Job-sharers may be incompatible;
- Job-sharers may be perceived as 'second class' employees;
- Communications become more complex;
- Difficulties if one sharer leaves in replacing with compatible partner;
- Allocation of overtime between partners and between job sharers and full-time staff will need careful handling; and
- May not attract male unemployed because of the relationship between part-time salary and state benefits.

The operational advantages referred to above make no reference to the social implications of job sharing, but these are in themselves important. With the population of the UK that is available for work increasing by ¾ million between 1980 and 1986 and 1¼ million by the end of the decade, job-sharing presents an opportunity for job creation. Job-sharers, particularly if they are school-leavers, can get a foothold into employment, receive training and have the opportunity of progressing to full-time employment.

One question still remains for the organization convinced of the merits of job-sharing in principle – which jobs are most suitable for job-sharing? This can be answered by taking account of the following factors:

- Is the job structured such that different individual contributions have little influence on results?
- Does very little new information occur on a daily basis?
- Is there regular personal contact with suppliers/customers?
- Are initial and follow up training requirements minimal?
- Is little travel to work required?

Much has been written about the ways in which certain employers, notably GEC Telecommunications Ltd, have introduced job-sharing. At GEC Telecom job-sharing was aimed at school-leavers, who are required to attend a course of further education at a local technical college on one of their 'off days'. Within the production area, job-sharers work on a 'week-on/week-off' basis. Clerical workers however operate a two-and-a-half day week. One study of this arrangement referred to high attendance rates among job-sharing teams and added that

> they demonstrate a considerable degree of loyalty to each other, often covering for their sharer if s/he is sick or needs to take time off. The commercial benefits that the scheme can bring were amply demonstrated in December 1982 when, following a long running delay in the production of a telephone component due to the quality control problems of one of their suppliers, the company was able to catch up by inviting its job sharers to work on a full-time basis for a period of several weeks.[27]

The trade union reaction to job-sharing has generally been a cautious one. Many regard it as a poor substitute for a full-time job, though they may subsequently admit that a job-sharing opportunity is better than no job at all. Management tend to stress the social dimension of job-sharing, in particular the bias towards youth which may be a consequence of job-sharing. It is possible to guarantee no existing employees will be forced to job-share, and that terms and conditions of employment will be pro rata. And, of course, the fact that job-sharing can double the number of potential members for the relevant union is a further selling point.

Minimum hours contract

Another alternative form of contract which is related to part-time working (which we covered in detail in chapter 4) is the minimum hours contract, or minimum–maximum contract as it is sometimes called. This is a very simple concept which has considerable operational advantage. It involves specifying to an employee the minimum number of hours to be worked in a week; payment for these is guaranteed. This level is typically set at 20 hours. However, the contract in addition specifies the right of management to require the employee to work up to a pre-defined upper limit in any week. This is generally set at 25 or possibly 30 hours. Hours between the minimum and the maximum are paid at flat rate and a period of notice, 24 or 48 hours, is specified in the contract before the employee is asked to work the extra hours.

Such a clause inserted into part-time contracts provides obvious operational advantages to management who can vary the employees' hours of work within these limits to suit business requirements. In this, the minimum hours contract resembles the philosophy behind the annual hours concept described in chapter 4.

Given that over 20 per cent of the working population of the UK is part-time such a clause may have widespread application.[28]

'First call' contract

It is increasingly likely that many key individuals employed permanently by organizations will seek opportunities to exploit their marketability externally. This tends to be frowned on by employers who wish, understandably, to retain the full benefits of the person whose salary they are paying. Some of these specialists may as a result opt for freelance work; others will join organizations less restrictive in outlook. One consequence of such pressures is the development of a 'first call' contract. This provides an organization with the right to first call on an employee's time. If, however, the organization has no requirement at a particular point, the employee is free to undertake work elsewhere, subject only to the employing organization opting to apply the 'first call' principle.

It is unlikely that such a contractual term will ever be widely used, but given the market pressure on certain key skills, such flexibility for the employee may be attractive.

Conclusions

In this chapter we have explored self-employment, outworking, networking, homeworking, temporary employment, job-sharing, minimum hours contracts, first call contracts – and this is by no means an exhaustive list of alternative forms of contract. In chapter 4 we examined the development of a Saturday/Sunday contract as well as various forms of part-time shiftworking.

For the employer these options represent different degrees of flexibility – flexibility to match labour to operational requirements. There are also opportunities as we have seen for cost savings. There are cost-effective alternatives here for organizations. Competitors abroad, particularly in other parts of Europe and in Japan, are using such concepts and the onus is on UK management to be more imaginative in future in the deployment of alternative forms of contract.

For the trade unions and employees, the alternatives represent a movement towards a more casualized workforce. Self-employment, subcontracting, temporary employment – these provide opportunities for greater personal freedom and for freedom to exploit the labour market. For workers in short supply with scarce skills, this market freedom can produce high rewards. However, for most people in a context of high unemployment, market freedom is irrelevant and casualization leads to greater insecurity, of both job and income.

The trend toward homeworking and part-time work (including jobsharing) can lead to increased leisure and greater personal control over the timing of work and leisure. Part-time working has considerable operational advantages, and has major social overtones too.

The concept of the 'core' workforce of permanent staff and the 'peripheral' workforce of temporary staff may be too simplistic. Organizations will be more complex than this. The permanent staff will themselves break down into full-time and part-time, to suit the needs of the business and individual preferences. The 'peripheral' staff may include permanent temporaries with a continuing regular commitment for periods each year to the organization. They may even be paid a retainer for their services. It is a complex and dynamic picture, and a challenging one for managers.

References

1   C. Handy, 'The organization revolution and how to harvest it', *Personnel Management* (July 1984), p. 23.
2   Handy, 'The organization revolution and how to harvest it', p. 24.
3   J. Atkinson; quoted in 'The emergence of two new working nations', *Financial Times*, 23 April 1984.
4   N. Bosanquet; quoted in *Financial Times*, 23 April 1984.
5   'What is an employee', *IDS Brief* 272 (March 1984).
    P. Keighton, 'Employment and self-employment', *Employment Gazette* (May 1983).
    The official definition of self-employment is laid down in the *Social Security Act, 1975* (ch. 14, 1 (2) 1) as follows:

    Employed earner means a person who is gainfully employed under a contract of service, or in an office (including elective office) with emoluments chargeable to income tax under Schedule E; and self-employed earner means a person who is gainfully employed other wise than in employed earner's employment (whether or not he is also employed in such employment).

6   We are grateful to R. Goward for allowing us to see material in his unpublished thesis entitled 'Self-employment – small beginnings, big future?' (Polytechnic of Central London, 1982).

7   T. Austrin, 'The "Lump" in the UK construction industry', in T. Nichols (ed.), *Capital and Labour* (Fontana, 1980).
    Report on Construction Industry (Phelps Brown Report), Cmnd 3714 (HMSO, 1968), chapter 6.

8   'How many self-employed?', *DE Gazette* (February 1983), p. 55.

9   *Labour Force Survey* (HMSO, 1979).

10 C. Hakim, 'Employers' use of homework, outwork and freelances', *DE Gazette* (April 1984), p. 146.

11 C. Handy, 'Where management is leading', *Management Today* (December 1982), p. 51.

12 P. Judkins and D. West, *Networking – the distributed office* (Rank Xerox, 1982), p. 4.

13 P. Johnson, 'From redundancy to self-employment', *Personnel Management* (December 1980), p. 37.

14 J. Curran and J. Stanworth, 'Some reasons why small is not always beautiful', *New Society*, 14 December 1978.

15 Hakim, 'Employers' use of homework, outwork and freelances', p. 146.

16 Judkins and West, *Networking – the distributed office*, p. 9.

17 Judkins and West, *Networking – the distributed office*, p. 16.

18 Austrin, 'The "Lump" in the UK construction industry', p. 305.

19 Dave Lamb, 'The Lump – an heretical analysis', Solidarity Pamphlet (1975).

20 Hakim, 'Employers' use of homework, outwork and freelances', p. 149.

21 The national dock strike in mid July 1984 was ostensibly because criteria for the use of sub-contract labour was not adhered to by the British Steel Corporation at Immingham.

22 TUC, *Homeworking: a TUC Statement* (1978), p. 2. The TUC have also produced a Code of Practice on Homeworking (1978).

23 'Temporary workers', *IDS Study* No. 295 (August 1983).

24 Unless the contract was preceded by one entered into with the same employer and the interval between contracts was not more than 8 weeks and the total period of the previous and current contract exceeds 13 weeks.

25 For a detailed summary of the trade union position on temporary and fixed-term working see *Labour Research Department Bargaining Report* No. 26 (May/June 1983).

26 *Labour Research Department Bargaining Report* No. 26, p. 7.

27 M. Syrett, *Employing Job Sharers, Part-time and Temporary Staff* (IPM, 1983), p. 48.
    See also 'Why split jobs', *Industrial Relations Review and Report*, 287 (January 1983), pp. 2–8.

28 For more details on the extent of part-time working, see 'Part-time work – a survey', *Industrial Relations Review and Report* 320 (May 1984).
    O. Robinson and J. Wallace, 'Growth and utilization of part-time labour in Great Britain', *DE Gazette* (September 1984), pp. 391–6.

7
Forms of employee involvement

So far we have discussed the content of managerial strategies in key areas of industrial relations. Industrial relations is, however, as much about process as content and it is to developments in the key process areas that the remaining chapters are devoted.

In this chapter we examine communications and consultative structures and changes in the level of collective bargaining. The next chapter examines overall relationships with trade unions in detail.

The 1980s have seen a renewed focus on forms of employee involvement. In a context of rapid technical and organizational change, management has sought to involve trade unions and employees in business developments through direct communications and through consultative structures. Collective bargaining as a form of employee involvement remains predominant in UK organizations; over two-thirds of employees have their pay and conditions affected in some way by collective bargaining.[1] In the public sector, bargaining continues to be centralized, although developments in the direction of local bargaining are occurring. In the private sector, the evidence available suggests a move away from industry level bargaining to company bargaining and, within organizations, from central to local bargaining.[2] The issue of industrial democracy as described in the 1977 Bullock report receives less attention nowadays, although an interest in participation remains through the European Commission initiatives on the provisions 'for information and consultation' and on employee involvement, known as the Vrederling proposals and the draft Fifth Directive respectively.

This chapter will refer to these much maligned proposals, but will concentrate more on two aspects of employee involvement which reflect the key trends in vanguard organizations: communications and consultative structures and levels of collective bargaining.

Managerial objectives in these two areas, and in the overall relationships with the unions that we consider in the next chapter, will be no different from the cost-effectiveness criterion which we have stressed throughout. In these areas cost-effectiveness requires an emphasis on ensuring that management's messages are relayed to employees as quickly and accurately as possible; a mechanism for ensuring that employee concerns, fears and expectations are relayed up the managerial

DOI: 10.4324/9781003193043-7

chain effectively; approaches which release creativity and encourage innovation and flexibility amongst the workforce; but which do not involve a direct challenge to management on key policy issues.

Guest's analysis of the approaches to participation is useful here.[3] He distinguishes between 'individual' (or 'direct') and 'representative' participation. We follow this distinction below, beginning with a review of developments in the area of 'individual' participation. Guest also distinguishes between 'policy' and 'executive' issues, defining policy issues as

> such things as the goals of the enterprise, what markets the company should be in, what share of the market should be achieved, what sources of finance are appropriate, where . . . units should be located and what sort of personnel policies on issues such as employment, equal opportunity, redundancy and, indeed, participation should be pursued.[4]

Executive issues cover those subjects that ensure the effective implementation of those policies, and these in turn may be long-term (such as those relating to terms and conditions of employment) or more immediate task related issues.

We see a trend both towards 'individual' participation and away from policy issues towards this day-to-day task-related subject matter. The abandonment of the worker directors experiment in the Post Office is typical of this move in the level of participation;[5] the growing interest in quality circles is further evidence of a trend towards focusing on issues of day-to-day concern to the workforce.

This focus on task related issues stresses increasing communication and involvement but at an individual or small group level, and includes a new emphasis on local consultation through supervision and junior line management. The operational pressures on these levels of management, for example, to introduce new machinery, equipment or office systems means that organizations have increasingly seen the necessity to develop coherent communications policies and packages and to monitor their effectiveness. More organizations than hitherto are finding that time spent in the development of coherent approaches to communication and involvement is well repaid, even against the harsh criterion of cost-effectiveness.

Communication and consultative structures

Workplace communication

The continuing focus on efficiency improvements has led to much reorganization, rationalization and technical change. As we have said, management has increasingly recognized that employees need to be informed of the objectives of these changes in order that their greater understanding can lead to greater commitment. Through this process of communication, too, it is possible that problems that may have arisen in the implementation phase of any efficiency exercise can be minimized. Ideas will arise from the workforce on how efficiency improvements can be secured, and such cooperation from employees in tackling issues is fundamental to the future success of any organization.

There are other pressures creating this further interest in communications. The Japanese attention to communication processes is well known, and appears to offer a number of advantages, particularly in the speed with which changes seem to be implemented and the greater identification of employees with the business. EEC draft directives on the provision of information and consultation (about which more below) have also highlighted this area. The requirements of the 1982 Employment Act for all companies with more than 250 employees to include a statement in their annual reports on the steps they have taken during the year on information and consultation has also had some influence.

There is an enormous variety of approaches to workplace communication and we can do no more here than say a few words about mechanisms that have become increasingly widespread recently. These include to adopt Guest's framework 'individual' approaches:

- Direct communication;
- Mass communication meetings;
- Departmental meetings;
- Work group meetings;
- Quality circles; and
- Attitude surveys.

We will examine all of these mechanisms in turn.

Direct communication through management
Some organizations are now consciously encouraging their junior line managers to spend more time with employees to discuss work and industrial relations issues with them and to feed their reactions through to more senior managers. The need for such encouragement is surprising, but reflects the previous use by these organizations of the unions as the main 'alternative channel' of communications to the workforce. This certainly became widespread in some industries – particularly in the manufacturing sector – in the 1960s and 1970s. These industries are now beginning to examine the more individually oriented approaches in banking, insurance, health service and other sectors where highly unionized workforces still nevertheless expect direct communication from and to their management.

There are occasional problems in these industries, but in general, despite the fact that pay levels may not be high, industrial relations is good and the employee representatives often perform a more limited role in comparison with their counterparts in manufacturing.

The advantages to management of approaching their employees directly hardly need rehearsing. It not only minimizes the likelihood of employees hearing the 'wrong' message, it also reinforces the role of line management. Increasing and improving the relationship between the manager and his subordinates will further develop the individual orientation of workers.

This development, commonplace for most of Britain's more successful companies, is increasingly marked in both public and private sector organizations. Managements that have made such moves are enthusiastic about its value. It may be that this quiet, almost unnoticed, change in the role that managers play in communications has had a significant influence on industrial relations in this country. It is increasingly being noticed that even in very similar environments – comparing nearby social security offices, one small private port with another, or between road hauliers – relationships are often sufficiently varied even to affect responses to calls for industrial action. The ability of managers to communicate with their individual employees is central to the development of that relationship.

Mass communication meetings

One approach that has been adopted by a number of organizations includes the exposure of the most senior managers in an establishment to the workforce at regular intervals. This can be instructive – both for the boss and the employees! For practical reasons, these meetings are generally handled either functionally or according to grades – say all manual employees, then all 'staff' employees. The 'state of the union' meetings as they are sometimes called, are usually short and infrequent – two or three times a year. The aim of such meetings is to encourage an identification with the unit wider than the employees' own workgroup, provide an opportunity for the boss to relay certain key messages about the progress of the organization and, through questions, allow issues to be raised directly with senior management. Answers are subsequently provided through departmental management to avoid any danger of this group being bypassed.

Some companies now use video presentations by the MD, with questions taken by a local senior manager, to achieve these objectives.

Departmental meetings

Meetings of employees within departments are also becoming more common. The aim is usually to cover all employees; some organizations also include in their meetings the departmental shop stewards. The meeting is chaired by the departmental manager or supervisor and focuses on items specific to that department. There is usually an attempt to ensure that items 'in procedure', or which are part of the trade union consultation and negotiation framework in the establishment, are referred to the appropriate joint consultation or negotiating body. In this way, the departmental meeting does not develop into a negotiating body.

The purpose of such meetings has been summed up by one organization using this approach as follows:

> The intention is that the communication at these meetings should be two-way.
> Employees are expected to raise items which are of interest or causing concern.

It is accepted that not everybody will raise points at meetings, but, on the other hand if there are strong enough feelings about an issue, someone in the department will bring it up and everyone will hear what is said in reply.[6]

Workgroup meetings

Meetings of the workgroup, led by the supervisor, tend to take place more frequently than the departmental meetings – indeed in many cases they take place daily. They are generally short, and focus on practical day-to-day targets and problems; for example of quality or deliveries. Such meetings are useful in developing the cohesiveness of a workgroup, especially where it is multi-functional, consisting of technicians, craftsmen, semi-skilled, clerical and supervisory staff for example. The 'morning assemblies' found in many Japanese companies are typical of such workgroup meetings. A closely related technique, known as team briefing, has been defined as

> a system of communication operated by line management. Its objective is to make sure that *all* employees know what they and others in the Company are doing and why. It is a management information system. It is based on the leader and his/her team getting together in a group to talk about things that are relevant in their work on a regular basis for half an hour.[7]

This system has evolved from briefing groups, a technique which was often better in theory than practice. That system, which involved passing information down through the management chain, often suffered from information which was out of date, lacking in relevance and not understood by the manager handling the brief. The team briefing or workgroup meeting approach, focusing on local issues, largely overcomes these problems, and ensures that discussion is kept task-related.

Quality circles

Quality circles arose in Japan in the early 1960s; by the 1980s there were in Japan an estimated one million such circles covering 10 million employees. They consist of small groups (5–10) of employees who meet voluntarily for around one hour on a regular basis to identify and hopefully solve operational problems. In the UK a National Society of quality circles has stimulated further interest in this approach. Organizations introducing quality circles have claimed increased productivity, improved motivation, improved quality and the development of a team approach to problem solving. The record of quality circles is notably patchy, but the financial savings and efficiency improvements shown as a result of many quality circles are impressive.

Some recent research into quality circles has suggested that the following factors, amongst others, need to be taken into account:

- Before introducing quality circles full communications between management, shopfloor and the trade unions is necessary to explain the purpose and operation of quality circles.

- Circle leaders and members should receive training tailored to their individual needs.

- Circle members must be allowed complete flexibility in the projects they choose.

- Management commitment to the quality circle programme is vital to its success.

- The progresses, achievements and developments of quality circles need to be communicated and publicized throughout the company.[8]

    Of these, the evidence is that continuing public support of the top management is critical.

Attitude surveys
Many organizations now use forms of attitude survey, and many consultancies offer them. Establishing employees' concerns and opinions is central to the vanguard organization's approach. They attempt to do this through a range of mechanisms; avoiding reliance on just local management or trade union channels because of the special pleading and filtering of information involved. Attitude surveys have been more common in non-union companies; but unionized organizations are finding that, provided they are presented in an acceptable way, union members are usually happy to be able to express their views.

Representative approaches to participation
The focus on task-related issues and the increasing development of alternative channels alongside collective bargaining has also led to a renewed emphasis on *representative* approaches to participation. One senior manager in a local authority told us that as cash limits had been restricted and bargaining issues reduced in number the unions had

> gone back, really, to where they started in this authority – the old nitty-gritty ground-level consultation. Of course, we're very happy with that – the only problem is that its time-consuming. We've regenerated consultative committees in several departments.

This is not an isolated development. There have been significant changes in two areas – the more widespread use of joint consultation through trade union representatives, and a newer concept, 'advisory boards'. We review each in turn.

Joint consultation through trade unions
Joint consultation committees were initially seen as vehicles for tackling the necessity for increased production between the wars and particularly after the Second World War. The growth of collective bargaining in the 1960s and 1970s led to the relevance of such committees being questioned and they were summed up, somewhat dismissively, as covering 'tea and toilets'. In the 1980s, in a new context, there has been renewed interest in

this approach – primarily as a mechanism for discussing 'non-negotiable' matters of general interest to the workforce. The changed bargaining relationship of the 1980s has meant that in some organizations the ability of trade unions to negotiate every issue has diminished. In this context trade union support for joint consultation makes sense, since it provides information of general interest, an opportunity to comment or question and an opportunity to 'negotiate' in practice. The unions have emphasized the importance of consultation at the earliest practicable opportunity; for example, at the planning stage of the introduction of 'new' technology.

A number of points of detail in the area of joint consultation have also changed. There is firstly increasing reliance on departmental consultative committees, consisting of departmental managers and departmental stewards. As we will explore in chapter 8, management have been keen to develop the role of the departmental steward, to avoid problems becoming too centralized around the senior steward and personnel manager or senior manager concerned. Secondly, joint consultation committees are more integrated with each other – with clearer reporting lines between central and departmental committees, and clearer definitions of roles. Thirdly, management are understandably keen that joint consultation occurs with all the recognized trade unions in an establishment or department. This saves time and money, and is a more effective mechanism for consultation. In many instances, managements are stating as a pre-condition to the establishment of a committee that all trade unions must be represented.

Company advisory boards
Company advisory boards in the UK are of relatively recent origin, and have been associated with 'no-strike' clauses and 'pendulum' arbitration. A number of electronics companies, including some Japanese organizations operating in the UK, have signed such agreements with the EETPU.[9]

Company advisory boards in this context consist of employees who may or may not be trade union members. An example of the terms of reference and composition of one such Board is shown in Table 7.

In this example, elections take place by a majority vote amongst the members of the constituencies, in a secret ballot. The board generally meets monthly. In another example members of the board are required to report back to their constituencies, and no member may be mandated on any issue but must be free to reach a conclusion based on the arguments propounded. Two observers, who are changed for each meeting, sit in to avoid any accusation that something is going on behind closed doors.

The attractions of such company advisory boards include the coverage of the workforce, the refusal to allow mandated views and the link in one forum between pay negotiations and discussions on the organization's performance and plans. These approaches deserve serious attention, but are more readily achieved in a 'greenfield' site rather than one where joint

Table 7 *Terms of reference and composition of a typical advisory board*

Terms of reference

The company advisory board will be charged with the responsibility of reviewing the performance and plans of the company and with recommending to the company policies, procedures and practices which will be to the mutual benefit of the company and its employees.

The advisory board will keep itself informed of appropriate legislation, codes of practice and trade union information, so as to make recommendations which will best satisfy the aspirations of the majority of employees whilst protecting the rights of minority groups. In making any recommendation the CoAB must also recognize that the company must meet its commercial obligations and objectives at the same time as fulfilling its responsibilities to employees, its customers and society at large.

Composition

'Constituencies' will be identified covering coherent sections of the Company's total workforce. Employees in these groups will be invited to nominate candidates for election as representatives on the advisory board for a two-year term of office. In the setting up of the advisory board terms of appointment will range from six months to two years so as to provide for elections every six months.

---

consultation and collective bargaining is already well established along more traditional lines.

Summary

In developing its relationship with employees, organizations have a wide range of options available in the fields of communication and consultations, from mass meetings of the workforce to quality circles and to company advisory boards. The focus may be the individual, the group or the trade unions. In choosing a particular approach, much will depend on the attitude of senior management, on the culture of the organization and on what management is trying to achive. In practice there is usually a combination of these options and a wide variety of non-verbal, written and audio-visual options. There is we believe a move to individualize communication and involvement and to keep them focused on task-related issues. This means that, certainly for the all-important verbal communications, individual, often junior, line managers develop an expanding role. They require coherent policies to guide them. These policies have to be internally consistent, and consistent with management's approach to collective bargaining. It is to this second key area that we now turn.

Collective bargaining

In the 1960s the Donovan Commission emphasized the importance of collective bargaining in achieving and maintaining a constructive approach to industrial relations and throughout the 1970s management were focusing on the need for 'formal, comprehensive and authoritative company or factory agreements'. Management discussed the implications of the formal and informal system and pondered upon the loss of managerial control, to which the Commission drew attention. 'Informality', 'fragmentation', 'chaotic wage structures' ... the Donovan analysis is indeed well known, and its influence substantial. Although not all managers were convinced by the trend towards greater formalization in industrial relations, the momentum was irreversible, and new or revised procedures covering disputes, grievance handling, shop stewards' functions and so on became – and have remained – one of the main preoccupations of most Personnel Managers.

Focusing on collective bargaining in the 1980s, the concern is less about informality or fragmentation than about achieving organizational objectives in the most cost-effective manner. Hence emphasis is now being placed on local rather than national agreements and on decentralizing bargaining in both public and private sectors.

Levels of bargaining

For all but the smallest companies there are essentially four options in the level at which they bargain:

1 Bargaining at national level (multi-employer bargaining);
2 Bargaining at Group level (central bargaining);
3 Bargaining at establishment level (local bargaining); and
4 Bargaining at both Group and establishment level (multi-level bargaining);

The theoretical range of options is much wider than this, and it is often necessary to complicate the discussion by introducing additional variables such as the manual/non-manual nature of the workforce and the focus of negotiations, general pay increases, conditions of employment or productivity bargaining. With these provisos however, we will discuss each option in turn.

Multi-employer bargaining

Bargaining at national level through employers' organizations has declined in importance in recent years, although it still remains significant. The CIR found that

> in most industries covered by an employers' organization, the majority of firms are in membership.

The main advantage of multi-employer bargaining was that

> it offered a possible counter to Trade Union power and therefore a possible protection against a tendency for trade unions to employ leap-frogging tactics ... and it provides a framework of wages and conditions as a reference point for domestic arrangements. [10]

In a more recent study, 75 per cent of establishments covered said they were members of an employers' organization. [11] However, in this study, the overall picture was one of establishments who were members of employers' organizations, using them primarily as sources of advice, particularly on legislation. It is possible that this research, conducted in the late 1970s, overestimates membership of employers' organizations. In engineering, the national dispute in October 1979 – the dispute which culminated in the concession of a 39-hour week from November 1981 – led to resignations from the Engineering Employers' Federation. Some of these resignations were companies who had decided not to adhere to negotiations on minimum rates of pay, and on conditions of employment, but only to avail themselves of advisory services. However, with a national dispute, these companies become involved even though the dispute had no direct relevance to them, and therefore many of these companies decided to sever their links altogether.

Even in the public sector, which for many years has been held to be the apotheosis of centralized national bargaining, the pattern can be seen to be breaking down. In a series of negotiations in the fire service, the local authorities and the health services at the end of the 1970s and the beginning of the 1980s there were real and very apparent splits in the employers' ranks. The traumatic decentralization of the water industry occurred in 1983. [12]

The relevance of 'two-tier' bargaining arrangements, whereby national negotiations determine minimum rates of pay, which are supplemented by domestic discussion at an individual employer's annual review date, has certainly been questioned in recent times. [13] The introduction of national negotiation of *minimum* rates was, of course, related to the desire of companies to have more options with regard to their own labour costs whilst not allowing competitors to undercut them. Even minimum rates, however, can affect shift and overtime premia. The enhanced aim of companies to control their own increases to labour costs is likely to lead to greater questioning of the value of multi-employer organizations, especially of the 'minimum agreements' type.

One major issue for the 1980s is, then, the value of remaining in membership of employers' federations as against the advantages which would be likely to result from leaving it.

Companies are questioning their membership more frequently: taking account of the following issues:

Advantages of remaining in membership:

- Advisory services are often of a very high standard, helpful at, for example, industrial tribunals.
- Information is collated and summarized by the employers' organization: information which small companies find hard to obtain and which in larger organizations takes a lot of time.

- Companies *may* be protected from leap-frogging claims, especially on conditions of employment.
- There is a possibility of influencing national issues through membership of employers' organizations.
- A procedure for resolving disputes is usually available.
- Substantive and procedure agreements establish the 'sets of rules' which govern industrial relations within the plant; these are well known and largely accepted by the parties.

Disadvantages of remaining in membership:

- Officials of employers' organizations do not always understand the policies and practices of particular companies.
- Companies may find federation rules restrict them from negotiating with full-time officials of the trade unions as often as they would wish. It is not unknown for companies to conduct 'informal' negotiations to avoid such rules.
- Companies in industries where minimum rates are set find that national negotiations set a floor for further domestic increases – which they may not be able to afford.
- Conditions of employment may be improved without the individual company being able to secure appropriate 'trade-offs'. Given our earlier analysis of the importance for company managements of securing flexibility of task and other initiatives, this may be critical to the organization's ability to 'buy in' changed practices.
- Concessions granted by employers' organizations may not be perceived as being paid for by the employer since the true relationshhip between the employer and the negotiating group may be obscured.
- Many companies become frustrated at the conservatism of some of the employers' organizations, and the feeling that they cater for the 'lowest common denominator'.
- There is a cost of membership of employers' organizations.

To summarize, membership of employers' organizations can minimize the dangers of sectional claims being pursued and provide valuable informa- tion. On balance – and there is little statistical information available either way – more companies apparently believe that they may be better placed to control costs and secure productivity improvements by develop- ing bargaining arrangements directly geared to their own circumstances.

Central bargaining
The issue of the centralization of industrial relations continues to be debated in the 1980s. The origins of a trend towards central bargaining can

again be seen in the Donovan Report which said 'a company agreement will be more effective than a series of factory agreements', although admittedly the evidence to support this trend in the 1970s was contradictory.[14] What is central bargaining and why did the conventional wisdom of that decade believe it should be developed?

A company bargaining centrally has been defined as seeking

> to determine at group level basic pay and conditions in its plants with interpretative issues settled at plant level within the framework of the main substantive and procedural agreements.[15]

Centralization of industrial relations within a multi-plant organization is related to a number of factors of which two will be highlighted – the structure of the organization and industrial relations pressures.

The structure of the organization is fundamental in the determination of bargaining levels. In manufacturing, for example, the technical interdependence of the operation is the key. Companies are seeking – for economic reasons – to manufacture their own components, or at least to control the supply. Materials and components are being moved between sites of the company, and staff are often moving between the plants too. Integrated production processes, developed through acquisition or mergers, generate pressures for all employees to be treated equally, and that can lead to pressures for central bargaining. We see the same sort of influences in service industries, where the demand for an identical service and image in all locations has created similar pressures. The development or extension of central accounting and computer systems covering all sites in an organization is also contributing towards unification and a group philosophy, and hence fostering pressure towards central bargaining over pay and conditions.[16]

Other issues concerning organizational structure are also relevant. In the 1980s the need for organizations to respond quickly and effectively to changes in both production and information technology is paramount if competitiveness is to be maintained. Management at local level finds itself under increasing pressure to devote maximum time to managing the introduction of such changes and to be freed from the time and effort associated with negotiation over basic pay and conditions. This is not to say that local management can spend less time on industrial relations; far from it, since 'managing change' and 'managing IR' are almost synonymous processes. Local management can, however, spend less time on the negotiation of terms and conditions which may be known to be centrally determined anyway. The managers locally are then less involved in handling conflicts associated with pay and conditions, although managers are as likely as before to be involved in those conflicts associated with the day to day handling of IR in a company. The difference is, however, that they are more able to concentrate on key business issues, rather than concentrating on substantive issues of basic pay and conditions. Finally, with the pressure on controlling labour costs which characterizes industrial relations management in the 1980s, some senior managements believe that central bargaining best facilitates tight control of labour costs. This involves of necessity setting up systems to control and monitor local arrangements. The wider implications of this will be discussed below.

Turning to industrial relations pressures it has been evident for some time that trade unions are seeking to bargain with companies at the 'right' level, i.e. the level at which crucial business decisions, which have a substantial effect on the workforce, are taken. This is particularly so in the context of recession, where the union seeks information, consultation and negotiating opportunities on rationalization plans, closure plans and investment and commercial policies.

Trade unions have also sought to orchestrate their approach to organizations by pursuing identical claims in different parts of the company. The development of combine committees within trade unions has assisted this process. The decentralized company can put considerable time and resources into handling each claim locally. This, however, is artificial and distracts management from its prime task of running the business. If establishments are being 'singled out' in this way, especially on conditions of employment on which it is simpler to mount a concerted campaign for improvements, an organization might determine that a central dimension in collective bargaining may be more cost-effective. It has to be said, however, that such approaches from trade unions were more typical in the 1960s and 1970s than in the changed environment of the 1980s.

Central bargaining may also have the effect of separating members and shop stewards at local level from the officials, lay or full-time, conducting the central negotiation. While this may create process difficulties, decisions on the outcome of central bargaining have to be considered by the members of each union involved across the company as a whole, which reduces the likelihood of small groups disrupting the process of collective bargaining. Such disruption from powerful work groups is of course always possible notwithstanding central decision-making processes.

In the 1980s workgroup power has, for reasons we have already identified, been constrained. In this context certain policy options have become more accessible to management. While central bargaining can provide for greater control over labour costs, minimizing wage drift, certain costs may in fact be higher in a centrally bargained organization. These can arise in a number of ways:

- Where there have been pressures in pay bargaining to 'level up' to the highest paid in the company, with the result that terms and conditions of employment are paid in certain locations which are higher than would be justified by local labour market or business cost considerations.

- Comparative wage levels are of obvious importance to employees and often have a more direct effect on negotiations than absolute wage levels. Central bargaining adds to the consciousness amongst employees and trade unions of pay levels in different sites. The result is that further pressure for parity and complete harmonization is a product of central bargaining, and this may be irresistible once the centralized process has begun.

- As was the case with multi-employer bargaining, central bargaining can reduce the opportunity for improvements in pay and conditions to be directly paid for by productivity improvements unless each improvement is conditional upon local improvements in efficiency. This is difficult to negotiate centrally.

- The discretion of local management to reward staff may be felt to be more constrained. This can be demotivating for managers who may perceive opportunities to gain improvements in efficiency lost because increases in pay are not 'allowed'; if this is the case this may hinder efficiency improvements rather than encourage them and this thereby can add to unit costs.

For some managements, these will be good reasons for avoiding central bargaining in the 1980s!

Local bargaining
Much that can be said about decentralized bargaining patterns is the converse of the factors associated with central bargaining, and therefore does not need to be discussed in detail. Plant bargaining is consistent with the type of business structure which is associated with the existence of profit centres. With business accountability at plant/divisional/product group level, industrial relations accountability resides at the same level, subject only (generally) to centrally determined budgetary control. While this budgetary control may in theory undermine the process of local bargaining, as long as employees are unaware of the nature of this central control, the perception of true plant bargaining can be successfully maintained.

This approach clearly provides a certain degree of managerial discretion to meet particular local labour market requirements. The needs of the local business in terms of ability to pay, or the requirement to recruit and retain scarce skills, can be emphasized. A more direct link between productivity returns and improvements in terms and conditions is also possible. For the unions, decentralized bargaining

> maximizes the scope for plant level union representatives to represent and negotiate about the local needs and interests of their members. It also enhances the position of strategic work groups.[17]

Because of the widespread existence of decentralized patterns of bargaining in the UK it is necessary to explore further why companies such as

GEC, Plessey, and STC adopt such an approach. Some of the main reasons can be categorized as follows:

- Problems can be handled without having to follow central rules and procedures as is often the case in central bargaining.
- Issues can be dealt with by the people most closely associated with them, who have detailed knowledge of the circumstances.
- Terms and conditions can be designed for the particular circumstances of the establishment, and as such, it is argued, are more likely to optimize the use of resources.
- There is greater freedom to reward staff in relation to the changing circumstances of the local labour market, and the ability of the organization to pay.
- It is in line with attempts to keep negotiations away from the policy issues of the organization as a whole, and to concentrate on local 'performance'.
- It is more likely that employees can identify with their particular local unit and its problems rather than with the organization as a whole. This identification may facilitate cooperation since the workforce can more easily see the outcome of their endeavours reflected in the local company's results.
- There may be greater opportunities to focus on detailed improvements to operational efficiency when negotiating pay and reward improvements than may be the case with centralized bargaining.

Whilst all this is true, there are of course many well-known disadvantages of decentralized bargaining arrangements. Considerable time and resources have to be devoted to bargaining at local level on issues which in many cases the negotiators at least know to have been determined at the centre. Establishments are exposed to parity claims quoting precedent from within the same organization. By linking pay directly to productivity locally, management can find itself 'buying out' practices which the workgroup generates just to have bought out. For the unions, the main disadvantage is their inability to gain an input at the level that the 'policy issues' are decided.

Multi-level bargaining
One more innovative approach to the centralization/decentralization debate is to bargain centrally on conditions and at establishment level on pay. This separation provides an organization's management with certain opportunities. Under such a system policies on conditions of employment can be pursued without being influenced by tactical considerations associated with the pay review. Thus a programme of harmonization could be pursued in its own right, and phased according to the policy rather than the pay round. Also the forum which negotiates changes to conditions can be

used as a mechanism for communicating with employees on the situation of the business. This has the advantage of distancing such communications from the pay review negotiations where such information is likely to be seen as part of the negotiating process.

Multi-level bargaining in this way can provide some of the advantages of local bargaining in terms for example of relating pay to local ability to pay and local labour market considerations. It can also provide some advantages of central bargaining in terms of consistency and 'equity' in treatment of conditions of employment.

In organizations where domestic bargaining has been well established, or where the organization has grown by merger or acquisitions, this separation between pay and conditions is likely to be attractive.

For other organizations, however, this option may be viewed as a 'halfway house': an unsteady compromise. These organizations will argue that central bargaining over conditions will in itself lead to a greater awareness amongst employees of the role of Group HQ and central bargaining over pay then becomes almost inevitable. In addition, many a pay review has been settled by marginal adjustments to conditions. Why reduce negotiating flexibility by this separation? If the organization is seeking predictability over labour costs in the year ahead then there will be a reluctance to allow separate negotiating forums on conditions of employment to occur once the pay review is settled. Nevertheless, the opportunities provided by this separation are real enough, and this option deserves more serious consideration than it currently achieves.

Centralization or decentralization?

The debate about bargaining levels is a very practical one for many organizations in both public and private sectors. We have tended to focus on manufacturing organizations here as this is where the issues are seen at their most apparent. In this sector, there are certainly examples of moves toward decentralized bargaining, including BL (Cars) and Pilkingtons. Looking more broadly we can also identify some interesting trends. In the public service sector, for example, there is a move to push many industrial relations decisions out and down the structures. The rapid resurgence of plant bargaining on productivity bonuses at British Steel (which are described in chapter 5), and the development of bonus schemes within local authorities are typical examples of this trend. For these public sector organizations, at least, decentralization is viewed as the most cost-effective approach to collective bargaining in the 1980s.

For some organizations, bargaining structure will be determined by the management organization or the technology and there will be little to debate. For others – we believe the majority – the management structure, technology, economic development, geographical factors and the rest, will not lead conclusively toward one type of approach. We have stressed throughout this book our conviction that management is not in practice, and should not be in theory, tied to 'inevitable' ways of running their organization. There is always a choice, though it may be wider for some organizations than others. There is evidence that shows the importance of understanding and managing in order to cope with the technological and other constraints that we identified in the first two chapters – but there is no evidence that different bargaining structures cannot be made to work in similar contexts. The decisive factor lies in their integration with the overall business policy of the organization. We believe that in the public sector the moves towards an inevitable concentration of key business decisions at the centre, will place limitations on any proposals to decentralize collective bargaining. In the private service sector on the other hand the scope is very wide. Many organizations here, we believe, will develop bargaining structures in a way which provides the best opportunity to relate pay directly to productivity.

Any move from central to local bargaining, or local to central bargaining will be a radical change for the organization: for this reason it is rarely attempted. It requires two basic ingredients. First, management must be clear of its overall objectives prior to entering into discussions, though the details may change during negotiations. Second, change is best introduced by joint working with representatives of recognized trade unions within the organization. There will be much suspicion from employees and trade unions of the motives for changing bargaining structures:

> Change must be accepted as being in the interests of both sides. An employer wishing to change the bargaining structure must therefore have a 'quid pro quo' for the unions.[18]

Without searching 'after areas of mutual acceptability'[19] with trade unions, change will be difficult to achieve. This remains true even in the changed circumstances of the 1980s.

Summary

Management requires a communication, consultation and bargaining structure which best facilitates the achievement of business objectives. More specifically, management are seeking through their choice of bargaining structure to maximize operational efficiency, particularly through maximizing control over labour costs. Through its communication and consultative structures, the organization is also seeking to maximize the cooperation and commitment of the workforce to business objectives. It can do this through the wide range of communications and consultation mechanisms that we have described. In practice, most organizations will use a combination of these options, including, for many, a continuation of a substantial emphasis on collective bargaining in one form or another.

The objectives of all this activity are being clarified. The purpose is to develop a multiplicity of direct and representative channels enabling senior executives to get messages down to non-managerial employees and to have an accurate assessment of their expectations and concerns. It is also intended to release the creativity and energy of the workforce in order that their immediate tasks are carried out more effectively. Overall the method will be to reduce the number of what Guest (see page 123) calls the policy issues on the agenda, to use collective bargaining as one of a number of channels to discuss long-term executive issues and to develop a range of direct and representative structures at the workplace which concentrate on more immediate task related issues.

References

1   ACAS, *Collective Bargaining in Britain*, Discussion Paper No. 2 (1983), p. 41.
2   See, for example, *ACAS Annual Report 1983*.
3   D. Guest and K. Knight (eds), *Putting Participation into Practice* (Gower, 1979), pp. 19–39.
4   Guest and Knight, *Putting Participation into Practice*, p. 27.
5   E. Batsone, A. Ferner and M. Terry, *Consent and Efficiency* (Basil Blackwell, 1984).
6   Quoted in 'Employee communications' *IDS Study No. 318*, (July 1984), p. 11.
7   IDS, 'Employee communications', p. 4.
8   S. W. Brown, 'An evaluation of the effects of quality circles in five north west companies'. Unpublished MSc dissertation; quoted in B. G. Dale, *Research in Quality Circles* (UMIST, 1982).
    K. Bradley and S. Hill, ' "After Japan": the quality circle transplant and productive efficiency', *British Journal of Industrial Relations*, vol xxi, 3 (1983), pp. 291–311.
9   See the survey in *Industrial Relations Review and Report* 324 (July 1984), pp. 8–10.
10 Commission on Industrial Relations, *Industrial Relations in Multi-plant Undertakings*, Report No. 35 (HMSO, 1972), p. 14.
11 W. Brown, *The Changing Contours of British Industrial Relations* (Heinemann, 1983).
12 See 'Public sector bargaining', *IDS Study No. 303* (December 1983), pp. 36–7.
13 D. McIntyre, 'Inquest on the engineering dispute and the future of two-tier bargaining', *Personnel Management* (December 1979).
14 See A. W. J. Thomson and L. C. Hunter, 'The level of bargaining in a multi-plant company', *Industrial Relations Journal*, vol. 6, (1975).
15 Commission on Industrial Relations, *Industrial Relations in Multi-plant Undertakings*, p. 30.
16 Thomson and Hunter, 'The level of bargaining in a multi-plant company', pp. 27–34.
17 Commission on Industrial Relations, *Industrial Relations in Multi-plant Undertakings*, p. 35.
18 Thomson and Hunter, 'The level of bargaining in a multi-plant company', p. 38.
19 W. J. McCarthy, 'Changing bargaining structures', in S. Kessler and B. Weekes (eds), *Conflict at Work* (BBC, 1971).

8
Management and the trade unions

Managerial action, both directly and indirectly, is such a central influence on the unions that it is in some ways surprising that it is only in the 1980s that many organizations have realized that they can manage, rather than merely react to, the unions that they deal with. Increasingly, managements are now moving away from ad hoc reactive responses to the unions towards a process of managing the unions in the same way that other aspects of the environment are managed. The establishment of long-term policy goals, the development of appropriate styles and tactics, is becoming more widespread. Inevitably this process is constrained by attitudes and cultures, by history and technology and by managerial ability. But where managements have a coordinated approach to the unions, integrated with other aspects of management policy; where that approach has been disseminated through the management team and their commitment to it obtained; in such organizations management will be able to influence the unions more successfully than they do now.

The logic of the argument in this book is that management is in a position to manage the unions strategically – just as it can manage other aspects of the human resource. This chapter therefore reviews the position of the unions in Britain and examines the pressures they are under and the problems they face. It argues that the unions are currently experiencing a period of stress and substantial upheaval but that they nevertheless have opportunities to change and the ability to adapt. A key role in the development of that change will be played by managements and at the end of the chapter we suggest some of the options that management now has.

Changes in trade unions

The popular press likes to portray the image of the trade union movement as a carthorse: slow, unchanging despite the changing surroundings, strong but simple, and anachronistic. An objective examination reveals a different picture.

In the first place, the trade union movement in Britain is remarkably varied and adaptable. Thus it is extremely difficult to make any valid generalizations about the unions. Blanket statements always need to be qualified by referring to unions that approach things differently. In the

DOI: 10.4324/9781003193043-8

UK the unions have an immense variety in size, membership, financial arrangements and wealth, in organizational structures and in political links and policies. No other country has such a diversity of unions.

This variety is influenced by and affects the circumstances in which the unions have operated: and the circumstances in which they now find themselves. It is not accidental. The unions are, to coin a phrase, 'adept at adapting'. Throughout their history the unions have changed to meet changing pressures. The pressures are more varied now than ever before, and the unions are changing faster than ever. Whether they can change fast enough, and what influence strategically thinking managements can have upon the direction of that change, we will discuss once we have examined in greater detail the pressures, and the problems and opportunities that face the unions.

The pressures on the unions
In the last 15 years of the twentieth century the unions are facing the mutually reinforcing pressures of declining membership and declining influence.

The reasons for these declines are not hard to find. We group them under the headings of

- economic circumstances;
- structural changes in industry;
- the climate of opinion;
- union policies;
- managerial action;

and discuss each in turn.

Economic circumstances
These were examined in chapter 1, in an attempt to ascertain the influence on Britain's economic performance of industrial relations. The point was made there that the two are interdependent. It has been persuasively argued that the growth or decline of union membership correlates with the economic cycle.[1] There can be little doubt that there is a broad relationship between, for example, increasing levels of unemployment and declining union membership. There is also a relationship between the volatility of both earnings and prices, and changes in union membership.[2]

Britain's economic problems and the high and continuing level of unemployment have created a new situation for the unions. The 'fear factor' is believed by many union officials to be increasingly potent. Employees are less ready to join trade unions if they feel that economic factors make their own employment expendable. They are less likely to take collective action once they are in the unions. They are less prepared to take up exposed positions as employee representatives, and less willing to press for negotiations over issues beyond the normal pay and benefits package.

Structural changes in industry

Structural changes will reinforce the economic trends. Our consideration of these changes in chapter 1 emphasized the decline of traditional large-scale manufacturing organizations, the reductions in the size of employing establishments, the increase (comparatively at least) in non-manual employment and the more diverse tasks to be undertaken in employment. We have in succeeding chapters discussed the blurring of the distinctions between jobs, the trend to relate rewards more to individual performance and the introduction of new patterns of work and employment relations.

Each of these changes puts pressure on the unions. They are faced with an increasingly disparate group of organizations employing fewer people than in the 1960s or 1970s. There is evidence that below a certain number of employees in a workplace trade unions find it difficult to maintain the 'self-sustaining' structures that have been their backbone.[3] In smaller establishments, and more diverse ones, there is less possibility of creating and sustaining strong, confident lay representative systems. Of course, it has traditionally been these representatives who have maintained membership, handled day-to-day issues and linked the members to the union.[4]

Changes in the nature of the workforce have added to the pressures on the unions. In the 1970s they were very successful in spreading membership to numerous previously unorganized groups. They are now finding it more difficult. There are fewer jobs for the male, manual workers whom unions have traditionally recruited. The 1970s surge in membership of women, clerical and supervisory staff, public sector employees and professional and managerial workers[5] – amongst other groups – is proving difficult or impossible to sustain. The individual orientation of many of these employees, possibly working in a self-employed context with a reward system geared to their and the organization's needs, means that the collective approach of most unions will become less relevant.

The climate of opinion

This has changed too, and will not be reversed easily. There have been continual criticisms of the trade union movement throughout its history but, at least over the last few decades, these have been against a background of substantial and growing union influence. This background was taken as given: managers might mumble about unions challenging their authority, particular companies might refuse to recognize the unions, and the newspapers fulminate against growing union power. But the unions' role in industry was unchallenged and their influence with government through an enormous range of agencies was accepted. Only a minority of larger employers thought that collective bargaining was other than a realistic and just process for settling terms and conditions. Few thought that recognition, once granted, could be withdrawn.[6] The unions could be reformed, might need controlling – but they were an established and appropriate part of the British industrial and even political scene.

Recent events, and a clear and consistent lead from Margaret Thatcher's government, changed that. The unions are now operating in a climate of public opinion which is manifestly hostile. Not only are Conservative politicians, and the press, ever ready to criticize. Well informed and sympathetic specialists are raising questions about the role and future of the unions.[7] The unions themselves have become more defensive and less confident.[8] Most significantly, perhaps, opinion amongst some managers is changing. There is a growing list of organizations in the public and private sectors that have threatened to replace recalcitrant workers by non-union labour[9] or have withdrawn union check-off facilities[10] and even recognition.[11]

Union policies
Union policies are undoubtedly another factor contributing to the growth and decline of particular unions.[12] Though, as Bain and Price argue, they may make little difference to the overall extent of union membership.[13]

Unions that restrict their recruitment to particular sectors are limited by the success of those industries – when the sectors decline, so will the union's membership. The Mineworkers and Railway unions and the Steelworkers have shrunk in just this way. And there are other unions which, whilst not restricting themselves to particular sectors, are nevertheless so identified with areas of declining employment that they are coming under pressure. In this category could be placed unions as diverse as the Amalgamated Union of Engineering Workers (with the decline of manufacture), the Banking, Insurance and Finance Union (with the increase in new technology in those areas) and perhaps some of the public sector and civil service unions, with the trend towards demanning and denationalization.

Managerial action
Managerial action is also adding to the pressures on the unions in both public and private sectors.

> Whether workers decide to become and remain union members . . . will also be significantly influenced by the attitudes and behaviour of employers. The greater the degree of recognition which employers confer upon unions the less likely employees are to jeopardize their jobs and career prospects by being union members, the more easily they can reconcile union membership with their 'loyalty' to the company, and most important, the more effectively unions can participate in the process of job regulation and thereby offer employees service and benefits which will encourage them to become and remain union members.[14]

And as we shall argue, managers can decide to influence much more than this.

Table 8   *Union membership 1966–1983*

	Numbers (millions)	Density (%)
1966	10,260	42.6
1967	10,188	42.8
1968	10,189	43.1
1969	10,468	44.4
1970	11,174	47.7
1971	11,120	47.9
1972	11,391	48.7
1973	11,570	48.5
1974	11,755	49.6
1975	12,184	51.7
1976	12,376	51.8
1977	12,846	53.3
1978	13,112	54.3
1979	13,447	55.4
1980	12,947	53.6
1981	12,182	51.0
1982	11,445	48.7
1983	11,338	47.0

Density based on employees in employment and unemployed (June).
Sources: Historical Abstract of British Labour Statistics 1886–1968 (HMSO, 1971); *DE Gazette*, various.

The union decline

These pressures have resulted in a decline in union membership and union influence. The decline in membership is readily quantifiable. Table 8 shows that the proportion of employees who were trade union members increased steadily from the end of 1960 to the end of 1970, topping 50 per cent in 1975 and remaining above that figure till 1981. The trend, however, then reversed – and reversed dramatically. The year 1979 was the last of growth. Reported membership dropped 3.7 per cent in 1980; and 5.9 per cent in 1981. From a peak of over 12 million members in 1979, TUC-affiliated unions' membership dropped to below 10 million by 1984. This trend is continuing. The unions in some areas are suffering from this more than others. We have already referred to the position of those unions whose membership is restricted to industries where total employment is seriously reduced as a result of structural changes. Unions in other declining sectors are losing membership much faster than their industries are losing employment. This is happening in the agriculture, forestry and fishing, textiles, clothing, footwear and allied industries and in construction. But all unions are facing this threat.

The decline in influence is more difficult to illustrate. At the national level the unions have found that the continual involvement in the development of all aspects of economic and social policy which they experienced in the 1970s had, by the 1980s, changed to a process of heckling from the sidelines. There can be some debate about the extent of their involvement in the 1970s, or the degree of exclusion in the 1980s, but it would be hard to argue other than that a significant shift had occurred.

At organizational level there is a similar change. A survey in 1983 found that nearly 100 per cent of both managers and unions recognized a toughened managerial attitude to negotiations;[15] and the Confederation of British Industry reported at the start of the decade 'signs that management gradually is regaining the confidence to take the necessary actions [which will include] constructive but firm relationships with individual trade unions'.[16] An example can be drawn from the 1982 Employment Act, which required successive ballots to maintain 'lawful' action in support of closed shops. This has not so far generated significant numbers of ballots – those that occurred have in general been strongly in favour of the closed shop, especially where the unions have been prepared to campaign for its retention[17] – but did cause managements to reappraise their closed shop policies; and in some cases to terminate the agreements.[18]

Problems for the unions
For organizations that have been built to positions of some power by their ability to speak for large numbers of workers the decline in membership and influence poses severe problems.

At the national level unions are faced with increasingly disparate membership, grouped in small numbers and needing more attention from the formal union institutions if they are to retain membership. Fewer members means fewer subscriptions. With more of their members on the retired and unemployed lists, and with the reluctance of any organizations to strike off members as soon as they fall into arrears, union incomes are falling faster than their memberships.

This means, immediately, that the unions, which have always been far from wealthy, are now virtually 'broke'. They are beginning not to replace full-time officials who leave, they are reducing dispute and other benefits, spending less on circulars, on research, on officials' expenses. Most unions over the past few years have actively considered the possibility of merging with one or more other unions as a means of sharing costs and reducing overall expenditure. The number of unions dropped from 481 in 1977 to 401 in 1982, mainly as a consequence of mergers.[19]

At the local level trade union officials face a gloomy situation. They have fewer members – but the number of local officials may also have been reduced. Members are found in smaller units, and there may well be no shop steward or employee representative in the group. The officials are spending more time in their cars to get to smaller groups of members, facing reduced subscription income and working with fewer lay activists. They may find themselves competing more aggressively (perhaps even overtly) with other unions for the members that there are.[20]

Table 9 *Stoppages in years 1970–83*

Year	Stoppages beginning in year	Workers* involved in stoppages (000s) Beginning in year Directly	Indirectly	In progress in year	Working days lost in stoppages (000s) Beginning in year (a)	(b)	In progress in year
1970	3906	1460	333	1801	10 854	10 908	10 980
1971	2228	863†	308†	1178†	13 497	13 589	13 551
1972	2497	1448†	274†	1734†	23 816	23 923	23 909
1973	2873	1103	410	1528	7 089	7 145	7 197
1974	2922	1161	461	1626	14 694	14 845	14 750
1975	2282	570	219	809	5 861	5 914	6 012
1976	2016	444†	222†	668†	3 230	3 509	3 284
1977	2703	785	370	1166	9 864	10 378	10 142
1978	2471	725†	276†	1041†	8 890	9 391	9 405
1979	2080	4121	463	4608	28 974	29 051	29 474
1980	1330	702†	128†	834†	11 887	11 965	11 964
1981	1338	1326	173	1513	4 188	4 244	4 266
1982	1528	1974†	127†	2103†	5 258	5 276	5 313
1983	1352	500†	71	574†	3 736	3 981	3 754

(a) The figures in this column include days lost in the year in which the stoppages began.
(b) The figures in this column include days lost both in the year in which the stoppages began and also in the following year.
* Workers involved in more than one stoppage in any year are counted more than once in a year's total. Workers involved in a stoppage beginning in the year and continuing into another are counted in both years in the column showing the number of workers involved in stoppages in progress.
† Figures exclude workers becoming involved after the end of the year in which the stoppage began.
Source: DE Gazette, July 1984, p. 310.

The face that the officials present to their members will also have to change. The traditional approach is one which relies on finding out 'what the members are prepared to do about it' (what industrial action they are prepared to take) and then expressing a view to management. In the 1980s unions are finding approaches based on 'what the members will do' less relevant, since in many cases it is clear that the members would not be prepared to take collective industrial action. Table 9 suggests this by showing the way the number and extent of strikes has changed since 1970.

The positive side
The picture is not entirely gloomy for the unions. Managers hoping for a 'collapse' of the unions will be disappointed. The unions have three advantages. The first is that they are already heavily involved in an enormous

range of British social structures; they are embedded in most industries and in a long list of organizations at local, regional and national level. Unlike the United States' unions, for example, which at their peak only ever held sway in a minority of industries and regions, the British unions are an integral part of the broad spectrum of employment and civil administration.

The second advantage that the unions have is their variety and flexibility. Amongst the different union forms there are likely to be some that are more fitted for the new environment, and some that can adapt relatively easily to it. There can be little doubt that over the next decade there will be major changes in the union movement. Equally there can be little doubt that although some unions will survive only by merger and others will struggle, some unions will be well placed to adapt and re-organize, and prosper.

The third positive feature for the unions' involvement is that there are already people within it who are facing up to the problems that the unions will have to overcome. Many sympathisers, and officials, are retreating into a defensive posture. There are already, though, those who are indicating a new road to survival.

These individuals argue that the need for trade unions is beyond dispute. They point to myriad examples of unfair treatment of employees, of discrimination, of exploitation; to all those doing boring and mindless jobs and to the millions on low wages. And they argue that new forms of unionism will develop, presenting a different face to members, a different organizational structure and different involvement at national level.

It is difficult to be clear about the way the unions are likely to develop, especially since the arguments presented by these commentators run counter to the current 'crisis management' of most unions. In their assumptions of increased resourcing they also go against present trends. Nevertheless, the claims for such a 'new unionism' will be influential in the next decade or so, and it is worth devoting a little space to pulling together the main themes of these thoughtful, if still highly speculative, approaches.

'New Unionism'

The new unionism requires full-time officials to become more active and more visible, calling in to workplaces frequently, rather than waiting to be called in. The officials will continue to be involved in the operation of grievance and disciplinary procedures, but will be more involved in discussing such issues as new technology, merit pay, multi-skilling, equal opportunities, training and retraining and health and safety. Policies will be needed on such issues. The union will have to improve its communications system to keep up morale amongst smaller groups and to show 'value for money'. The unions might develop more general services of the 'professional body' kind: some unions, like TASS, already issue technical publications or, like BALPA, hold conferences and seminars on technical issues not directly related to pay and conditions. The new unions will also develop new negotiating tactics. Strikes will be more often replaced by other tactics such as slow working or taking days off 'sick'.

At the organization level the new unions will need to increase subscriptions (perhaps moving to a percentage of salary as with BALPA and ACTT) in order to provide more full-time officials backed up by better research and support systems. They will have to broaden their activities, introducing technical training, as the EETPU has done, and providing more social meetings, opening up their offices to members during the day and in the evenings. They will have to establish policies on the newer issues that we cover elsewhere – such as alternative patterns of work and alternative forms of contract. They may have to take a more imaginative approach to pay bargaining and to work seriously at 'no strike clauses' (as the EETPU has done).

Eventually they may have to look at new organizational structures. Many of the unions have developed or added to their organization the concept of workplace based branches. As workplaces become smaller this may become inappropriate. Some union officials are already thinking the not-so-long-ago unthinkable and imagining a move from individual union cards based in particular skills or jobs to a 'TUC card'. As particular skills and jobs become blurred and people increasingly change jobs and retrain several times during their working life the old union boundaries and jealousies will lead increasingly to more people dropping out of the movement. The unions may have to develop single union arrangements within organizations by transfer of engagements rather than just on 'greenfield' sites. 'Bridlington' (the TUC's rules to stop unions taking each other's members) will have to be abandoned.

Changes such as these – and no one claims to have a comprehensive list – will be accompanied by changes at national level. The new unions will move towards community enterprises, to involvement with other crusading organizations on joint ventures and shared campaigns. They will be bargaining with local companies and local media for cash and resources for community projects. These unions will be using publicity far more than they do now. They will be making active use of law in employment and in the community and they will increase their involvement in policies over a wider field. The TUC will become more important organizationally, as a focus for individual union activity and as an active political lobbyist. The new unions and their officials will have a broader role.

The voices in the trade union movement that are discussing such changes are still few. The likelihood is that moves will be made towards this 'new unionism', but that they will be slow and patchy. Union membership continues to decline, but will not collapse. Union influence in particular workplaces will be dependent, amongst other things, on the way managements behave.

Trade unions – managerial objectives

Managements are becoming more conscious of the trends described above. Some few are planning and controlling their relationships with the trade unions in a strategic manner. There is now less credit given to the idea that the unions are just there – like the weather – and have to be coped with in the same way. Many of the changes in employment that we have discussed so far have shown a significant effect on the unions but many organizations are starting to manage their union relationships more directly.

Managers in these organizations have a series of linked objectives. These are aimed not at the destruction of union influence but at ensuring that it is channelled into issues that in the management's view will contribute to the better functioning of the organization that employs both managers and union members. Thus the unions' role in grievance and disciplinary issues is seen as positive, their role in improving the workplace encouraged and their challenge to management on pay and conditions is accepted in the context of the mechanisms we discussed in chapter 7. The lay officials' role in wider organizational issues is generally discouraged.

The objectives that these managements have include:

- clarification of union recognition;
- fewer plant level and organization level bargaining groups;
- fewer shop stewards;
- a different role for union officials; and
- emphasis on departmental stewards.

We will consider each in turn.

Clarification of union recognition
This is a first step in the strategic management of trade union relationships. We identify four stages of recognition: appropriateness, individual representation rights, bargaining rights and UMAs (union membership agreements – or closed shops).

'Appropriateness' is a declaration by the management that there is one union organization with which it would be prepared to deal in certain conditions. It was uncertainty about this phase which led to the proliferation of unions in some workplaces in the 1960s and 1970s. Private sector companies are increasingly prepared to take the line that much of the public sector has traditionally adopted and to be quite firm about which unions they will deal with and which they won't. Some companies are now going much beyond this and nominating – at an early stage – the single union that they would be ready to countenance if it can recruit sufficient members. At the same time, however, they are being much firmer about insisting that the union proves that it has at least half of the potential members on its books before it is recognized. A declaration of appropriateness may encourage that union to continue its recruiting activities; it certainly makes the position clear for those who might be thinking of joining a union and yet, importantly, it is clear to line managers that it confirms no rights even for the union selected.

'Individual representation rights' is a second category. This stage is perhaps the most difficult for line management to control. Because of the way the law is framed in the UK, with certain union rights dependent upon recognition 'to any extent', it is a stage which management will want to approach carefully. It has the merit of being variable across the organizations as some individuals or groups prefer to use or not use the union in this capacity. It has the merit of focusing the union on individual issues and ensuring that these issues are channelled constructively and independently. Provided that the representational rights are framed to include only union representatives from the workplace (so as to exclude external union officials) there is no automatic development into collective bargaining. Indeed many workplaces have operated 'individual representation rights only' for many years. Such rights however do confer additional legal options on the unions and can be developed into collective bargaining. Managements using this as a strategic option will seek to monitor it carefully.

'Negotiating rights' on collective issues forms a third category. During the 1970s, in particular under the promptings of the Commission on Industrial Relations and ACAS, recognition was seen as a one-way development and companies often allowed collective bargaining rights to unions who had in membership far less than half the workforce of a particular unit. This view of recognition has come under increasing challenge and a handful of notorious cases have shown that employers can resist demands for recognition, even when those demands are supported by the entire labour movement.[21] Increasingly management is saying to the unions 'when you can prove to us that 50 per cent of employees in a potential category have in fact joined the union *then* we will recognize you for collective bargaining'.

'Union membership agreements' are an extension of collective bargaining rights and are found widely in Britain. It is worth noting not only that these are circumstances in which all employees in a grouping are required to be union members, but also that they are agreements. Management has accepted such agreements – under pressure in some cases, certainly, but in others because the advantages of certainty, of a voice and a vote for non-activists and of single-channel communications seemed very real.

The changes introduced by the Employment Act 1982, effective from 1 November 1984, requiring closed shops to be approved by 80 per cent of those entitled to vote or 85 per cent of those actually voting, has already had an effect on the position of union membership agreements. In some cases unions have refused to take part in the ballots. This has led some organizations to state that they will not dismiss employees if they either do not join or resign from union membership, since to do so risks 'fines' of up to £30,000. For employers, the legal change provides a number of potential problems. Some employees may seek the opportunity to join other trade unions, leading to demands for recognition and the proliferation of bargaining arrangements. Inevitably, there will be instances of employees resigning their union membership – leading to threats of industrial action if they are not dismissed. Management may be caught again in the dilemma of facing legal sanctions on the one hand or industrial sanctions on the other.

Reducing the number of bargaining units
Doing this at each location is a widespread managerial objective. A multiplicity of unions at a workplace has been seen as an irritant by managers – and perhaps particularly by personnel specialists. The ever more rapid pace of change, decreasing union membership (and concomitant increasing inter-union competition), and the overriding need for flexibility amongst the workforce, have turned an irritant into a major problem for many managers. It is much more than coincidence that such a high proportion of companies moving to or setting up at 'greenfield' sites choose to negotiate with a single union. Managers with long established bargaining machinery have fewer options.

We can aggregate these options into two broad and often complementary approaches. The first involves a policy of encouraging one or two unions at the expense of others, with a view eventually to withdrawing recognition from those not deemed appropriate. Such a policy, carefully thought through in line with technological changes, can lead to a 'decreasing influence, decreasing success, decreasing membership' spiral for some unions – to the point at which recognition can be withdrawn. There is significant evidence from around Europe, for example, that managerial unionism can be stemmed in this way.[22]

Either alternatively, or at the same time, many managers and industrial relations specialists spent much of the early 1980s persuading groups from different unions to work together on an in-plant basis. Such groups often operate relatively independently of the formal union structures and are in many ways more like a 'plant' or 'office' union than a disparate group from several unions. The success of such arrangements may mean that multi-unionism is less of a problem than would otherwise be the case.[23]

Fewer shop stewards
There has already been a considerable decline in union membership but the numbers of shop stewards has not declined to the same extent. Fewer bargaining units would increase this disparity. Numbers of stewards have stayed high because managements have been understandably reluctant to tackle an issue which might be misinterpreted as an attack on the functions of the trade unions. Increasingly, however, it is becoming difficult for

managers to accept a shop steward organization which bears little relationship to the size and shape of the membership. In this, considerations of
cost, travel, time off and other facilities for large numbers of stewards play
an important part. This cost cannot be borne by the trade union either.
Opportunities are being taken to review the shop steward organization
either across the board (after a major re-organization or redundancy) or on
a personal basis when particular stewards leave.

A different role for union officials
This is implicit. Full-time officials continue to be involved in procedural
discussions, particularly with personnel departments, locally and centrally. These focus on the pay review, new job evaluation, salaries or redundancy announcements. The few full-time officials continue to be a hard-
pressed group, difficult to contact at the best of times. However, lay representatives are increasingly involved in local arrangements associated
with added value salaries, productivity bargaining, working time initiatives, and with individual and small group concerns. The full-time officials
are being forced, as we have indicated, to concentrate more on policy
matters – advising lay representatives on retraining, new technology,
level of pay settlements and the like.

Fewer full-time stewards
Cost pressures, reduced size of work groups and declining union membership will also lead to fewer full-time convenors. In large establishments,
senior stewards will continue to be virtually full-time on union business,
but most organizations are looking more critically at this and attempting
to limit time off work. This was, for example, the origin of the debate in the
civil service about the 'facilities agreement', an issue which still rumbles
on. It is to be expected that organizations recognizing unions for the first
time, those on 'greenfield sites' for instance, will impose limits from the
outset in order to avoid the development of the full-time lay official.

Emphasis on departmental stewards
One effect of having full-time representatives was that issues tended to be
passed on to them rather rapidly: they had the time and experience to deal
with any problems. This meant, generally, that the personnel manager or
equivalent was pulled in on the other side. This process had two main
consequences. Firstly, issues quickly reached the end of domestic procedures by virtue of the seniority of the people handling the early stages.
Secondly, this undermined the position – and confidence – of departmental
managers and shop stewards. Handling issues close to their source has
become a management policy in many organizations, and a corollary of
this is that departmental stewards are fully involved. This has meant
building up the role of the departmental stewards, particularly through
setting up or reforming the departmental consultative committees which

we considered in chapter 7 and through shop steward training. The latter is being done more frequently on an in-company basis, where their role within the organization can be stressed.

Management action

In summary, then, the unions are changing and managers are taking conscious steps to influence that change in their workplaces. Taken with the development of the communication, consultation and involvement approaches that we considered in the previous chapter it would seem that management is able to develop a union organization within the workplace which is responsive to organizational objectives, and more aware of the pressure for organizational success and efficiency. This has undoubtedly been helped by the economic context, and there is evidence from the motor car industry in the mid 1980s, for example, that some claimed changes in attitude may be just a response to hard times. In those organizations with coherent and well-planned approaches, the development of relationships with trade unions which foster cost-effectiveness is more likely to be a long-term change.

References

1 G. S. Bain and F. Elsheikh, 'Union growth and the business cycle: a disaggregated study', *British Journal of Industrial Relations*, vol. XX, 1 (1982), pp. 34–43.
   G. S. Bain and R. Price, 'Union growth: discussions, determinants and destiny', in G. S. Bain (ed.), *Industrial Relations in Britain* (Basil Blackwell, 1983).
2 Bain and Elsheikh and Bain and Price, ibid.
3 Bain and Price, ibid. p. 27.
   W. Brown, *The Changing Contours of British Industrial Relations* (Basil Blackwell, 1981), chapter 4.
4 I. Boraston, H. Clegg and M. Rimmer, *Workplace and Union* (Heinemann, 1975).
   R.Undy, V. Ellis, W. E. J. McCarthy and A. M. Halmos, *Change in Trade Unions* (Hutchinson, 1981).
5 'Managers' unions in decline', *Financial Times*, 4 September 1983.
6 C. J. Brewster and C. P. Heaton, 'Recognition: an explanatory framework', *Employee Relations*, vol. 3, 1 (1981), pp. 28–32.
7 J. Edmonds, 'Decline of the big battalions', *Personnel Management* (March 1984), pp. 18–21.
8 Instructive examples are found in the 1983 TUC Annual Report which suggested that the movement must at least temporarily abandon wider programmes and concentrate on issues 'of direct interest to trade unionists and which unions could influence'; the discussion paper issued by the TUC at the beginning of 1984; and an article by David Basnett, General Secretary of the General, Municipal and Boilermakers Trade Union in the August edition of the union's journal. He argued that the basic assumptions of the union were 'under serious challenge, not only from employers and a hostile Government, but also from our own members'.
9 See for example, Highlands Fabricators dispute (*Financial Times*, 22 August 1983) and British Telecoms dispute (*Financial Times*, 26 October 1983).
10 As the Birmingham City Council did from NALGO in 1983 (*The Times*, 11 August 1983).

11 For example, in the cases of ICI threatening to withdraw recognition from AMPS (*Guardian*, 24 April 1984); Birds Eye, Walls withdrawing recognition from ASTMS (*Sunday Times*, 29 May 1983); National Mutual Life from ASTMS (*Financial Times*, 6 August 1983) and most notoriously in the case of the Government Communications Headquarters in Cheltenham in 1984.

12 Undy *et al.*, *Change in Trade Unions*.

13 Bain and Price, 'Union growth: discussions, determinants and destiny'.

14 Bain and Price, 'Union growth: discussions, determinants and destiny', p. 18.

15 EPIC, *Industrial Relations Opinion Survey* (EPIC, 1983).

16 CBI, *Trade Unions in a Changing World: the challenge for management* (CBI, 1980).

17 See, for example, Steetley Brick Co ballot (reported in *Personnel Management*, April 1984, p. 11): 93.8 per cent in favour of closed shop.

18 *Financial Times*, 14 June 1984.

19 *DE Gazette* (January 1983), p. 27.

20 See, for example, article in the *Financial Times*, 22 May 1984; *Sunday Times* 28 August 1983; *Financial Times* 9 January 1984 – detailing the battle for membership in 'foreign investor', 'new technology' and 'greenfield site' areas.

21 Brewster and Heaton, 'Recognition: an explanatory framework'.

22 *Financial Times*, 4 September 1983.

23 The argument has been put succinctly by Willy Brown: W. Brown, 'Britain's unions: new pressures and shifting loyalties', *Personnel Management* (October 1983).

9
Conclusions

We have emphasized the importance for management of improving the cost-effectiveness of labour in dealing with the economic pressures facing organizations in the last decades of the twentieth century. We have shown, in the examples from organizations taking initiatives to enhance the efficiency of labour, that such improvements are possible. The areas with most scope for change include flexibility of task, working time and the development of alternative forms of contract. Payment systems are being changed to encourage and reward factors of more relevance to the organization. There is scope, too, for improvements in the processes of managing industrial relations. In chapters 7 and 8 we outlined some approaches to communications, to collective bargaining and to the trade unions, which can contribute to improving organizational effectiveness.

While economic and technological pressures lie behind many of the initiatives we describe in this book, they all raise critical industrial relations issues. For example, extending an individual's range of tasks across traditional job boundaries may be very desirable in the interest of efficiency improvements, and entirely logical as technology blurs the distinction between jobs. For the employees, however, it may imply job losses; not everyone may feel able to cope with the flexibility required; there will be questions about the pay implications of such changes. For other employees, by contrast, the extra satisfaction which may derive from a broader job will be an influential feature of such a change. What is clear is that few will be unaffected by initiatives of this kind. When a number of initiatives are occurring together – task flexibility, introduction of shift-working, de-manning . . . – then the implications on industrial relations are enormous.

In the successful planning and introduction of cost-effective initiatives within organizations, there appear to be several key issues. This concluding chapter considers in turn questions of managerial style; the role of line managers; the role of specialists; the need for policies to be integrated and consistent, not only within the manpower area, but also with the overall objectives of the organization; the role of senior executives in industrial relations and how policies can be developed. Finally, we pull together under the three main themes of the book – cost-effectiveness, strategies and industrial relations – the issues we have discussed.

DOI: 10.4324/9781003193043-9

Management style

Employees have little difficulty in identifying a managerial style for their own organization and comparing it with that of others. In very few cases is the managerial style developed consciously; it is an amalgam of the behaviour of a wide range of different managers. The fact that for many organizations a coherent and identifiable style can be detected, and which varies between otherwise similar organizations, shows the influence of the systems and controls adopted by top management.

There are therefore two aspects of establishing managerial styles: determining the style in relation to organizational objectives, and ensuring that managers adopt the chosen approach.

A number of analyses of industrial relations style have been developed; one example of which is shown in Table 10.

Table 10 *Styles of IR Management*

'Traditionalists'	Adversary style, opposition to trade unions/overt 'exploitation' of employees
'Sophisticated paternalists'	Non-union, unitary philosophy/great attention to employee commitment
'Sophisticated moderns'	Legitimating and involving trade unions
'Standard moderns'	Pragmatic, fire fighting approach

Source: J. Purcell and K. Sisson, 'Strategies and practice in the management of industrial relations', in G. S. Bain (ed.), *Industrial Relations in Britain* (Basil Blackwell, 1983).

These styles in turn have been described in more detail, for example the 'sophisticated moderns' style includes sub-groupings such as 'consultors' who work through recognized trade unions but alongside this also focus on non-union channels.

Which of these styles enhance or detract from organizational effectiveness? We believe that the vanguard organizations are adopting elements from several of these 'ideal' type approaches in order to facilitate desired organizational outcomes. When these outcomes stress efficiency improvements, and enhanced productivity in a context of recognized trade unions, then many organizations have adopted the 'consultative' approach – legitimizing the union role but seeing them as only one channel of communications.[1] In chapter 7 we discussed some of the other forms of communications being adopted by the vanguard organizations. Here they resemble the 'sophisticated paternalist' style – a 'caring' approach aimed at enhancing the satisfaction and commitment of the individual employee. At other times the imperative of cost-effectiveness will demand pragmatic action; and a blunt response to any working group reaction. It is certainly the case that the development of a coherent 'company philosophy' has been a recognizable feature of many successful organizations.[2] None the less it is likely that in management style, as in so much else connected with complex organizations, the 'correct' approach will vary within and between organizations. Such variations are in part determined by the environment within which the organization operates, but only in part. The right approach may also rationally vary with issues, with workgroup and with managerial choice.

This is not an argument for ignoring questions of policy and style. The more attention and clarification that an organization has devoted to these issues the freer it is to make detours, to vary its approach and still to get back on a consistent course as efficiently as possible. This is why so many vanguard organizations have developed coherent, clearly expressed, but flexible company philosophies.

Once the style has been determined senior executives have to ensure that the chosen approach is adopted by the management team. One implication is that recruitment into and selection for management, which is absorbing increasing amounts of time in many organizations, will be seen as crucial. The motivation, reward and, in particular, training and development of managers have become key concerns for senior executives. In this, organizations are consciously using the measurements and control systems within management. This includes the use of more sophisticated recruitment processes, with psychometric testing, attitude assessment and the use of highly paid consultants for internal and external recruits into management. It also includes the wider use of performance appraisal systems, and of courses and other training activities which concentrate on man management issues as a means not only of improving managerial competence but also of persuading the managers that the organization's approach is correct.

Line managers – key resource, with problems

The focus of such activity is line management. Line managers are any organization's key resource – in industrial relations as much as in other fields. They it is who must handle pressures for cost savings and operational improvements on the one hand, and motivation and effective communication on the other.

Are they equipped for this? In the 1970s, one study reported:

> If management is going to be able to take initiatives in industrial relations, it must become much more professional and sophisticated.[3]

This meant, amongst other things, managers preparing for negotiations more thoroughly, within the context of the organization's industrial relations policy. It meant spending more time on the strategy and tactics appropriate to negotiations to effect changed practices. While this was desirable, other writers doubted more fundamentally whether managers wanted a role in taking such initiatives:

> The trouble with the greater part of the best of line management in British

industry from top to bottom is that it does not want to accept the responsibility for the human aspects of the job. . . . By training and inclination it prefers the greater security it experiences in dealing with the more calculable technical or commercial problems. Labour policy it is quite willing, even eager, to leave to a personnel department with the necessary expertise.[4]

Given the rapid developments of trade unionism, particularly white-collar unions, in the post-war period, many managers were faced with shop stewards and union officials for the first time and, understandably, preferred in many cases to let the 'experts' in personnel handle this new and organized dimension to industrial relations. Significant developments in labour law, particularly the unfair dismissal provisions introduced in the early 1970s, further weakened managerial confidence and strengthened the role of the personnel department in industrial relations. The speed with which issues were passed to the senior stewards meant inevitably that the personnel manager and senior line managers became involved. This centralizing tendency within organizations left first line supervision and middle management in many instances remote from the industrial relations implications of organizational changes. Often by-passed in procedure, often with less knowledge of events than the trade unions and rarely trained in industrial relations, it was not surprising that many line managers abrogated industrial relations and employee motivation to the personnel department. Some first line supervisors as a result identified more with their trade union than with their managerial role.

By the mid-1980s, pressures to improve the cost-effectiveness of labour has placed the emphasis firmly back on line managers – particularly middle managers at departmental head level within organizations. These are the managers responsible for translating improvement plans into practice; for controlling the costs of the product or service, for introducing and maintaining new equipment and machinery, for handling the manning implications of such changes. With the increasing complexity of technology in many cases, and the more widespread availability of information on the critical components of the business, line managers are better placed than before to resume a central role in managing change. Many may still prefer this role to be handled elsewhere, and may still not be equipped with the necessary skills and knowledge for this IR role. But as the economic and technical changes proceed with great rapidity, so these middle managers and first line supervisors are required to handle the operational and industrial relations implications of these changes. Personnel departments, even if they wanted to remain involved in these day-to-day activities, will not in many cases have the time or the technical experience to be involved in detail. This is not to detract from the role of personnel in the overall planning of change, and in developing and maintaining an industrial relations policy framework which facilitates the achievement of organizational objectives. We return to this changing role for personnel departments below.

Of course, such a change in emphasis from personnel to middle and junior levels of managers in the day-to-day handling of industrial relations is not occurring without problems. For example, many line managers are themselves feeling under pressure as a result of the pace of technical and organizational change. The developments in technology are increasingly requiring 'technical' managers, often needing software engineering skills, who are able to handle man-management, rather than 'generalist' managers who may have been more skilled in man-management rather than technical matters. These technical developments, too, are putting pressure on the numbers of managers within organizations, and therefore line managers may be working in a context of redundancies amongst their own group. The IR skills and knowledge of managers increasingly involved in handling change assume increased importance. Whilst many large organizations have placed some emphasis on industrial relations training in recent years, this continues to be focused on law and procedures, rather than on planning and negotiating complex technical and organizational changes.[5] It is to this subject of industrial relations training that we now turn.

Industrial relations training for managers

Management development and training are vital parts of the organization's strategy to improve operational efficiency. Through career development programmes, and formal training courses, individuals can be developed to improve areas of key skills and knowledge which are important to the future needs of the business. As we have indicated, styles of behaviour can also be influenced in this process.

Industrial relations training will continue to have a role in equipping managers with the skills and knowledge to enable them to handle industrial relations issues effectively. Four particular aspects are being emphasized under this heading.

* policy development;
* the broader view;
* the motivational effect; and
* cost-effective training.

Policy development through the training process is an attractive option for many organizations. It enables line managers to make an input to the policies and goes some way towards ensuring their understanding of and commitment to the necessary action.

A broader view of industrial relations is an inevitable corollary of the emphasis on increasing line management's overall responsibility for its department or section. To argue that the effective management of change means that line managers must accept greater responsibility for upward and downward communication, for carrying out policy decisions, for motivating staff and for handling most union issues is to argue for them to be adequately prepared and supported in all these areas.

One important industrial relations training objective is to influence managerial commitment. As we have said it is important to convince managers of the organization's approach to its employees. The increased confidence that results from successful training and the chance to understand and even influence the organization's policies contributes to the process of motivating the managers.

Finally, here, the pressures for cost-effectiveness will apply to industrial relations training as elsewhere. This implies tailor-made courses, developed for the organization on the basis of a detailed needs analysis. It implies training and development that is integrated with other changes to the managerial approach to labour costs and labour output. And it implies a rigorous evaluation of the impact of the training.[6]

The role of the specialist
We have already indicated that as the role of the line manager changes, so will that of the personnel specialist. The ambiguities of the personnel manager position have been well documented.[7] It is possible to identify varying levels of specialization. At the lower levels it is worth remembering that in many organizations the personnel role is not carried out by a specialist at all. For many small and medium-sized companies it is the office manager, the administration manager or someone in the finance department who deals with personnel issues such as recruitment, pay and conditions and grievance handling.

Where there are full-time personnel specialists the role can become successively differentiated. At one extreme the specialist may handle only personnel issues, but handle the complete range. At the other extreme some of the largest organizations have complete departments specializing in recruitment, training, management development and industrial relations. This occurred, as we have indicated, as organizations began to employ larger numbers, and with the growth of trade union membership, the influence of employment legislation and the effects of industrial training, health and safety, anti-discrimination and other statutory bodies.

Some of these managers will be only, almost incidentally, in personnel for a while, as part of a managerial career progression. They are not 'professionals' in terms of seeing personnel management itself as their chosen career path although they may be equally 'professional' in the performance of their job. It is a minority who have Institute of Personnel Management qualifications, a majority who have moved into personnel from within the organization rather than from personnel jobs elsewhere. They are, as a general summary, managers doing personnel jobs rather than personnel specialists.

The emphasis on the role of line managers in industrial relations which we have described in this chapter clearly affects the role of personnel, for

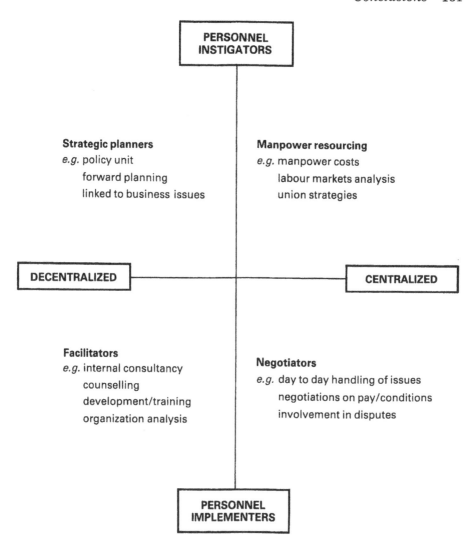

Figure 5 *The personnel role in industrial relations*

both the generalist and the specialist. Figure 5 shows how the roles of personnel might vary. The horizontal axis indicates degree of centralization of the organization. The more centralized it is, the more likely is a central personnel department to be directly involved in industrial relations: the more decentralized, the more the group will adopt a 'facilitating' advisory and coordinating role. The vertical axis indicates hierarchy. Those specialists at the top of organizations are, or perhaps more accurately could be, doing rather different tasks from specialists lower down. At the top level they have become almost generalists again, involved in board level decisions in all major areas of the business; though obviously

Example 9.1   *The Personnel Planning Unit*

The personnel planning unit (PPU) of one decentralized company consists of just four people: a high-flying personnel specialist, an older experienced line manager with a finance and production background, an industrial relations specialist brought in from a university and an administrative assistant. The PPU receives reports from a traditional hierarchy of personnel managers and officers at regional and plant level and produces confidential 'state of play' summaries for them. It occasionally provides direct advice and support, but is specifically excluded from involvement in negotiations – though informal contacts with union full-time officials are maintained.

The major role of the PPU, which is located at headquarters on the 'directors' floor', is to monitor developments in industrial relations, establish company industrial relations policies and comment on all issues discussed at board meetings. It reports solely to a senior director. In broad terms the PPU looks ahead at industrial relations issues that the board needs to take into account, and checks the industrial relations impact of decisions in other areas of the business.

more aware of and emphasizing the manpower options and implications of business strategies.

Organizations may well have a need for many of these roles. In general, however, we believe there is a growing movement away from the bottom right-hand of our diagram – the traditional day-to-day negotiating role being increasingly handled by line managers – towards the top left-hand corner. The 'Manpower Resourcing' and 'Facilitator' roles are relatively recent developments but are now widely accepted. The strategic planning role is rarer, but is spreading, as Example 9.1 illustrates.

It is an interesting aside to note that competitor nations such as West Germany and Japan expect such labour specialist input at the highest levels as a matter of course. Indeed in West Germany, the involvement of the labour director in all major executive board decisions is required by law.

For personnel this emphasis on the strategic management of industrial relations, with most managers and all first line supervisors involved in day-to-day issues, represents, we believe, the most appropriate allocation of responsibilities for organizational efficiency as we near the twenty-first century.

Integration: the role of senior executives in industrial relations
Such an allocation of responsibilities is, in ideal terms, as well as in the practical reality of an increasing number of organizations, the answer to the conundrum of consistency. If, as we have argued, policies have to be

flexible to take account of circumstances, and if the cost-effective approach is to push responsibility for much of industrial relations out to line managers, how does the organization ensure coherence and consistency?

Part of the answer lies, undoubtedly, in the role of the industrial relations specialists. If some of them are involved in this strategic management role they are in a good position to monitor action, and proposed action, in the industrial relations arena. They can ensure, as examples, that recruitment policies and payment systems are compatible, that proposed new working practices and objectives *vis-à-vis* the trade unions do not clash, or that new approaches to employment contracts and new communications methods do not cancel each other out. Perhaps more importantly, however, the strategic specialist can play some part in ensuring that industrial relations objectives and the overall organizational objectives are broadly compatible.

Whilst the role of the strategic specialist is important, however, its major impact may often lie in bringing the manpower perspective to the attention of other senior executives. An essential element of effective industrial relations strategies is that they originate in the requirements of the organization's overall objectives.

> The starting point of a company employment policy must be *corporate* policy: The employment policy must stem from the business policy and be an integral part of its implementation.[8]

In a more political environment such as the public service sector such policies are more complex, and perhaps more crucial to success.

Manpower is a major cost and a central opportunity area for most organizations. It is commonplace that the senior people in many British organizations have been concerned with the product (engineering, service or whatever) of their organization rather than with such complex and unsatisfying areas as manpower. That is changing. Company directors with manufacturing, marketing and, even, finance bases are recognizing the crucial role that industrial relations, in the wide and practical sense that we have discussed it in this book, has on success.

Developing the strategy
How do they do this? It is important to begin with the identification of operational priorities for the senior line management in the organization. What are the outcomes which are necessary to improve the effectiveness of the organization? While sophisticated diagnostic aids can be deployed to identify such priorities, in our experience senior line managers (and junior ones too) generally know only too well what needs to be achieved – their difficulty lies more in finding solutions and implementing them effectively. In this, the industrial relations framework of substantive agreements and procedures, of custom and practice, is a crucial environmental consideration.

Of course, many priorities for senior line managers will focus on improvements in engineering or project management or purchasing which do not have a direct IR implications. However, as we have said often in this book, pressures to improve cost-effectiveness are meaning that increasingly it is a priority for management to improve the flexibility of labour, to seek forms of contract which are more appropriate to the nature of the work or to better harness the ideas of the workforce.

Once senior line management has clearly identified the operational priorities, there is a key role for the personnel specialists, including the IR specialists, to develop policies to meet these organizational objectives. This stage is essentially a period for senior management to evaluate the options, including examining the costs of various approaches, the advantages and disadvantages and gauging the trade union reaction. Multi-function working parties, including line and personnel expertise, remains the most effective mechanism for such considerations.

Such joint study groups may well concentrate on any of the subjects we include in this book – changing patterns of reward, initiatives in working time, flexibility of task, alternative forms of contract, forms of employee involvement – or on detailed aspects of them. There is, however, a considerable degree of interdependence of these subjects. Improving flexibility of labour may involve changes to task flexibility, patterns of work and payment systems. Extending the use of 'peripheral', as distinct from 'core', employees may have implications on the shape of the organization and on patterns of communication. Most of these initiatives have implications on pay and conditions, some have implications on union recognition. In coordinating these different policy developments, the senior personnel specialists will play a key role. The senior line managers – essentially at board level – are responsible for ensuring that the policies that emerge from these studies remain relevant to and consistent with the organizational priorities which were the startingpoint.

While there are many issues to be dealt with in this process of managerial review, we believe it is important to distinguish between initiatives which are consistent with current organizational policy, and initiatives which break new ground. Clearly, the latter group requires very careful consideration at the most senior levels of the operational and industrial relations implications for the organization as a whole. Much of what we have covered in this book falls into this category – one thinks of the annual hours contract or the extension of homeworking or changing bargaining structures.

Concentrating on initiatives which for the organization are novel, i.e. not provided for by existing arrangements, agreements or customs, and assuming managerial commitment to the initiative has been secured through this process of management consultation, then consideration must be given to how such outcomes are going to be achieved. Too often in organizations, tactical IR issues are considered before strategic priorities have been defined. Such tactical questions as 'will the unions agree' are often met by the answer 'No' long before ideas have been developed from the organizational perspective. Of course, this question does need to be in the background, otherwise time could be wasted pursuing utopian ideas. However, putting the question always at the forefront can stifle constructive debate.

Consideration of how to secure a desired change raises the issues of management style which we discussed earlier in this chapter. Although each organization will respond differently, we can identify some general approaches including

- consult the workforce and persuade them of the desirability of the change; for them and for the organization as a whole;
- consult, but be prepared to 'buy in' the change in the form of extra basic pay, shift allowance, one-off payment, productivity deal, and so on; and
- link the desired change to a trade union claim as a quid pro quo. Thus new patterns of work could be introduced in conjunction with an hours of work reduction; alternative forms of contract as a trade-off for fewer redundancies; flexibility of task in conjunction with an annual review increase.

Assessing these options is another key role for the personnel specialist. It involves consideration of likely developments in terms and conditions of employment over the short and long term.

This overall process of management review followed by consultation and negotiation with employees and trade unions is likely to involve considerable time periods prior to effective implementation. Much will depend, of course, on the size and complexity of the organization and the number of initiatives being introduced. What can be said is that if managements do not start developing such strategies in the short term they may find themselves being led by events and responding in a generally unplanned ad hoc manner. For those organizations who have not already moved on, the opportunity to begin at least managerial considerations of the issues we raise in this book is now.

Concluding remarks

This book has been about three key elements in the management of employees. First we have stressed *cost-effectiveness* as the touch-stone against which management are being judged. Second, we have argued that this criterion requires coherent managerial *strategies* that apply to industrial relations in much the same way that organizations adopt strategies in other areas. Third, we have emphasized that *industrial relations* is being considered more widely and being more closely related to the overall objectives of the organization.

Cost-effectiveness

The notion of cost-effectiveness involves reduction in costs on the one hand and performance improvement on the other. The tension between these twin objectives has been analysed most lucidly by the radical school of writers on industrial relations,[9] but is well understood by every manager asked to reduce overtime and increase output, or restrict manning levels and improve customer satisfaction. We have suggested that there are a significant number of areas where vanguard companies and public sector bodies are managing in ways that do achieve increased cost-effectiveness despite this tension.

The ground is continually changing and the target moving, but the ultimate arbiter, in the private sector at least, will usually be achieving sufficient gross margins to provide for a tangible return to investors whilst also allowing for investment for the future. Responsiveness to customer or client demands, and the development of sufficient flexibility in the work-force to meet such demands, are critical. We have shown how advanced management have increased flexibility in task – developing workforces capable of operating in a wider variety of environments. There have been a number of spectacular deals in this area, but we have concentrated on the evidence that small-step, pragmatic progress has been successful too.

There have also been intriguing developments in working time arrangements which have moved many managers away from the view that working hours should remain fixed even where operational requirements vary. Flexibility in working time, through alternative shift patterns including part-time shiftworking, 'minimum–maximum' contracts or annual hours arrangements for example, is proving that it is possible to reduce unit costs, improve flexibility and increase employee satisfaction.

Managements are also seeking to encourage and reward different factors in pay systems and emphasizing quality and flexibility rather than such criteria as output or 'time spent'. To reflect such changes, the structural parameters of pay systems are changing, with the increasing use of multi-factor schemes and with the desire for greater freedom in pay structures to accommodate individual needs in the interests of the business.

More generally, the breakdown of the strict correlation between work and employment may yet come to be seen as the most appropriate approach to alleviating high levels of unemployment. There has been a marked increase in the number of people who work without being in full-time employment: work and reward are more widely shared, the stigma of not having a job is lessened, the pressure for conformity reduced.

These developments have occurred largely in response to economic and competitive pressures on management. Whilst a few managements may have tried to use the current high levels of unemployment to exact maximum concessions from the unions, most have recognized the continuing need to work with the unions and their members.

Flexibility as a key concept for the organization – in task, working time and contractual arrangements – has as a corollary an increasing flexibility and variety in social arrangements. This can be exaggerated; most people will continue to be employed on full-time contracts at the end of the century. But individuals will be less tied to specific jobs, working hours or employers and freer to develop their own patterns of living.

We have also described how pressures to improve cost effectiveness have led to a renewed emphasis on forms of employee communications. Here it is recognized that spending time communicating and consulting employees may actually prevent many of the problems of implementation which so often beset new initiatives. In addition, there is a greater recognition of the amount of knowledge amongst the workforce which through forms of employee involvement can be made available to management. Developing direct communication mechanisms alongside trade union channels, for example, can enable a focus on day to day task related issues with real gains for management.

Alongside developments in communications and consultations, cost-effectiveness in industrial relations may also require a focus on bargaining structures and trade union facilities. Bargaining within the organization rather than through an employers' association may provide more control and predictability over substantive terms and conditions of employment, for example. We described in chapter 7 the implications of central versus local bargaining where cost-effectiveness is a real consideration, alongside more frequently discussed issues of organization and technology.

Strategic planning
The key managerial objective of cost-effectiveness can only be achieved if the issues that we have discussed in this book are addressed in a coherent and consistent manner. There are innumerable reports from the NBPI, CIR, ACAS, NEDC and other bodies, and numbers of academic and consultancy studies, which show how easy it is for clear rational policies in one area of industrial relations (such as pay and rewards, or trade union relationships) to be undermined by policies in other areas (such as recruitment or task flexibility). There is a need for all these areas to be moulded into a coherent and consistent plan if they are to be successful.

Industrial relations policies developed to encompass these issues are no more predictive and fixed than policies in any other aspects of business or public service. Marketing, customer service and financial plans are adjusted to changing circumstances – but are still seen to be central to rational organization. Equally industrial relations policies and plans must be adaptable and capable of adjustment. And equally, in this major operating cost area, a coherent plan is a prerequisite for success. The process of developing achievable objectives for labour relations in one, three or five years' time is becoming ever more vital – and increasingly widespread.

Alongside such truisms however, it is important to recognize that pressures on costs, especially, affect managers very directly – and usually require instant, often short-term, pragmatic action. Problems of increased manning and high overtime rates, wage-drift and extended or competitive union recognition often stem from this source. Again, there is no simple answer; there is a tension between longer-term planning and the need for action to resolve immediate issues. This is a tension familiar to line managers. We have argued that where they can take short-term remedial action within a context of a clear, coherent and well-understood industrial relations strategy, the problems will be reduced.

Industrial relations
The role of management in industrial relations has in recent years become an explicit concern of academic writers.[10] It has, however, tended to be the focus of calls for research[11] rather than the subject of empirical study. Batstone and his colleagues point out that

> the industrial relations tradition has not faced up to the question of how overall corporate strategies relate to labour relations strategies and practices.[12]

In partial defence of the industrial relations academics it should be pointed out that practising managers have been no clearer.

This divorce between industrial relations and overall corporate strategies may be to some extent semantic. It is apparent, for example, that Winkler's finding that boards do not consider industrial relations relies on a narrow definition of the subject.[13] They always have considered labour costs and manpower issues. What is happening now is that the homilies preached by such as the Donovan Report[14] and the CIR[15] – that manpower and industrial relations are a board level responsibility – are being acted upon. But in a different context.

Industrial relations analysts who pursue this aspect of the subject quickly find that they are stepping over disciplinary boundaries. The student of trade unions can, with some deference to historians and economists, claim the subject as entirely within industrial relations. The student of management's role can do no such thing. A measure of eclecticism – which mirrors the managerial situation – becomes necessary. The boundaries between industrial relations and personnel, manpower planning, organizational behaviour and related subjects have long been blurred. Now the line between industrial relations and management theory and corporate strategy is being crossed too.

This reflects industrial experience. Management teams within organizations now consider manpower and labour relations strategies explicitly. The accent is on the organization's business objectives (or perhaps service objectives in some of the public sector) and how carefully thought through labour relations strategies can contribute. The senior executives are looking at industrial relations in terms of costs, efficiency and flexibility;

developing policies appropriate to these aims; and establishing monitoring and controls to make the policies operational. Again there is tension. Traditional industrial relations specialists' values (natural justice, consistency, comparability, defensibility and so on) may be subordinated to more pragmatic, organizationally-oriented goals. But they cannot be thrown out altogether. One aspect of cost-efficiency is the development of a committed, motivated workforce; breaches of the traditional values will act against that possibility.

So the development of cost-effective strategies in industrial relations is not simple or straightforward. There will be tensions and divergent pressures. Some of the 'vanguard' organizations are handling these tensions and developing such strategies. We are conscious that in abstracting from these organizations and looking into the future we have taken a risk. Many organizations will undoubtedly end the twentieth century no clearer about their approaches to handling their employees than they were half a century before and for them the initiatives we describe in this book will remain words not actions. But the competitive and economic constraints and pressures will continue and the issues we have addressed will increasingly be seen to be crucial to organizational success.

References

1   A move towards this style has been detailed by K. Sisson. See 'Changing strategies in industrial relations', *Personnel Management* (May 1984), pp. 24–7.
2   These organizations include Marks and Spencer, ICI, IBM and Rugby Portland Cement. See also T. Peters and R. Waterman, *In Search of Excellence* (Harper and Row, 1982).
3   W. H. Cuthbert and K. H. Hawkins (eds), *Company Industrial Relations Policies – The Management of Industrial Relations in the 1970s* (Longman, 1973), p. 23.
4   A. Flanders, *Management and Unions – The Theory and Reform of Industrial Relations* (Faber and Faber, 1975) p. 62.
5   See C. J. Brewster and S. L. Connock, *Industrial Relations Training for Managers* (Kogan Page, 1980), chapter 1 for more details.
6   Brewster and Connock, *Industrial Relations Training for Managers*, pp. 186–97.
    C. J. Brewster, 'Evaluation of management training: a focus on change', in C. Cox and J. Beck, *Advances in Management Education* (John Wiley, 1980).
7   A. Crichton, *Personnel Management in Context* (Batsford, 1968).
    S. R. Timperley, *Personnel Planning and Occupational Choice* (George Allen and Unwin, 1974).
    T. J. Watson *The Personnel Managers* (Routledge and Kegan Paul, 1977); K. Legge, *Power Innovation and Problem Solving in Personnel Management* (McGraw Hill, London, 1978).
    S. Tyson and A. Fell, *Evaluating the Personnel Function* (Hutchinson, 1986).
8   S. Rothwell 'Integrating the Elements of a Company Employment Policy', *Personnel Management* (November 1984), p. 31 (emphasis in original).
9   A. Fox, *Beyond Contract: Work, Power and Trust Relations* (Faber, 1974).
    A. L. Friedmann, *Industry and Labour: Class Struggle at Work and Monopoly Capitalism* (Macmillan, 1977).
    M. Burawoy, *Manufacturing Consent* (University of Chicago Press, 1979).
    C. Littler and G. Salaman, *Class at Work* (Batsford, 1984).

10 The evidence can be seen in conferences and papers devoted to the topic:
    K. E. Thurley and S. Wood (eds), *Managerial Strategy and Industrial Relations* (Cambridge University Press, 1983).
    M. J. F. Poole and R. Mansfield, *Management Roles in Industrial Relations* (Gower, 1980).
    See also review articles.
    D. Winchester, 'Industrial relations research in Britain', *British Journal of Industrial Relations*, vol. XXI, 1 (1983), pp. 100–14, and
    J. Purcell, 'The management of industrial relations in the modern corporation, agenda for research', *British Journal of Industrial Relations*, vol. XXI, 1 (1983), pp. 1–16.
11 S. Timperley, 'Organization strategies and industrial relations', *Industrial Relations Journal*, vol. XI, 5 (1980), pp. 38–45.
    S. Wood, 'The study of management in British industrial relations', *Industrial Relations Journal*, vol. XIII, 2 (1982), pp. 51–61.
12 E. Batstone, A. Ferner and M. Terry, *Consent and Efficiency: Labour Relations and Management Strategy in the State Enterprise* (Blackwell, 1984), p. 2.
13 J. T. Winkler, 'The ghost at the bargaining table: directors and industrial relations', *British Journal of Industrial Relations*, vol. XII, 2 (1974), pp. 191–212.
14 *Royal Commission on Trade Unions and Employers Associations, 1965–1968* (Donovan Report) (HMSO, 1968).
15 *The Role of Management in Industrial Relations*, CIR Report No. 34 (HMSO, 1973).

Index